Christina Marsden Gillis

THE PARADOX OF PRIVACY

Epistolary Form in Clarissa

A University of Florida Book   *University Presses of Florida*
Gainesville

University Presses of Florida is the central agency for scholarly publishing of the
State of Florida's university system. Its offices are located at 15 NW 15th Street,
Gainesville, FL 32603. Works published by University Presses of Florida are evalu-
ated and selected for publication by a faculty editorial committee of any one of
Florida's nine public universities: Florida A&M University (Tallahassee), Florida
Atlantic University (Boca Raton), Florida International University (Miami), Flor-
ida State University (Tallahassee), University of Central Florida (Orlando), Uni-
versity of Florida (Gainesville), University of North Florida (Jacksonville), Univer-
sity of South Florida (Tampa), University of West Florida (Pensacola).

Library of Congress Cataloging in Publication Data

Gillis, Christina Marsden.
  The paradox of privacy.

  (University of Florida monographs. Humanities; no. 54)
  "A University of Florida book."
  Bibliography: p.
  Includes index.
  1. Richardson, Samuel, 1689–1761. Clarissa.
  2. Epistolary fiction, English—History and criticism.
  I. Title. II. Series.
  PR3664.C43G5 1983   823'.6   83-14568
  ISBN 0-8130-0761-5 (alk. paper)

Typesetting by G & S Typesetters, Austin, Texas
Printed in U.S.A. on acid-free paper

Contents

Introduction

Perhaps the starting point for discussing a novel, even a great and important novel like Samuel Richardson's *Clarissa*, is one's own reaction as a first-time reader. I remember being drawn in by *Clarissa*: by the heroine herself, an individual pressed and impinged upon, first by her own family, then by the rake Lovelace; and by the "history" of Clarissa Harlowe, an account told in letters of a woman seduced from her father's house, forced to endure the trial of incarceration in a London brothel, raped when she refused to yield to either ruse or demand, and finally, completing her journey "in the world" with a return to her father's house and a burial vault within it. I was struck also in that initial reading, like so many readers before me, with the power of setting in Richardson's novel. Here too I felt drawn in: into enclosed rooms and a story which could unfold only in small details and individuated letter spaces. Perhaps that is why I responded to *Clarissa* like one of Richardson's own coterie of correspondents/readers and expressed my first reactions to the novel in a letter to a friend.

Subsequent readings of the novel led me to qualify my sense of enclosure within it. At Roy Strong's exhibit on the English country house at the Victoria and Albert Museum in 1974, I would peer into an eighteenth-century architectural model and find in this structure a Palladian symmetry and an open-ness—central hall flanked by double suites of rooms on either side—which, I now saw, reflected another dimension of Richardson's enormous work. As each space in the balanced pattern of the Palladian model invited examination of itself and its complementing other, so too each letter in Richardson's novel brings another into being. An architectural description—"reception rooms were arranged in pairs"—might apply to both a house and an epistolary novel where letters are exchanged.[1] The "small Circumstances" of an individual room or letter are not in themselves enough. Visibility, in house and novel, requires that rooms open

1

one out of the other in stagelike sequence, that letters gradually arrange themselves in a pattern. Perhaps it is the slowly evolving pattern, our being forced to wait for the door to be opened, that explains at least in part our sense of being drawn in when we read *Clarissa*. The pattern manifests itself in a continued tension between enclosure and open-ness, or, as I came to call it, the private and the public. The tension is both an architectural and a literary problem. Both have to do with form and how it is read; both have to do with this study of privacy in *Clarissa*.

My interest in houses and letters is not unique of course. Providing in *The Rise of the Novel* what is probably the most well-known reading of *Clarissa* as an exploration of the private, Ian Watt interprets the letter as a key to the private world of consciousness, and the epistolary novel as exemplar of a "new, subjective, individualist and private orientation" in life and literature.[3] In Watt's analysis, our accessibility to the houses in Richardson's novel figures our admission to the minds of the characters as well. Like Watt, I was intrigued with how a "private orientation" could be traced in both houses and letters; but I felt that Richardson himself, novelist, printer, letter writer, would more likely have seen in the letter the peculiar ambiguity between private and public, the perhaps anomalous process that Elizabeth Eisenstein describes as "speaking privately for publication"; the "urge to scribble" merges into the "itch to publish."[4] It is ambiguity itself, even the convergence and blending of real and fictional words, which marks, for example, Richardson's own correspondence. Although it is generally agreed that the novelist's correspondents effected no essential influence on the novels, John Carroll has suggested that the plethora of detail in Richardson's work may have been encouraged by his real-world letter writing activity.[5] An influence the other way, from fiction into the world, is evident when one of the novelist's favorite correspondents, Lady Bradshaigh, writes a Pamela-like "to the moment" style. Lady Bradshaigh emphasized the private function of letter writing when she pointed out that the letter should "appear extempore, and just as the thoughts flow'd at the time of writing"; but when Richardson explained to her the arrangements he was making for the publication of his correspondence, Lady Bradshaigh highly approved the scheme. She admitted that she "all along had a view to these letters becoming publick."[6]

How private, then, is this so-called unpremeditated scribbling? Is the "extempore" necessarily more authentic, more true? Malvin Zirker and John Carroll, commenting in different contexts on Richardson as real-world letter writer, have cautioned against the assumption that letters are "artless" outpourings which allow readers to "confront directly the correspondent's personality."[7] Just as the line between fiction making and auto-biography is not always clear, so the letter is not the "confessional."[8] The notion of authenticity in letters and letter writing will be treated in more detail in chapter 5 of this study. It is an essential issue in the reading of epistolary fiction, because how we read the novel will correspond in part to how we read the letters that compose it.[9] This may be ultimately to question the transparency of letter language and its reliability as a depiction of individual consciousness.

Yet, for Watt, the private letter is the "nearest record of . . . consciousness in ordinary life."[10] Letter language is a window into the mental processes of fictionalized individuals—"window into the heart," the epistolary manuals say—and consciousness a part of the realistic tissue of the novel as a whole. Watt's reading of "private experience" in *Clarissa*, his pointing to the growth of the suburb in eighteenth-century London as reflecting an increased emphasis upon privacy, firmly attaches the novel, its characters, and its mode to the social and economic world he seeks to describe. Students of Richardson, including myself, have found these insights highly relevant and valuable; but the topographical and architectural metaphor is complex in *Clarissa* because letter language is more ambiguous than Watt suggests. If private space reflects consciousness and the world of experience, it is also an integral element in the experience of creating written language. To this degree, the authenticity of the private text created within the closed room may be multidimensional in ways that Watt does not explore.

What is "real" is difficult to define in epistolary literature. How are we to speak of realism when language imitates not reality but letters? At the furthest extreme from Watt, John Preston's reading of *Clarissa* suggests that the novel points toward an existential void.[11] Letter texts for Preston spell not communication but barriers. Quite rightly Preston reminds us that the epistolary novel is really about writing and reading; but the medium is opaque according to Preston; its message "attests nothing but itself." *Clarissa* is a novel of isolation and estrangement.

Privacy in Richardson's novel is thus unremitting for Preston. There is no way in. If letter language is deemed unreliable as communication, the novel is a closed structure. To note that *Clarissa* is about writing and reading, however, is not necessarily to accept the conclusion that Preston presents. Alan McKillop, writing much earlier than Preston, provided the important notion of paradox, which, built into the letter-writing process, underlies the fiction in letters: the letter documents may emphasize the isolation of the heroine, but they also connect her to the world.[12] Anthony

Kearney, similarly, sees *Clarissa* as a "study in isolation" but notes too the tension between isolation and a "reading out for contact."[13] Countering directly Preston's thesis, Mark Kinkead-Weekes accepts letters as "barriers" but argues too that through letters, Clarissa, confined through the major part of the novel, is ultimately freed.[14] Clarissa is not Tristram Shandy, who is, as James Swearingen argues, enclosed in subjectivism, part of a household where language is broken up in "provinces of quasi-private meaning."[15] Epistolary fiction, by contrast, depends upon an addresser and addressee who share a symbolic system. Richardson's letter writer is confident that turning experience into language "to the moment" will in fact capture that moment for all time; the attention that epistolary "editors" give to collecting and arranging—and the faith that Clarissa has in her own collection or "story"—attest to a confidence in order itself. Letter texts are finally to be read, reliably, within context, by a community of readers.

To emphasize the ways in which readers are admitted to the novel is to attend to the very fictiveness of the epistolary effort. Leslie Stephen was one reader who accepted the fictiveness and, seemingly, even grew impatient with it. Richardson, he wrote, "is constantly trying to account by elaborate devices for the fertile correspondence of his characters, when it is perfectly plain that they are simply writing a novel."[16] More recent commentators have sought to demonstrate Richardson's "artistic and moral purpose"—McKillop's phrase—by examining how the mechanics of letter writing and sending are integral elements in the fiction, how complex the letter-writing process is, and how difficult the attempt to categorize letters.[17] These are issues that I will address also in this study; for, like my predecessors, I want to underline the ultimate open-ness, and public-ness, of Richardson's great epistolary work. But I will go further than previous readers in looking at form as a spatial construct and examining the tension between private and public in spatial terms. Spaces literally open up in *Clarissa*; closed rooms are transformed into stage space. I will not be the first to point out that the dramatizing tendency in Richardson counters the privatizing.[18] My purpose, however, is to align rooms and rhetorical modes in letter writing, in order to contrast writing and acting (even teaching) spaces and to indicate how the tension between the closed and the open, private and public, is also one between writing for the self and creating an instructive "story" for an audience.

Ironically, the epistolary novel, a compendium of letters which in themselves may be laden with ambiguity, lends itself particularly to a consideration of form as a concrete construct. Form, in this sense, is not synonymous with what Frederick Hilles calls the "plan" of *Clarissa*;[19] taking into account the pattern of letter writers and delineating three major divisions in the text according to whose letters dominate, Hilles tends to equate pieces of acting in the novel with pieces of telling in letters, always a dangerous assumption in epistolary literature, where the telling may run against action conceived of as events occurring in chronological order (this may be what Dr. Johnson was responding to when he said we would "hang ourselves" if we read *Clarissa* for the story). The epistolary world is to this degree a world of its own, a paradox of patterned disorder: spatial design against temporal. In a valuable new study entitled *Epistolarity: Approaches to a Form*, Janet Altman uses the term "mosaic" to describe the epistolary novel.[20] The whole cannot be examined without regard for the individual parts. In epistolary synecdoche, text stands for writer; the letter writer, Jean Rousset has said, does not *have* a style, he *is* the style.[21] The so-called literature of the heart is one of distillation, concretization, as writers transform themselves into letters, each delineated text ultimately becoming a building block in an emerging design, a house of texts.

"It is when he becomes an individual that a man lives more and more in private rooms," Lionel Trilling has written;[22] but in the world of Clarissa Harlowe, individuals inhabit not only private rooms but private texts as well. Rooms and texts image each other. This point has not been stressed in preceding studies of privacy and private space in *Clarissa*: neither in Watt, who connects the house and consciousness in terms of the privacy of individualism, nor in Margaret Doody, who cogently urges a multiplicity of readings for "house"—mansion, estate, brothel, prison—and the connection between all such imagery and the psychological states of a character.[23] In my own reading of *Clarissa*, I am searching for a shaping principle, or what Jonathan Culler calls a "model";[24] I am concerned with the product of the building process and with the "manner of construction."[25] "The basic convention which governs the novel," writes Culler, is "our expectation that the novel will produce a world." Words, he continues, "must be composed in such a way that through the activity of reading there will emerge a model of the social world, models of the individual personality, of the relations between the individual and society, and, perhaps most important, of the kind of significance which these aspects of the world can bear" (p. 189).

As components of the form, and as individuated spaces, letters produce the emerging model. Spatial form is always metaphor, one recent commentator has written; narrative must be temporal.[26] But such rubrics are surely less tenable in epistolary fiction, where the reader is presented with overlapping, often disjunctive "times"—writing time, reading time, experiencing time, and so on—where temporal discordance may be itself an element in the plot (how can Clarissa act on her confidante's advice before she has received it?), and where the physical (spatial) arrangement of letters is integral to our perception of the novel.

The spatial construct is ultimately more than metaphor as we attempt to explain *Clarissa* as "model." We attend to the telling as well as the told—or, perhaps more exactly, to where the telling takes place: first, in what kind of space was the text ostensibly composed, and, second, in what spatial context are we now reading it? The first may be an architectural, the second a textual question. Yet the two are hardly totally separate. In both houses and novels, both constructs, we find evidence of worlds we have lost and hope to reconstruct through experiencing them anew. A 1763 visitor to Chatsworth who remarked rather testily that the rooms were "of little use, except to be walked through" was, like the novel reader, expecting something more: perhaps that each room tell its own part of the story, that each be important for its own sake as well as that of the whole. Yet, the tendency to "walk through," to move on to the complementing spaces, impels the novel reader too. We seek out the patterns in which individuated spaces are delineated and made available to us as components in a total structure. The Palladian model in the Victoria and Albert exhibit made this clear; but Palladio and Samuel Richardson were both interested in the relationship between the individuated unit and the whole. Palladio, for example, put forth the perhaps bizarre notion that private houses were the nuclei of public buildings because "man formerly lived by himself; but afterwards, seeing he required assistance of other men to obtain those things that might make him happy . . . [he] naturally sought and loved the company of other men; whereupon of several houses, villages were formed, and then of many villages, cities, and in these, public places and edifices were built."[27] Despite the fallacies of Palladio's theory, in its dichotomies of private-public, solitary-social, we have the broad outlines of Clarissa Harlowe's epistolary world. Houses are both spaces in which individuals create identities and formal units in a communal topography.[28]

Like Palladio, let us begin with the private. Raymond Williams, in *Keywords*, defines privacy as a state of being "withdrawn from public life" and, like sociologist Richard Sennett, points out that a growing emphasis upon privacy and the "private life" was deeply connected with corresponding changes in the sense of both individual and family. Similarly, in his work on marriage and family in the years 1550–1800, Lawrence Stone labels privacy a "profound psychological shift" in the middle and upper middle classes in England in the seventeenth and eighteenth centuries, a shift that accompanied what he calls the rise of "affective individualism."[29]

It is difficult to describe privacy without recourse to concepts of individualized self, space, and visibility. Privacy is the capacity to control the degree to which one will be exposed; it is a "self-space" wherein one enjoys the right to "determine when and how much of oneself is to be known by others."[30] Privacy is usually viewed as a zone, physical and spatial. For example, an eighteenth-century Quaker autobiographer refers to physical withdrawal to a specific locality when she records that even as a child, dissatisfied with her own spiritual condition, she would seek out the "privatest place."[31]

My own interest in privacy was first piqued by Philippe Ariès's statement that in the eighteenth century the family "began to hold society at a distance, to push it back beyond a steadily extended zone of private life [and] the organization of the house altered in conformity with this new desire to keep the world at bay."[32] Particularly concerned with the physical organization of space, Ariès explains that the eighteenth century witnessed the beginnings of the modern type of house, "with rooms which were independent because they opened on to a corridor. . . . People were no longer obliged to go through them all to pass from one to another." Interestingly enough, those developments in the use of private space that Ariès discusses have only recently received full attention from architectural historians. Mark Girouard's *Life in the English Country House* represents a major step in constructing the social life of the house; and in Girouard's diagrams of floor plans we see the increased compartmentalization of the house into its private and public zones.[33] Here too is the house in which Richardson found his model.

When we consider attack upon private space in *Clarissa*, of course, we think not so much of a private family as a single individual. Members of the Harlowe family press upon Clarissa in their efforts to force her acceptance of the dreaded suitor Solmes; Lovelace, the "encroaching" rake, forces his sexuality upon her. The heroine retreats, first to her own room, then to the still more confined and interior writing closet, finally to the private space of the letter. She is pressed further and further within; her room, her body, her letters—all attacked.

That the individuated room, in its multiplicity of meanings, is so often depicted as the object of attack from without only underlines the crucial significance of creating space and self-space in *Clarissa*. The heroine's experience is akin to that of monologuists, real and fictional, who have frequently expressed the equation of privacy and writing for the self. Room and journal space conflate, for example, in Doris Lessing's *The Golden Notebook*, a novel that tells its own creation; Katherine Mansfield recounts in her real-life journal: "I have changed the position of my desk into a corner. . . . Yes, this is a good place for the desk, because I cannot see out of the stupid window. I am quite private."[34] In a rather different vein, Marianna Alcoforado, the Portuguese Nun in the famous (fictionalized) love letters, pours out her passions in a "pseudomonologue" to an absent lover who remains far beyond the confining convent walls.[35] There is no "stupid window" here either, little reference to the world outside the cloister cell—or outside the writer's own consciousness. The Nun writes in the tradition of the confined solitary: the emphasis here is upon process and self, not the communication that can free the writer to a company of readers.

Particularly in chapters 1 and 2 of this study, I will examine how Clarissa's letters also represent a personalized spatial order; we are not to consider these letters as "premeditated." Rather, they are merely "scribbled," ostensibly the products of a private activity which Anna Howe, Clarissa's primary correspondent, connects with female domestic life: "Our employments are domestic and sedentary; and we can scribble upon twenty innocent subjects. . . . [The strange thing is] that such a gay, lively young fellow as this [Lovelace] who . . . frequents the public entertainments . . . should be able to set himself down to write for hours."[36] Private scribbling also suggests, of course, the suppression of form in the creation of jotted note or even fragment. The tendency of sentimental literature to refuse completion, to endow fragment with authenticity just because it is mere fragment, to deny art of plan, is thrown into relief in *Clarissa*.[37] Even though Clarissa realizes that letter writing, no matter how familiar and "easy," is not "prompt speech" (IV, 288; II, 432)—and is hence more subject to design—letter writing is countered to premeditation. The very negation of premeditation and story making in epistolary fiction exalts the private and the separate, the isolation of language within time, text, and consciousness endowing separateness itself with moral value: what is separate is the "real thing," the authentic. Letters, according to this rhetoric, are documents, faithful records of the individual heart. John Hughes's preface to his translation of *The Letters of Abelard and Heloise* (1713) is typical: the letters comprising his volume, Hughes writes, are more moving than any that "flow from the Pen of a Writer of Novels" and full of "sentiments of the Heart which are not to be imitated in a Feign'd Story."[38]

If the language of sentiment ostensibly cuts itself off from connection in a "story," however, it also bespeaks a writer whose identity is at best tenuous and whose institutional ties are either nonexistent or unacknowledged. Seduced from her father's house and the identity that she held there—albeit an economically defined identity: a commodity in the marriage market—Clarissa fears that she is become a "cypher." In her flight to London she renders herself anonymous. London may be the "world" (as Anna Howe tells her), but it is also the place "to be private in." One may even be forced to experience a forced withdrawal from a social identity. Mrs. Sinclair's house, in whose inner space the heroine will be incarcerated at the hands of Lovelace, is a locus of lost identities.

In such circumstances as these, the act of validating the private self through letter writing, of seeking verification ultimately through one's addressee, achieves existential significance; writing, continued writing, is the only means of negating anonymity. "We are not being led into a story, but into the process of writing a story," Northrop Frye has pointed out.[39] This point, to some degree, explains the great length of *Clarissa* and Richardson's own apprehensions that the "World is not enough used to this way of writing, to the moment."[40] The letter is a genre of detail, even trivia, carefully recorded, sent out, perhaps then to be re-recorded at the reception point. It is as if the prolongation of detail will postpone the ending, the completion of the form, and the termination of the writer's own existence.

And yet to maintain existence through epistolary communication is a risky endeavor. Despite assertions of authenticity, we are struck with the fragility of letters; they are so clearly vulnerable to attack. John Preston is correct, too, in indicating how words themselves may precipitate isolation, imprisoning the writer who is surrounded by physical emptiness.[41] Barriers of salutation and closure, limits which in an actual correspondence shut out outside readers, may function like the actual walls that keep Clarissa from gaining access to the public street outside Mrs. Sinclair's London brothel/prison. That the world beyond the personal remains murky is borne out in the fact that except for footnoted information, readers of epistolary novels are never directly addressed, the gap between the specified addressee of the letter and the unknown reader beyond the text underlining the latter's distance from the letter texts. Perhaps in an attempt to break down that distance, Richardson sought "attentive" reading in his readers. Attentive reading, like its twentieth-century counterpart, "active listening," focuses attention upon the speaking/writing subject; language is to this degree totally personalized.[42]

But attention to the personal is not in itself adequate to the sentimentalist strategy. Sentimental literature contains contradictions within itself: what is most personal may be also the most exemplary; the most private language demands public form. A literature that eschews design is, at the same time, promoted as a vehicle for the moral reformation of readers.[43] Instances of Clarissa and Anna Howe's "blaming, praising, and setting right the other . . . are strongly to be recommended to the observation of the younger part . . . of female readers," says Richardson in the preface to *Clarissa*. The private does accommodate itself to the public, the novelist argues; "parts" that "are proposed to carry with them the force of an example ought to be as unobjectible as is consistent with the design of the whole, and with human nature."

Attentive readers will see, then, the interconnection between part and whole, private language and public example.[44] Attention belongs to a didactic enterprise also; it is not simply a matter of "feeling," as John Preston suggests when he calls it "an encounter which is not a meeting . . . full of feeling, but the feeling . . . not reciprocated."[45] Attention figures strongly in later eighteenth-century pulpit rhetoric, for example—particularly in Hugh Blair and James Fordyce—to describe audience accessibility to didactic texts whose composition and design will emerge only through experiencing the "parts."[46] It served writers (and speakers) for whom notions of rhetorical persuasion were reduced, in Locke's terms, to the "artificial and figurative application of words Eloquence hath invented, and for nothing else but to insinuate Wrong Ideas, move the Passions, and thereby mislead the Judgment."[47] It protected the centrality of the "heart" and feeling by positing a notion of audience behavior in which eye, heart, and intellect are all interdependent. No less than Richardson, psychologically oriented rhetoric exalted the personal through emphasizing sincerity and the necessity of convincing one's audience of one's own faith in the message. This conviction was as true for John Wesley as for the Earl of Shaftesbury, the latter stating his confidence in the efficacy of the personal when he said that "others [will] partake [in the promotion of universal good] by being convinced of the sincerity of our example." The feelings so touched, a tear is evidence of the efficacy of language: "What comes from the writer's heart," writes Edward Young in *Conjectures on Original Composition*, "reaches ours," and "a single tear does the writer more honor than the rattling thunder of a thousand hands!"[48]

Those "others" who are convinced by "sincerity" to promote the general good belong, ostensibly, to a community of kind, loving hearts. Sincerity is a quality of voice that translates the heart of the speaker and speaks to the feelings of the audience. Speaker and voice, in this scheme, carry the burden of inculcating moral behavior in listeners. When Blair and Fordyce specifically addressed the didactic function of pulpit language, they too stressed the significance of sincerity and personal example—the cleric comes to his pulpit not like a "feigned character," writes Fordyce[49]—but, like Richardson, they emphasized also the necessity of gaining "attention" and appealing to the audience's own role in putting the text together. Likening the sermon to a garden stroll, Fordyce explained that attention is gained when a "succession . . . in intellectual prospects is opened from time to time." By this analogy, we experience a text "step by step, from one Reflexion and Discovery to another."[50]

In Clarissa's world, where the norm is not so much a loving human family as a collection of "familiars," a term connoting neither the kinship group nor a network of social and institutional connections, the individual voice, or heart, will be protected ultimately only in a collection of texts that call forth reader attention.[51] That is why individuated letters, viewed as signifiers of isolation and separation, do not provide the only linguistic model in Clarissa. Neither are sincerity and authenticity in themselves enough for the novelist who saw the limits of personalized language: letters in isolation are unreadable to a public audience. Those very letters that both Pamela and Clarissa are compelled to write, to seal, to hide, even (as in the case of Pamela) to wear in one's clothing as protective identity and shield —those documents that ostensibly describe the heart in the process of re-creating itself—must ultimately be separated from their creators to enter the world themselves as readable texts. Clarissa's letters, created in an interior, heart or inner room, achieve validity only when released to the external audience.[52]

Despite, then, the sentimentalist's avowal of individuality and authenticity, Richardson overcame the limits of personalized language through the formal character of his novel and the techniques he used to transcend the language of the self. He drew upon the conventions of conduct books, spiritual autobiography, domestic drama; he played with verbal motifs in Clarissa, creating what Irwin Gopnik has called a "network of verbal intricacies."[53] Still more important, the novelist was aware that letters are themselves codes, that they have both form and tradition. We have only to look into an epistolary manual to note the kinds of letters that can be written, to see that letters are written discourse within which writer, message, and addressee may be manipulated to define a particular mode of communication. Richardson himself controls the letters in Clarissa so that the three major letter writers of the novel—Clarissa, Lovelace, and Belford—represent, in order, three kinds of writing, all interdependent but all tracing a movement from private to public.

Yet, this is not to suggest that the transition from private to public in

Clarissa is ever simple or smooth. Here is a novel that images and explores, rather, the tension between private language and public form, part and whole, individual and outside world. It is a novel in which the central incident is a violent rape, a forced breaking of the private. The rape of Clarissa Harlowe in the inner house of a London brothel differs from the many fictionalized seductions and rapes that preceded it because it destroys not only the privacy of the body but the individual letter as an image of that privacy. The torn "papers" or fragments of letters that the heroine writes in her delirium after the sexual death indicate not only the rending and subsequent disintegration of the earthly woman, but the breaking of the letter as an enclosed, individuated text, as a separate whole. The letter is opened, rendered accessible to reconstitution and exposure within public form. From this process derives another wholeness, the new reality that is the book.

In my own attempt to describe that reality, I have divided the present study of *Clarissa* into two major sections, "Spaces" and "Letters." An investigation of the opening of private space in Richardson's novel demands both a spatial and a literary/historical approach to its epistolary form. The structures of architectural and dramatic space that I discuss in part I provide their own model for the examination of letter and monologic narration in part II. Each part depends upon the other, together providing a framework for our understanding the wholeness of *Clarissa*. If, for example, we ask why the wholeness that we sense at the end of *Humphry Clinker*, the completion that results when the Bramble family complete their journey, is so different from that Richardson achieves in *Clarissa* (who also completes a circular journey in the world), Wolfgang Iser's suggestion that the letters comprising Smollett's novel do not depend upon the introspective power of language is well taken but not in itself adequate.[54] Both *Humphry Clinker* and *Clarissa* are collections of letters; not only the kinds of letters, however, but the dynamic that they trace, and finally the kind of reading that they call forth, are fundamentally significant in our reactions to these novels. That the journey keeps up its pace in *Clinker*, that letters move only away from the axis of that journey, that addressees do not write letters, that letter writers are not literally confined—and that the titular hero never writes but remains an objective focus or unifying principle within the Bramble group and their letters—are all increments in the difference between Smollett's and Richardson's deployment of epistolary form. Wholeness in *Clinker* derives from principles outside of letter texts. In *Clarissa*, dominated as it is by barriers, walls, and representations of private spaces, wholeness evolves from the collecting of texts themselves. The more the letters trace the ordering of self, the more they need active readers; if language ostensibly works against form in *Clarissa*, neither can it be divorced from form. Language, letters, novel: all suggest the process of opening in *Clarissa*. Rooms are opened, stage flats drawn apart, letters collected and connected. Words, Geoffrey Hartman has written, "expose" both "private dreams" and "public illusions."[55] Words, in letters, join private and public, perhaps building public illusions out of private dreams.

1

Spaces

HARLOWE PLACE | 1

The Privacy of Separateness

> The relations of the rooms to each other
> are in fact the relations of their doors.
>
> Robert Kerr,
> *The Gentleman's House,*
> *or, How to Plan English*
> *Residences*

Unlike earlier experimenters in the epistolary form, Samuel Richardson thinks in terms of the shape and pattern of things. A private place, a place of introspective experience controlled by an individual who decides himself under what circumstances and to what extent he will expose himself, is depicted in Richardson's *Clarissa* in the isolated and enclosed space: the differentiated and interior room. For almost three-quarters of the novel, Clarissa Harlowe is "enclosed," first by her family at Harlowe Place, and then, in Mrs. Sinclair's brothel, somewhere in or near St. James's Parish, London. She is raped by the libertine Lovelace within the "fatal inner house" of Mrs. Sinclair's establishment, forces her way through a narrow passage out of the "vile house," sets her life—and her correspondence—in order, and dies in a room above a public shop. The death and posthumous praises of the heroine take up more than a third of the novel and are reported mainly through the letter-writing pen of Belford, one-time confidant/correspondent of the seducer Lovelace, and now, more important, audience *ab extra* to the events surrounding Clarissa's death.

Richardson takes us in *Clarissa* from letter-writing settings that are separated and interior spaces (Harlowe Place and Mrs. Sinclair's house) toward "scenes" (the room above the shop and ultimately the burial vault) that are described by outside observers like Belford or Colonel Morden and that

17

stress the heroine's emergence from the individuality of self toward a wider, public identity. Although we are always aware of rooms within this epistolary novel, then, it matters considerably whether the setting is a locus for the creation of the letter or whether it functions as part of a static picture of public moral example.

The writing place is particularly important in *Clarissa* for its relationship to the writer and to the letter she writes.[1] In Henry James's *The Portrait of a Lady*, a complex variation of the "persecuted maiden" theme that also underlies *Clarissa*, R. W. Stallman has found that Gilbert Osmond's house "interprets [its] inhabitants metaphorically"; when Isabel Archer is cornered by Osmond at an angle of the terrace, James's setting, according to Stallman, suggests Osmond's "moral obliquity."[2] A metaphorical use of setting is seen in *Clarissa* too, when Richardson places his heroine in a locked room, completely cut off from a public street, and indicates that Clarissa's moral struggle will be played out within her own consciousness. But there are important differences between James and Richardson: James's setting conveys a detailed objective reality that Richardson's rarely affords. In Richardson's epistolary art, a range of writers presents a kaleidoscopic pattern of points of view or perspective. Pattern itself dominates over what might be called physical "landscape." In James's own early experiments with "epistolarity"—*A Bundle of Letters, The Point of View*—it is exactly "point of view" that dominates his interest too;[3] but in those works, setting, in the metaphorical sense, is irrelevant. James provides no epistolary mechanism, none of that emphasis upon the writer's location in a particular space. Unlike Clarissa, and many of her predecessors, James's letter writers are compelled neither to write nor to find secure, isolated places in which to do so. The generalized settings in James's epistolary works do not point, then, toward the imaginative act or the form in which that private act is rendered communicable or public.

The importance of the internal space in *Clarissa*, however, is an integral element in Richardson's exploration of the private act. What might be called external landscape is rare in *Clarissa*, the most outstanding example appearing mainly in a footnote (II, 303; I, 446). Clarissa describes the back entrance of the Harlowe Place garden to Anna Howe:

> Then, perhaps, they [the family] have no notion of the back door; as it is seldom opened, and leads to a place so pathless and lonesome. If not, there *can* be no other way to escape (if one would) unless by the plashy Lane, so full of springs, by which your servant reaches the solitary Woodhouse; to which lane one must descend from a high

bank that bounds the poultry-yard. For, as to the front way, you
know, one must pass thro' the house to that, and in sight of the parlours and the servants' hall; and then have the open courtyard to go
through, and, by means of the iron gate, be full in view, as one passes over the Lawn.

What Clarissa stresses within the text of her letter is the geography of
Harlowe Place as it is relevant to her possible escape. The family, by this
point, has increased its pressure upon Clarissa to marry the "odious
Solmes," and she has already told Lovelace that she has "no way to avoid
the determined resolution of [her] friends in behalf of Mr. Solmes, but by
abandoning this house by his [Lovelace's] assistance" (II, 298; I, 443).
Clarissa seeks the most private route, that which will not be visible from
the house.

But if the heroine describes the plan of her family's estate only in terms
of what is within sight of what—and that gate, lawn, and courtyard will all
figure importantly much later when Clarissa's coffin enters the familial residence by the *front* entrance and in full view of the gathered family, servants, and villagers—Richardson as "editor" fills in with quite other details in the footnote:

> This [door], in another of her Letters (which neither is inserted) is
> thus described:—"A piece of Ruins upon it, the remains of an Old
> Chapel, now standing in the midst of the Coppice; here and there an
> overgrown Oak, surrounded with Ivy and Mistletoe, starting up, to
> sanctify, as it were, the awful solemness of the place. A spot, too,
> where a man having been found hanging some years ago, it was used
> to be thought of by us when children, . . . with a degree of terror (it
> being actually the inhabitation of owls, ravens, and other ominous
> birds) as haunted by ghosts, goblins, spectres. (II, 303; I, 446–47)

Richardson wants the full emotive effect of the gothic landscape, complete
with owls, mistletoe, and goblins: evil events will occur if one ventures out
of this gate. Although ostensibly emanating from Clarissa's pen, the lines
only contrast with the usual descriptive mode of the novel. The very juxtaposition of footnote and text underlines our sense that the effect of setting in *Clarissa* depends not upon gothic ruins and old legends—what we
would call "atmosphere"—but rather upon the value of such a setting
within the shape of the entire novel.

Clarissa's letter, on its own, without the footnote, supplies evidence of
danger and difficulty in both a moral and an epistolary sense. In telling us

that the proposed escape route is not within view and that it leads to a "pathless and lonesome" place, the letter suggests the image of the weary wanderer/pilgrim trying desperately to keep to a path but suffering "in the world" the trials of the isolated individual. And at the same time, Clarissa's emphasis upon the door looks toward all the doors and doorways which are so often the *foci* of important scenes in the novel. In the epistolary novel, doors are both barriers and passage points. As Clarissa emphasizes the privacy of this back door, we are recalled to the private letter-writing situation and the realization that the heroine will follow through this door the route of her own letters; she will begin her route toward her role in the public world. When she returns to the family house through the front door, she will be a public figure enclosed in a coffin. To this degree, the gate or door is a checkpoint between private and public, internal and external. The release provided by this back door will at first be ambiguous, of course, for the way leads almost directly to the more difficult confinement of Mrs. Sinclair's brothel; but when we have the whole novel before us we will see more exactly how Clarissa moves, like her letters, from a private and toward a public existence.

The description of the garden gate is about as far "outside" as one ever gets in *Clarissa*: so far outside that it is placed partially outside the text of the letter. Letters describe interiors, not in the sense that they reveal color, texture, or furniture design (as in *Sir Charles Grandison*) but rather, as they tell us the shape of a room, how—or whether—it connects with other rooms within the total interior plan of the house, and how one gets in and gets out. Richardson looks not outside the walls of the entire structure, but rather inside, into the consciousness of the letter writer and into the letter as product of that consciousness. The enclosed room suggests that the privacy necessary to the letter-writing process, as Clarissa experiences it, belongs to the unseen, internal space where the self may get on with its own business of introspection—and composition of the letter. The locked door is essentially related to what the French critic Maurice Blanchot has called the "need to write" (*besoin d'écrire*).[4] Letter writers in epistolary fictions are often solitary characters when they are about their chief pursuit; they inhabit not the gardens and rural retreats of seekers after retirement, but closets and cloisters where no audience is present save that which can be brought into presence through the act of writing.[5] Clarissa is one of that large company of epistolary heroines, in the tradition of the Portuguese Nun, whose letters represent the only release from the confinement of the closed room. Such release is, moreover, essential to maintaining the integrity of the self. Lovelace is able to consummate his rape of Clarissa's body only after he has intercepted her correspondence with Anna Howe and hence denied the persecuted heroine any communication with, or escape to, the world outside the "vile house."

On the one hand, then, the letter demands the privacy of solitude, but on the other, it implies by its very nature the importance of communication. Unlike the pen that writes the diary or journal, the letter-writing pen works toward the breakdown of privacy; it attempts to create its audience even as it asserts the distance that necessitates that creation.[6] The elaborate business of getting the letter to its proper recipient underlines further that outward movement not associated with the diary written for the self: Pamela's day-to-day letter/journal is transformed into a letter when Mr. B., an external audience, reads it.

But Clarissa, her predecessor Pamela, and real-life eighteenth-century correspondents all attest to the difficulty of epistolary communication, the riskiness of sending written words to a distant receiver. What great attention to the opening and reading of letters the Countess of Hertford recounts: "It was almost impossible to know how to set about opening the letter; for it had been in the water, and the cover was entirely off at one end. The letter itself was made into a kind of pasteboard. . . . I, however, preserved the pieces so carefully that I do not believe I have missed a single word."[7] That Richardson well understood the vulnerability of letters too is clear when he shows us Lovelace's exploitation of Clarissa's epistolary difficulties early in the novel: the rake coerces the heroine into what turns out to be a fateful meeting simply by not picking up the letter she has written informing him she will not go off with him. Believing her letter has not been received, Clarissa makes the significant error of appearing in person, substituting herself for the letter, at the secret meeting place. Clarissa herself moves out through the back gate, taking the route her letter should have taken. Lovelace's ruse succeeds, moreover, because experience committed to the letter is no longer the sole province of the writer; it takes on a life of its own when it is read, or pieced together, by its reader. Hence, the document that comes into being in an enclosed and private space insists upon its own public identity.

The investigation of private space in *Clarissa* begins with rooms as metaphors for private consciousness and the process of ordering personal experience. The shapes and patterns of rooms, their differentiation one from the other, whether it be in Harlowe Place or in Mrs. Sinclair's London brothel, signal not so much eighteenth-century architectural norms as Richardson's interest in the individual's attempt to fix the self upon a moral map and to separate the self from the communal space in order to carry on the duties of self-exploration. Because, however, the metaphor for self and creative process is ultimately indivisible from ongoing social processes in *Clarissa*, it is appropriate to consider that a house, real or fictional, suggests, first of all, a good deal about the kind of life lived within it. Harlowe Place, with its clearly differentiated private and public zones, is a house where family and family interests are important.[8] People like the Harlowes, a new but rich family, moreover, could well afford the privacy that differentiation makes possible, for privacy is particularly the prerogative of those who can afford a dwelling with separate rooms. The Harlowes easily had the means to build a partition within one large parlor making a separate sitting room for each of their daughters; and it is clearly apparent in Clarissa's descriptions of the suitor Solmes's visits to the house that the entrance hall is the public thoroughfare into the house and quite a different place from the inner sanctum of the parlor.[9] Clarissa's chamber and closet, we know from repeated textual reference, is located on the second floor, another nonpublic zone, at some distance from the parlor on the ground floor. This very distance between Clarissa and the rest of the family forces us to qualify Ariès's statement in regard to "public and private zones." In the Harlowe world, the differentiation of space within the house is really the expression of "mine and thine," an extension of the property ethos which so rules the family that it turns a favorite daughter into an outcast. In such a world, invasions of personal space will naturally be seen as invasions of one's own person and value as an individual. The divisions and barriers at Harlowe Place lie not so much between the Harlowes and the rest of the world as among the various members of the family itself.

No locus of intimacy and emotional support, Harlowe Place only heightens our sense of Clarissa's isolation as an individual, her need for privacy. In his treatment of the Harlowe's house in the first quarter of *Clarissa*, then, Richardson greatly intensifies tendencies toward privacy that are only hinted at in architectural commentators of the first half of the eighteenth century. My own examination of house plans in the period revealed that many houses were still without bypassing corridors and specifically differentiated rooms. The Victorian architect Robert Kerr, who was to call privacy the "first essential" in a gentleman's house, castigated the Palladian intercommunicating room system as a "serious defect": the "open central lines of thoroughfare rooms . . . must necessarily favour publicity."[10]

Far from a "first essential," the very word "privacy" is rarely seen in such writers as Vanbrugh, Robert Morris (*Rural Architecture*, 1750), or Colen Campbell (*Vitruvius Britannicus*, 1717). Even the closet, or small room attached to a larger, though amply provided for in the plans of the period, is not referred to as a private place. It is more common, in Vanbrugh for example, to find reference to publicness. When the architect of Blenheim, England's monumental gift to its public hero the Duke of Marlborough, wrote to the Earl of Manchester in 1707 concerning the construction of Kimbolton, he spoke of a "Noble Room of Parade" between the drawing room and bedchamber. Vanbrugh saw nothing improper in the juxtaposition of what we think of as a private room—bedchamber—with a public gallery. It is the publicness that dominates: the architect explains to his client that Kimbolton will look *outward* toward its gardens; the future owner is informed, in language suggesting the male-female, public-private dichotomies we find associated with the so-called retirement tradition, that his house will "make a very noble and Masculine Shew."[11]

The architect/writer Robert Morris, whose *Rural Architecture* represents an exemplum of the country house ideal Pope sets forth in *The Epistle to Burlington*, stresses the notion of organic unity—not that of privacy—within the house.[12] Consider, for example, Morris's statement on the exact differentiation and labeling of rooms:

> I have not set down the uses and distributions of the apartments of any Structure; because every different Room may be, by every new inhabitant, converted to a different use; so that what an Architect may design for a Parlour, may be, by another, metamorphosed into a Bedchamber. . . . My general Design has been to introduce Convenience, Proportion, and Regularity. (Preface, *Rural Architecture*)

In a manner perhaps suggestive of the novelist's craft, Morris depicts the rooms in his plans as simple blanks; however, the architect's interest is focused not upon separate spaces but rather upon "proportion" and "dignity" within the "little community" that constitutes the house: rooms are "proportional to the Dignity of the principal Inhabitant." Similarly, rooms are arranged in "gradation": "Parts should be so disposed, that, from the highest Station, all the subservient Apartments should be join'd by an easy Gradation, that every Link in the Concatenation should be justly regulated" (Preface). The house plan replicates the divine principle of order; every link must be "justly regulated," but each is important for the working of the whole. Rooms are joined in "easy Gradation"; there is no suggestion of a bypassing corridor that would obviate the notions of gradation and degree. In those instances where Morris's design does contain a "gallery . . . to communicate privately [that is, separately] with each Room and the Staircase" (Plate XXII, for example) the rooms are interconnecting also; the pattern of gradation will not be upset, for upon it rests the good of the community that is Morris's house.

The plans of the great and grand houses that constitute Colen Campbell's *Vitruvius Britannicus* also contain often unnamed, interconnecting rooms opening off a great hall space.[13] Again, a principle of unity predominates. As for private and public zones, Campbell explains that at Chatsworth (built in 1681), on the same floor level, "State is joined with great Conveniency." He applauds what he sees as a blending of a man's public and private roles, and an easy movement from one to the other: the "state" apartment lies in close proximity to the area of the private man as represented in his library or collections. He makes a special note of the fact that at Chatsworth, the third story is "entirely given to State." A similar juxtaposition of public and private is seen in Vanbrugh's house, Eastbury, in Dorsetshire (1718). Here, a room labeled "Bedchamber" opens directly off the great hall and corresponds in position to the "great eating Room," which lies directly opposite, across the hall.[14]

The principle of interconnection between zones, and rooms, is not altered even in those grand houses where there is a broad passage around a staircase area or a central court (as, for example, at Kings Weston, 1713). Cholmondely Hall in Cheshire, "rebuilt and finished in a sumptuous manner in the Year 1715," contains long corridors along three sides of a courtyard; and Beddington Place, in Surrey, whose owner had "spared no cost to rebuild and imbellish," is similarly enhanced by a long gallery along one wing, off which the various rooms open.[15] In a plan he designed himself for Lord Cadogan, Campbell explains that the broad passage around the central staircase is ten feet in width and is "of singular Use to the Whole House in passing from one apartment to another." This is the only specific instance of bypassing suggested in *Vitruvius Britannicus*; rather, these very large houses repeat the pattern of those smaller structures that Celia Fiennes described in the years in William and Mary: "You go thence into parlours, dineing rooms, drawing roomes, and bed Chambers one leading out of another."[16] Communication remains dominant also some fifty years later when Dr. Richard Pococke undertook his journeys through England with visits to country houses. Dr. Pococke writes:

> On the 30th I went to see Petersham, the Lord Harrington's house; the house is of good architecture, Lord Burlington's design. The back front is the grandest, in which there is a room at each end of a peculiar form, joyn'd to the main body of the house in front by a colonade, but the communication with it is from the house itself.[17]

In his use of "house body" to designate the main part of the house, Dr. Pococke uses the same terminology as an anonymous seventeenth-century architect who, also likening the house to a body, pointed out that the main room should be at the center and the lesser rooms at the extremities.[18] Like the physical body, the house is structured according to organic principle. The parts of a house, like the parts of the family that inhabit it, constitute an interconnected whole: what Morris called the "little community."

The principle of intercommunication that figures so importantly in the architectural statements of the first half of the eighteenth century is totally alien to the world of letter writing as we find it in the first quarter of *Clarissa*. Hence, the rooms of Harlowe Place, even if interconnecting, are also seen as closed off from each other. Epistolarity in this instance is allied with the barriers that block communication and threaten community, tendencies that architectural commentators do not necessarily acknowledge. That Clarissa must communicate by letter to members of her own family, within the same house, is evidence that something is amiss, that neither the Harlowes nor their house represents a community. Rather, the excessive self-interest that moves James and Bella Harlowe to inflict inhuman pressure upon their sister in the choice of her husband is imaged by Richardson in terms of particularized zones, each with a door that can be firmly shut. That is why the door is so often the point of visual focus in Clarissa's descriptions of her tempestuous encounters with her family and her attempts to ward off their increasingly strong pressure upon her. The statement of the Victorian architect Robert Kerr is strikingly apropos: "The relation of rooms to each other is the relation of their doors."[19] Clarissa, as we shall see, is usually trying to get out of the parlor door and into her own chamber upstairs, there to write the letters that are her main vehicle of communication both within and without her family.

This does not mean that a country house is a rare setting for an epistolary fiction, for works such as *The Honourable Lovers* (1732) or Mrs. Davys's delightful *Familiar Letters Betwixt a Gentleman and a Lady* (1725) use the framework of the country-to-city correspondence;[20] but unlike his predecessors, Richardson explores through the structure of Harlowe Place the complex of relationships of which the letters—and the house—are the model. Cynthia Griffin Wolff has already pointed to the breakdown of order, the excessive interest in money, and the "crumbling of the structure of power and authority" among the Harlowes (why, for example, does brother James command such power over his father and uncles?).[21] Certainly all these tendencies are apparent in the early letters of the novel, when Clarissa makes it quite clear to her friend Anna Howe that she is the victim of the Harlowes's "darling view . . . of *raising a family*"; this is the view "too frequently, it seems, entertained by families which having great substance, cannot be satisfied without rank and title" (I, 78; I, 53). It is the plan of James Harlowe, the heroine's brother, to provide the two sisters with ten or fifteen thousand pounds apiece and then see "that all the real Estates in the family, to wit, my Grandfather's, Father's, and two Uncles, and the remainder of their respective personal Estates, together with what he had an expectation of from his Godmother, would make such a noble fortune . . . as might entitle him to hope for a Peerage" (I, 79; I, 54). This plan has gone awry, however, since Clarissa's grandfather willed to her what her brother had expected would fall to him; and neither the younger nor the older James Harlowe (Clarissa's father) could bear that the younger daughter be made so independent. Clarissa willingly gives up management of the estate to her father, but still the jealousy of her brother and sister is unassuaged, and "between them the family union [has been] broken, and everyone . . . made uneasy" (I, 85; I, 55).[22] All is not well in the Harlowe household.

The plan to marry off Clarissa to the "odious Solmes" derives, then, from a net of negative motives: jealousy, hatred, avarice—all posing under the rubric of "paternal authority." Just what "paternal authority" meant, particularly in regard to choice of marriage partner, was a matter of much discussion in Richardson's time. An elder sister remarks to a younger in one of the dialogues comprising Defoe's *Religious Courtship*: "But it is a Matter of such Weight [choosing a husband] and so irrevocable when done, that we ought to see with as many Eyes as we can; and a careful religious Parent is a good Scout to look out for us."[23] But that all parents are neither careful nor religious is seen in one of Eliza Haywood's essays in *The Female Spectator*:

> I believe, if we look into the world, we shall find no Evils in private life, than what Marriages . . . in Defiance of the Will of those who ought to have the Disposal of us, have occasioned. . . . Obedience to Parents is an indispensible Duty. Decency and good Manners require it. Natural affection obliges to it. Yet . . . when a Parent through Avarice, Caprice, or partiality, would force his child to marry against Inclination, I cannot think Disobedience a Crime.[24]

Mrs. Haywood's advice to a marriageable daughter is not to marry at all if she cannot agree with the parents' choice; the "female spectator" does not treat the problem of what the daughter should do if her parents, through "avarice" and lack of principle, do not permit the alternative of remaining single. The behavior of the Harlowes transcends the bounds of decency as outlined in the domestic conduct manual. Clarissa, who wants to believe in parental authority, finds herself in the "unhappy situation" that "obliges her, in her *own defence* as it were, to expose *their* failings" (I, 90; I, 61). The act of reporting to Anna events within the house is, in her terms here, an act of betrayal of family solidarity; she makes public what might be seen as private (familial) matters.

A marvelously executed coda that comes at the end of Letter I, no. 21 (both editions) provides a striking view of the world—social and epistolary—of Harlowe Place. Clarissa reports to Anna the family's reaction to her own encounter with Solmes that afternoon, a scene that has ended in an impasse: the mother supplicating with the daughter to "give hope" to the suit of Mr. Solmes and finally, in frustration, flinging herself away "with high indignation," the daughter retreating from the battlefield to the solitude of her room with a "heavy heart." There is nothing left to say. A space appears upon our page (and Clarissa's letter). And then:

> My Father is come home, and my Brother with him. Late as it is, they are all shut up together. Not a door opens; not a soul stirs. Hannah, as she moves up and down, is shunned as a person infected.
> (space, indicating time)
> The angry assembly is broken up. . . . I am ordered not to go to bed.
> (space)
> This moment the keys of everything are taken from me. It was proposed to send for me down: But my Father said, he could not bear to look upon me. . . . Shorey [mother's servant] was the messenger.
> (letter ends, and Letter I, no. 22, begins)
> Hannah has just brought me, from the private place in the garden wall, a Letter from Mr. Lovelace, deposited last night. (I, 158–59; I, 108–9)

I include so much of the text here because the juxtaposition of fragments, with spaces indicating time gaps, points up the three important but separate loci of Harlowe Place. Time gaps appear also as space gaps in the description of a family whose members align themselves in particular areas to impose pressure upon the outcast member: Clarissa is clearly alien to the rest, who are "shut up together." They plot their strategy, and she, presumably in her room, will have to answer as she can. There is no direct communication between the two places; servants function throughout this sequence of the novel as intermediaries, often bringing and taking the written letters that pass between the family and Clarissa. The hushed silence of the house—"not a door opens, not a soul stirs"—bespeaks the lack of human communication that Clarissa underlines when she tells Anna that the only fault of the Harlowes is that they are "*uncommunicative*" (II, 89; I, 300).

Finally it appears that some sort of plan has been formed: Clarissa's keys are to be taken away. It is the perfect Harlowe solution, of course, to keep the victim at a distance and out of visibility but to deny her her keys. That is, they can lock themselves up and cut off accessibility, but they will not allow her the same privilege. These keys must belong to her desk, because later (II, 247; I, 408) she is still talking about locking herself in to write; but in the epistolary world, the key to the drawer where one's letters are kept is analogous to the key to the room where one is—and ultimately, to one's own person. Ultimately in this Harlowe world too, having to give up one's key is giving up one's identity. Following the tumultuous scene with the family before Clarissa is supposed to be sent off to her uncle's "moated house," the heroine will be commanded to give up *all* her keys: to "cabinet, library, and drawers" (II, 223; I, 391). Certainly the key image maintains a strong sexual connection in *Clarissa* (particularly in connection with the rapist Lovelace, of course; note, for example, the involved ruse of the key in the escape from the garden [Letters II, nos. 16–17; I, nos. 61–62]), but Lovelace's sexual violation of Clarissa later in the novel is a crime of such enormity precisely because the key is already so closely related to attack upon individual identity.

If the first location referred to in Clarissa's letter is the enclosed parlor, and the second her own isolated chamber, the first sentence of Letter I, no. 22, indicates a third area related to the preceding two: the "private place in the garden wall." Here is Lovelace, of course, who in fact knows everything that goes on within the house through his hired spy and "pulls the strings" of the whole show by playing upon the Harlowes's worst impulses; the more the family pressures Clarissa toward Solmes, the more inclined will she be to go off with Lovelace. The "private place" is the place of secret communication between Clarissa and Lovelace, but it is closely bound up with the other "shut up" places of Harlowe Place because the family's attempt to confine Clarissa forces her to make use of the secret spot.

Because it is intimately connected with the transmission of Clarissa's letters, the secret place is even more importantly related to the private chamber where the letters are created. In a sense, the writing room is also invisible: we only know it by what is created there, who is in it, and perhaps where it is. Bourgeois drama focuses upon the room with every physical detail visible, a "locally human order of experience";[25] but we have, by contrast, no visual detail of Clarissa's writing place, and very little of the

parlor. We are aware of the chamber and the parlor as blank spaces awaiting their content in the same way as the room in Robert Morris's house
plan awaits whatever use the occupant desires.

We know when the heroine is "up" (in the chamber) and "down" (in the
parlor, the family's territory). "I will go down," "I thought I should have
been commanded down," or "I have been down" punctuate Clarissa's epistolary accounts of events. We know when she is alone and writing, and
when she is forced to encounter members of the family; this is an essential
division, reminding us that even when the epistolary character writes as
close "to the moment" as possible, there must always be gaps—of space
and of time. Letters record what John Preston has called the "Cartesian
moment," separated from past and future, enforcing a sense of isolation.[26]
Clarissa's writing place lies temporally and spatially between event (what
happened) and the recording of event as frozen within the letter space. Setting as referred to in Clarissa's statement, "I am in the ivy summer-house"
is not really simply defined; one frame of reference is juxtaposed to another: on the one hand, the past moment of the event recounted (even a
mental event) and, on the other hand, the place and moment that appear as
labels on the letter itself. In one sense the letter fuses the what happened
with the writing, but it also, of course, introduces still unknowable future
moments, future settings wherein readers will receive and read. "Don't
you see how crooked some of my lines are? Don't you see how some of the
letters stagger more than others?" (II, 335; I, 468), Clarissa anxiously asks
in the letter written in the ivy summer-house as she awaits the upcoming
interview with Lovelace; but Anna will only see after the fact, when the
present has become a past. Clarissa's depositing the letter away from herself—"I will hasten to deposit this"—already asserts that it belongs to a
different order of time and space. It will be read by Anna only after the
anxiety it contains has been realized in the fateful flight to St. Albans. By
that point, Clarissa herself also belongs to a different order: she has left her
father's house and followed the route of her letters.

If the writing chamber is necessarily isolated, it is, however, a very active
place in the first quarter of the novel. Of the first ninety-nine letters, for
example, sixty-nine emanate from Clarissa's writing place. The letters are
mainly narrative but are liberally interspersed with reflection: "my calamities have humbled me enough to make me turn my gaudy eye inward; to
make me look into myself.—And what I have discovered there?—Why,
my dear friend, more *secret* pride and vanity than I could have thought had
lain in my unexamined heart" (II, 264; I, 419–20). In a sense, of course,
there is no "inward" or secret examination within the epistolary form, be-

cause the letter must ever turn outward. In Clarissa's writing, nothing remains "unexamined." Our very reading of the product of the secret reflection is indicative that reflection has been transformed into public form. The writing process is apparently ceaseless. Even though Clarissa keeps very late hours—we find letters written at 3 A.M.—it may be argued that one day could not possibly contain within it the number of "experiencing" and "writing" hours that Clarissa habitually spends. She makes repeated references to her confinement (to her uncle: "[I am] confined, like a prisoner, to narrow and disgraceful limits" [I, 228; I, 156]; to Solmes: "I am confined, banished, insulted. . . ." [II, 212; I, 383]); but she is nonetheless an active force in this section of the novel. She writes, receives, encloses, edits, transcribes. It is, of course, because she is confined that she must write. Despite the supposed presence of her pert "gaoleress" Betty, she makes frequent trips to the secret places in the garden, and the letters flow unhampered. There is always another bottle of ink somewhere, even after the depredations of the family upon her writing supplies. For the family knows their victory cannot be complete until they have prohibited Clarissa from writing; even Betty the servant knows that: "Yet one hint I must conclude with; that your pen and ink (soon as you are to go away) will not be long in your power, I do assure you, Miss. And then, having lost *that* amusement, it will be seen, how a mind so active as yours will be able to employ itself" (II, 237; I, 401). Betty is right. A mind as "active" as Clarissa's must commit experience to the letter; she must remove herself from the parlor, her place of trial, to gain her own chamber and the only place that is truly hers: the private space of the letter.[27]

The private writing place is an active place because it is a locus of transformation: the transformation of mental event into language. The transmission of Clarissa's letter through the secret place in the wall—and then on, into the public world—analogizes the initial "transmission" that in Rilke's phrase "translates things" (*traduit les choses*). Rilke asks, "How can we endure, how can we save the visible, if it is not in the formation of the language of absence and of the invisible?"[28] In epistolary form however, while the notion of "absence" is particularly appropriate, we must speak of "translation" not into "invisibility," but rather into another kind of visibility. If the writing chamber lies between the world and the structured letter, it is, to this degree, an image for the writer's consciousness through which everything we read in the letter has already been refined and brought to birth. Roland Barthes makes a similar connection between the chamber and the "site of language" when he points out that the "antechamber" in Racinian tragedy is "a medium of transmission; it partakes of both interior and exterior. . . . It is between the world, place of action, and the Chamber, a place of silence."[29] In Racine's tragic locale, the "nontragic personnel" live in the exterior, site of "escape and event," and are the message bearers to the tragic character dwelling in the "antechamber." This notion of the coming and going of "messengers" is borne out also in the world of Harlowe Place, though not so much in terms of personnel (Betty, of course, does have that function) as in written messages or letters. In Barthes's words, these are the "fragments of the external world, distilled as *news*"; but there is always a "distortion" between the event and the event as reported, and the individual dependent upon such messages must always dwell in "irremediable uncertainty."[30]

The dilemma of being totally dependent upon the messages from the outside—and, we should add, *to* the outside—and being left only to oneself to deal with the dreadful uncertainty will be felt by Clarissa most acutely when she is confined within Mrs. Sinclair's inner house with free access to the outside world barred. She will not receive the letter from Anna informing her of Lovelace's perfidy; the privacy of consciousness and of the inner chamber will be threatened, and written communication will stagger to a halt. But if the room within the brothel represents the terminus of Clarissa's movement toward privacy, her direction is clearly established in the Harlowe Place sequence of the novel. In each of the three major instances of Clarissa's encounters with the family in the parlor (Letters I, no. 21 [both editions] and II, no. 33; I, no. 78) the heroine's movement is one of withdrawal from the relative publicness of the parlor to the privacy of her own room.

This is not to deny that the parlor is a room usually connected with privacy in the familial or domestic sense. Even by the early seventeenth century, the "hall" or "house body," once the dominant space of the country house, had become merely an entrance area to other parts; and the hall, with its public, communal associations, gave way in importance to the parlor, a more interior chamber, the place of the now more narrowly defined family.[31] In Richardson, however, where the privacy of the individual is at issue, the parlor may be viewed as a public place, even a stage set where the Harlowes attempt to direct the drama in which Clarissa is the major participant.

Who controls the acting space is integrally related, first of all, to who owns it. In Letter I, no. 21 (I, 152–58; I, 104–9), when Clarissa reports that Solmes "stalked in," the unwelcome suitor enters Bella's parlor. For this encounter, Clarissa has been caught in an alien place: "My Sister triumphed. I was vexed to be so caught," she later reports to Anna (I, 153; I,

105). Clarissa's only recourse is to behave with such rudeness that her mother is forced to lead her out of the room to *her own* parlor, where she reiterates her determination never to think of Mr. Solmes as possible spouse. It is fitting that Clarissa asserts herself in what is—or at least, *was*—her own parlor. Bella has not really triumphed after all. Her mother pleads with her to "go in again to Mr. Solmes, and behave discreetly to him," but the daughter tells Anna, "My feet moved [of *themselves*, I think] farther from the parlor where he was, and towards the stairs" (I, 157; I, 108). The staircase is the way to the upstairs bedchamber, movement thither a further assertion of self. Once the writer is in her own place, wherein the letter we read is being written, the particular room below can be subsumed into her own consciousness. Clarissa will no longer refer to "Bella's parlour" but, rather, to the place "where he [Solmes] was." In a sense, Bella's parlor is now Clarissa's also; it appears in Clarissa's letter and has relevance only according to the action that she has described.

The next two encounters in the parlor are both described within Letter II, no. 33 (I, no. 78), which Clarissa writes to Anna at a time of "excessive uneasiness." She begins her letter: "Well, my dear, I am alive, and here! But how long I shall be either here or alive, I cannot say. I have a vast deal to write" (II, 200; I, 375). This time Clarissa carefully explains at the outset the system of exits from the room; for as the total situation worsens, and the search for privacy more intensely dramatized, doors become increasingly important:

> There are two doors to *my* parlour, as I used to call it. As I entered at one, my friends [family] hurried out at the other. I saw just the gown of my Sister, the last who slid away. . . . And they all remained in the next parlour, a wainscot partition only parting the two. I remember them both in one: But they were separated in favour of us girls, for each to receive her visitors in at her pleasure. (II, 202; I, 377)

The "wainscot partition" does not really insure privacy, however, for the family remain as audience to Clarissa's meeting with Mr. Solmes. When the interview with the would-be suitor reaches an impasse—he, refusing to give up his suit, and she, pleading in vain that he not "have a young creature compelled in the most material article of her life, for the sake of [financial] motives she despises" (II, 205; I, 379)—then Uncle Antony bursts upon the scene: "So Niece, so!—Sitting in State like a Queen, giving audience! *haughty* Audience! Mr. Solmes, why stand you thus humbly?—Why this distance, man? I hope to see you upon a more intimate footing before we part." Typically, the physical distance at which Clarissa has held Mr. Solmes (for she had placed herself in one of the fireside chairs and begun busily to fan herself as soon as Solmes entered the room) spells her determination never to accept this man as her husband. Another verbal battle thus follows, with Clarissa finally declaring to Solmes: "Sir, you shall sooner follow me to the grave *indeed.* I will undergo the cruellest death—I will even consent to enter into the awful vault of my ancestors, and to have that bricked up upon me, rather than consent to be miserable for life" (II, 207; I, 380). To escape what she has already called being "circumscribed" in Solmes's "selfish circle" (I, 232; I, 158), she will choose the enclosure of the grave: the most private place. For the moment, however, her desire is to regain the solitude of her own room, privacy in another form. Hence she moves towards the door:

> I was going out at the door I came in at . . . and whom should I meet at the door but my Brother, who had heard all that had passed!
> He bolted upon me so unexpectedly, that I was surprised. He took my hand, and grasped it with violence. Return, pretty Miss, said he; return, if you please. You shall not yet be *bricked up.*

James does not want to see his sister "bricked up" and free of Harlowe influence; he will not allow such enclosure in a private place but will use even physical violence to return Clarissa to the control of the family. Thus the scene goes on, Clarissa attempting to move "with trembling feet towards the door" and gaining finally a brief hiatus in the garden.

Clarissa reenters the house for the second round, and once again the scene climaxes around the door. The dialogue this time is mainly between James and Clarissa, until Clarissa hears her father's voice thundering through the wall: "Son James, let the Rebel be this moment carried away to my Brother's" (II, 221; I, 390). Clarissa tries desperately to force her way into the other room, to make a visible contact with her father:

> Yet, not knowing what I did or said, I flew to the door, and would have opened it: But my Brother pulled it to, and held it close by the key. . . .
> I will not stir from my knees, continued I, without admission.—At this door I beg it!—O let it be the door of mercy! and open it to me. . . .
> The door was endeavoured to be opened on the inside, which made my Brother let go the key on a sudden; and I pressing against it . . . fell flat on my face into the other parlour. (II, 221; I, 390)

The humiliating fall through the door into an empty room, into a vacuum, yields nothing but pain; the others have all gone away to search her cabinet and drawers, and a servant informs her she must wait below. She cannot reach the family, but they continue to threaten her secret space. Concealment will become more and more necessary, and Clarissa will close her letter with "How lucky it was that I had got away my papers!" (II, 238; I, 401).

In order to protect herself, Clarissa must protect the papers, the recorded self. The relationship between the room, the papers, and the heroine herself will be drawn much more strongly in the section of the novel located in Mrs. Sinclair's house; but within Harlowe Place too, concealment (in the "secret place") is an integral element in the writing process. In those scenes where Clarissa is attacked upon her ground, within her own chamber, she moves further within, toward the writing closet. When the ever nasty Bella comes to Clarissa to taunt her, to dare her to tell her parents she refuses to go to her uncle's house, Clarissa reports:

> I want not to be led. . . . I *will* go [and tell them]: And was posting to the stairs accordingly in my passion, But she got between me and the door and shut it—. . . . But yet opening the door again, seeing me shrink back [at the news that James Harlowe is with his parents]—Go if you will! . . . [She followed] me to my closet, whither I retired . . . and pulled the sash door after me. (II, 47–48; I, 271)

There are two directions one can move from Clarissa's chamber: toward the staircase and hence down to the family's territory, or toward the yet more private place, the closet. Bella invades Clarissa's chamber as far as the closet door, but further than this she cannot penetrate: Clarissa enters the closet and closes the sash door. Neither Bella's person nor her eye will be granted access to this private space: "[Bella] looked thro' the glass at me. And at last, which vexed her to the heart, I drew the silk curtain, that she should not see me." The closing of the door, the drawing of the curtain, and finally the writing of the letter, all define private letter writing in the first volume of *Clarissa*. The curtain closing over the pane of glass makes its own striking commentary on the opening of both door and curtain in the final volume of the novel. But between these two interrelated acts lies the destruction of private space within Mrs. Sinclair's London brothel.

MRS. SINCLAIR'S HOUSE

The Destruction of Private Space

> I am a prisoner . . . in the vilest of houses.
>
> *Clarissa*

It is surprising that critics of *Clarissa* have not paid more attention to Mrs. Sinclair's London brothel, that "vilest of houses" in which Clarissa finds herself imprisoned in the second major sequence of letters comprising the novel.[1] More than mere setting, this double house, within which a sense of enclosure dominates over specific sensory detail, tangibly represents the action, and epistolary action of Richardson's novel. Clarissa's confinement at the hands of Lovelace signals that she has in fact lost control of the writing space of the book: she is both victim and epistolary subject of the rake who dispatches his spies, peers through the keyhole, invades Clarissa's private space—and writes most of the letters in this portion of the novel.

This is not to deny that Mrs. Sinclair's house is a moral statement. Just as its prostituted occupants don masks and costumes, the brothel itself is a corrupted house posing as respectable. Here too is the standard stuff of eighteenth-century seduction plots as Lovelace, arch play-maker, directs his tawdry cast of whores who play their assorted roles in the ruination of the innocent virgin.[2] In Richardson's novel, however, the condemnation of masquerade is related to what is also an epistolary problem: the exploration of the relationship of public/visible to private/interior. The inner house that is Clarissa's prison is also an interior stage upon which the heroine must wage alone the battle of virtue against corruption. Lovelace encroaches on her chamber, her correspondence, and her person; the struggle

35

to protect moral integrity is also one to maintain all private spaces intact. Like Harlowe Place, Mrs. Sinclair's house, the place of harlots, contains differentiated zones, supposed private and public areas; Clarissa's chamber, for example, is opposed to the dining room (where her meetings with Lovelace correspond to those with the Harlowes at Harlowe Place). Like the differentiated spaces that comprise the Harlowe family seat, too, the rooms of Mrs. Sinclair's brothel represent both process and product, individuated consciousness and isolated letter texts. When the rake accomplishes the rape of Clarissa, we witness not only the destruction of private space and private letter writing in the novel but also the opening up of the interior stage that analogizes Richardson's accomplishment in his own epistolary structure. Clarissa is broken as a private individual only to gain new identity as a public saint, just as the integrity of a single letter must be "broken" in order to become an element in a public form.

Well might Anna Howe warn Clarissa to beware of the city, for London is the world, a difficult and hard world fraught with the dangers of duplicity and anonymity. Mrs. Sinclair's house, a place of masquerade and play, is a microcosm of those urban evils that poets in the retirement tradition, writers of popular fiction, and domestic dramatists had all decried.[3] To step into the public sphere before the larger audience represented in the city is to enter into what Lady Mary Wortley Montagu was to call the "affectation of the mall."[4] The city is the place where one risks the loss of authenticity, of one's own identity; it is, as Richard Sennett has pointed out, a "gathering of strangers," where young newcomers especially were cut off from past associations "without even the marks of a past life as adults."[5] But if the twentieth-century sociologist Sennett tends to view positively the possibilities for role playing on this urban stage, Richardson does not. When Clarissa Harlowe is duped by Lovelace into leaving her family home and her position there, she is reduced to what she calls a "mere cypher." She is removed from that supposed inner world of feeling in which sentimental letter writers were wont to dwell. To carry on a search for personal meaning in the city the individual can only attempt to create his or her own inner world.

Because it is the inner world that occupies so much of Richardson's attention, we do not expect here the same kind of topographical realism that we find in a Defoe novel. To borrow Ian Watt's term, Richardson may be seen as the novelist of the suburb rather than that of the city.[6] Moll Flanders's London differs from Clarissa's. In *Moll*, for example, Newgate exerts an ironic force because it is a foul prison from which death or transportation are the major exit routes, and it is greatly to the credit of Moll's resourcefulness that the prison does become for her a gate to a new place; but Newgate is a real place and the streets that Moll traverses are real streets too.[7] It is impossible, however, to locate exactly Mrs. Sinclair's house on the eighteenth-century London map, because Richardson's realism is realized not so much through place names and association as in the shape and pattern of the urban landscape.

When Richardson does provide us with topographical hints as to the location of the brothel, it is within a framework that bespeaks moral confusion: the faked letter from Thomas Doleman (alias Lovelace) was planned to make Clarissa think she is making a choice according to her own will. She does not yet know that letters are not to be trusted in this world she has entered through Lovelace. The rake shows the letter to Clarissa ostensibly for the information it contains on rental lodgings in Hanover Square, Soho Square, Golden Square, and the "new streets about Grosvenor Square" (III, 196; II, 111). Clarissa reports to Anna that she has also considered lodgings in either Norfolk Street or Cecil Street. These are all eminently respectable areas that sprang into being in the rash of expansion that began in London after the great fire in 1666. Clarissa tells her friend, however, that she has decided to take up residence in the house of a widow on Dover Street, who

> rents two good houses, distant from each other, only joined by a *large handsome passage*. The *inner house* is the genteelest, and is very elegantly furnished; but you may have the use of a very handsome parlour in the *outer-house* if you chuse to look into the street. . . .
>
> The apartments she has to let are in the inner house: They are a dining-room, two neat parlours, a withdrawing room, two or three handsome bedchambers. (III, 194; II, 110)

We pass immediately from the apparent topographical fixity of the map to the bifurcated house that can exist in no real street because it is no real house. If the house were actually on Dover Street, as the letter suggests, it would be in the very respectable parish of St. James Westminster, a "dignified" though "not wholly exclusive" area, a place of "family domesticity" in the eighteenth century.[8] Anna Howe tells Clarissa, however, in the letter that never reaches its proper addressee, that the wicked house she inhabits is not really in Dover Street at all: "[If you ever went out and returned by another coach or chair], you would never have found your way to the vile house, either by the Woman's name, *Sinclair*, or by the Street's name mentioned by that Doleman in his Letter about the lodgings" (V, 32; III, 2). Clarissa is so readily confused and misled because she had no external referent, no connection with the outside world beyond that which the protean Lovelace provides. We may assume that she is in, or at least near, St. James's parish because she is seen attending services at St. James (V, 34; III, 4); but the exact location must be vague because the external world bears ultimately little relevance to the inner world of Mrs. Sinclair's house in which the heroine is confined.

Still, the map of London in the first quarter of the eighteenth century lends itself well to the novelist's exploration of inner depth and outer duplicity, the tension between private and public. In the map we see why the city is the place in which to be private (II, 267; I, 421–22); here is the city that an anonymous contributor to the *Ladies Magazine* (January 26, 1751) described as

> Houses, Churches, mix'd together;
> Streets, unpleasant in all weather;
> Prison, Palaces, contiguous,
> Gates; a Bridge, the Thames irriguous.
> . . . .
> Gaudy Things enough to tempt ye;
> Showy Outsides; Insides empty.⁹

The writer of these lines (who apparently shares what Watt would call the "suburban" fear of the multifaceted city) expresses through his less than successful poetry—"Thames irriguous"—an image of the city that we find presented graphically in Strype's edition of John Stow's *Survey of the Cities of London and Westminster* (1720).¹⁰ Commenting on the postfire building in St. James's parish, Golden Square, Soho, and Covent Garden—the areas mentioned in the Dolman letter—Strype says they are all "very populous, and full of courts and alleys"; there has been a great "encrease of Buildings, in converting of gardens and great Houses into *Courts, Squares*, and *Alleys* throughout the whole City" (p. 80). Although the building schemes such as those around St. James Square were laid out according to what John Summerson calls a "complete unit of development, comprising square, secondary streets, market and perhaps, church,"¹¹ Strype's map and commentary give the impression not so much of order as of what is "mix'd together," another form of moral emptiness ("Showy Outsides; Insides empty"). The intricate narrow passage is juxtaposed to the "good handsome Street." Consider Market Lane, for example,

> which also takes its Name from the Market near adjoyning, and lyeth on the Backside of the *Haymarket* [a "spacious Street of great Re-

sort"], into which it hath an ordinary and narrow Passage through Six Bell Alley, a Place for Stablings. In this Lane is *Salter's Court*, a small square Place, ill inhabited. Here is also another small Place called *Parson's Court*. (p. 81)

The same parish that contains Burlington House, with its "large Court Yard before, and a spacious garden behind, which fronts the Fields; and from thence receives a fresh and wholesome Air" (p. 83), is also the locale of Shrug Lane ("but meanly built, neither are its Inhabitants much to be boasted of," p. 84) and Knaves Acre ("narrow and cheeply inhabited by those that deal in old goods and glass Bottles," p. 84). Golden Square, "a very handsome open Place, railed round . . . and having very good Houses, inhabited by gentry on all Sides" stands in marked contrast to Maidenhead Passage just to the west of it (p. 84). Commenting on Strype's map, Summerson has written that although narrow-fronted houses form by far the most numerous units in London of that period, they

> do not cover the whole area. They are merely the breastworks of inner areas, where alleys, courts, yards and closes meet each other in an inscrutable topographical jig-saw. These hinterlands contained both the best and worse of mercantile London. At one extreme there was the long, broad, paved court, with a fine house fitting the end, equally good houses along the sides, and an entry to the main street wide enough for a coach or cart. At the other extreme was the miserable, unpaved alley, hastily built in the garden of a once affluent house as a means of producing rent from the labouring class which clustered around the advancing standard of capitalism. The hinterlands, in fact, belonged to the Londoner who did not require a shopfront.[12]

Summerson leads our eye to the "hinterlands" behind the broad spacious roadway or court, to what is not immediately visible; the map he describes, the city Richardson would have known, may have led the novelist, like our anonymous poet, to consider what is outside and what inside. There is something very vague about this nameless mercantile occupier of the hinterland; the brothel does not require a shopfront either. The landscape Strype provides is a fit setting for Mrs. Sinclair's house. The city, like the house, provides its own kind of privacy too, the privacy of anonymity.

As the events in Mrs. Sinclair's brothel demonstrate, Richardson was keenly aware of the danger in the narrow passage behind the broad thoroughfare, the invisible hinterland beyond the respectable row of houses.

The question of what is within dominates the treatment of setting in Mrs. Sinclair's house. This is why we do not find in Richardson—as we would in Defoe—specific use of street names. Angel Court, Maidenhead Passage, and Knave's Acre may all be fitting locations for the rape of Clarissa Harlowe; but if the names sit within the novelist's own imagination, it is shape, particularly depth, which dominates the creation as it comes to us.

Let us look again at the plan of Mrs. Sinclair's house, for the description Clarissa gives to Anna that she has received from the Dolman letter is not entirely accurate. Later, when the heroine is actually residing there, she will give a more exact account: "I told *him* [Lovelace] . . . that I desired that this apartment might be considered as my Retirement: That when I saw him, it might be in the Dining-room (which is up a few stairs; for this back house being once two, the rooms do not all of them very conveniently communicate with each other)" (III, 317; II, 193). Clarissa's room is once again a letter-writing setting; the heroine still tries to define a private place as a differentiated space. We learn here also, however, that the rooms do not "very conveniently communicate with each other," and there is no mention of the "large handsome passage" that supposedly (according to Dolman's letter) joins the inner and outer houses. We are reminded, rather, of the uncommunicative Harlowe family. Subsequent references to the passageway, as will be apparent later, convey a sense of neither breadth nor handsomeness. Mrs. Sinclair's house is an image in miniature of the city as we see it in Strype's *Survey*; it too contains its hinterland, its interstices that contrast with an open respectable facade. The lack of communication between inner and outer, private and public, suggests, moreover, Clarissa's own position in the house. Ultimately she will not be able to "communicate very conveniently" either: she will not be able to send out her private letters into the public world.

Once again, Richardson blends the real and symbolic in specifically spatial terms, providing in the epistolary setting (and action) the analogue to the urban landscapes he would have known so well. For Richardson was—Ian Watt to the contrary—a city person, spending many years after 1721 in a house in Salisbury Court (off Fleet Street), a "stronghold of City respectability."[13] He would be well aware that the typical construction of the London house was based on the principle of the use of depth: narrow-fronted houses were situated on sites stretching back to twice their width or more. The pattern goes back to the later Middle Ages, when with the crowding of the street fronts it was only natural that builders take advantage of the space behind. In describing the city, the area Richardson would have known so well, Summerson writes that "the houses turned inwards, here in the form of a 'court' or 'yard,' there lining an alley. . . . By the time of the fire this process of increment and involution had reached its ultimate stage; every square yard of the City was utilized. And when the City was rebuilt this old land utilization was perpetuated in the new structures of red brick."[14] Again, Summerson's description emphasizes the turning inwards, penetrating into the space behind or within. Economic factors forced the development of such housing, and the pattern of the narrow front and extension to the back is repeated over and over in the houses of London, in the city and in the newer areas, such as St. James Westminster, opening up to the west.[15] In the imagination of the novelist, however, surely housing such as this provides a suitable locale for privacy—the exploration of one's own being, which in Clarissa's words "turns the gaudy eye inwards" (II, 264; I, 419–20). When Clarissa tells Lovelace that her apartment is for her own "retirement" she really means *privacy*: being alone in a room that does not "conveniently communicate" with any other room. Privacy as sought by the heroine is the need of the soul in distress; it has a distinctively spiritual character. Lovelace will mock his victim's writing in her closed chamber as a "holy ritual," and the letter itself as the "sacred" artifact (III, 176; II, 97), but the private space *is* a holy place in Clarissa, a place for looking "inwards" and away from "worldly objects." It has a character similar to that described by a young woman dissenter in Gloucestershire in the 1750s, wrote:

> O love thy closets, send thy cares away,
> And to thy heavenly Father daily pray!
> Here, worldly objects do not tempt thy sight,
> But heavenly things appear in strongest light.
> . . . .
> Retire for converse with thy subtle heart,
> Enquire what once thou wer't, what now thou art.[16]

Mrs. Sinclair's house, located within the highly ambiguous and anonymous precincts of eighteenth-century London, proves a "body" for Richardson's epistolary art: in one sense a corrupted body hiding a morally rotten interior, its very bifurcation underlines Richardson's exploration of the relationship between private experience and public expression. The novelist must, like Lovelace, enter the interior space and break it open. That is why the action of *Clarissa* moves even further inward in the London brothel sequence and why, too, Richardson contrasts Clarissa's letter writing with the false publicizing, the duplicitous use of imagination, which marks the inmates of Mrs. Sinclair's infamous house.

In the terms I have used throughout this study, the "family" of harlots represents the perversion of privacy: they function within the interior, pseudodomestic space but comprise a microcosmic picture of public, social, and moral chaos. They point up the fragility of a so-called authentic identity where the presentation of self in the external world balances, reinforces, and justly represents those feelings and values known only to the private self. The split identity that Richardson images in the harlots and their house really underlines, then, the difficulty of authenticating private feelings and judgments in the world without. The sisterhoods that populate the brothels of eighteenth-century drama and fiction are not women of the street but, rather, empty role-players acting out their parts on an interior stage. They don masks because they have no real identity of their own. When Clarissa is tricked by Lovelace into returning to Mrs. Sinclair's house (after her temporary escape to Hampstead), she is led, partially drugged, by two supposed ladies, whores posing as relatives of Lovelace. Similarly, the female victim in Johnson's *Caelia* is told by the bawd Mrs. Lupine to put on her mask (I, ii); with the assistance of prostitutes, Fielding's debauched cleric Commons (*The Letter-Writers*, 1731) plays at being Alexander the Great; and a woman in one of Richard Steele's essays from *The Theatre* (1720), seduced through the dissimulation of a lover, finds herself in a city brothel where "whores take names of such Women of Beauty and Quality, as they resemble in Air, Shape, and Stature."[17] Ronald Paulson's comment on Hogarth's harlot (in *The Harlot's Progress*), that she "has no character of her own [and can only reflect] the society in which she finds herself," is particularly apt.[18] So too the pseudo ladies in Mrs. Sinclair's house, Sally Martin and Polly Horton. Sally, a mercer's daughter of no very great sense, originally met the rake Lovelace at a masquerade (VIII, 289; IV, 539) we are told; enthralled with the attentions of the "presumptive heir of Lord M.," she has allowed her pride to outweigh her discretion. She has attempted to rise above herself, and a fateful fall is inevitable. Ironically, she is left only playing at the role of lady.

Even more specifically, Sally plays at being a member of Lovelace's family. If the prostitutes only reflect characteristics of society, as Paulson asserts, they can also be designated only according to family roles. Clarissa interprets the sisters of the brothel within the categories she has always known: components of the family unit—aunt, mother, sister, cousin; and hence her most terrifying moment, that in which she is raped, is also the moment in which "Mother Sinclair" drops all her feminine guises: gone is the feminine "obsequiousness" and in its place Clarissa sees a "masculine air, and fierce look" (V, 312; III, 195). Those destructive tendencies that Richardson has already explored in the Harlowes are thus borne out fully in the harlot "family." The supposed domestic sphere in which feelings are to be nurtured and understood does not protect the authenticity of the individual self.

In the epistolary world it is ultimately to letters, the created documents, that we must look for validation or authentication of the individual self. Authenticity, a term used in epistolary rhetoric to indicate the "real" or actual document, acquires also the sense of "real" as accurate record of consciousness. In *Clarissa*, and the London pre-rape sequence in particular, authenticity stands in marked contrast to the harlot's mask and that world where sexual and imaginative play each highlight the other.[19] Clarissa suffers no moral death, no bifurcation between inner and outer, private and public. She is always seen in the same white dress because her clothing is part of her identity. By the same token, the "ample repository" that Lovelace describes as having been formerly used to "hold the richest suits which some of the nymphs put on, when they are to be dressed out, to captivate, or to ape quality" (IV, 47; II, 268–69)—this chest becomes the storage place for letters written to preserve the wholeness of the inner self.

Certainly the thrust of the action within Mrs. Sinclair's house is the emphasis on the reliability of the heroine's letters as encapsulations of private experience, a so-called real self; but this is not to deny Richardson's keen awareness of the function of visibility in familiar letter writing: letters are always visible acknowledgement both to the self and to the audience/addressee, and acknowledgement is an important element in the world of *Clarissa*. Even Lovelace is aware that some things ought not to be public and visible when he tells Belford: "But have not you and I, Belford, seen young wives who could be thought modest . . . permit freedoms in public from uxorious husbands which have shewn that both of them have forgotten what belongs either to prudence or decency?" (IV, 348; II, 472–73). Public acknowledgement takes on an even more serious significance, however, when it becomes exposure. After the rape, Clarissa must face the question of whether to expose herself to public view in order to satisfy her family's demands for a public prosecution of Lovelace. Dr. Lewen, the family's old cleric, puts the case to Clarissa:

> And can indignities of any kind be *properly pardoned* till we have it in *our power to punish them?* [and] . . . how will injuries be believed to grieve us, that are never honourably complained of? . . .

It is a terrible circumstance, I once more own, for a young lady of your delicacy to be under the obligation of telling so shocking a story in public court: but it is still a worse imputation, that she should pass over so mortal an injury unresented. (VII, 227; IV, 182)

Dr. Lewen explains to Clarissa the simple fact that she must publicly acknowledge the "injury" if Lovelace's guilt is to be believed: "Little, very little difference is there, my dear young Lady, between a *suppressed* evidence, and a *false* one (VII, 227; IV, 182); if Clarissa really wants to punish Lovelace, then she must bring the "shocking story" to public visibility. Clarissa will be driven to examine her own motives also, to acknowledge her own error in leaving her father's house with the rake. Hence, she connects "private guilt" and "public shame" when she answers Dr. Lewen, "It is certain, that creatures who cannot stand the shock of *public shame* should be doubly careful how they expose themselves to the danger of incurring *private guilt*, which may possibly bring them to it" (VII, 229–30; IV, 184). Clarissa had already acknowledged to herself her own role in events: "It would, no doubt, have been a ready retort from *every* mouth, that I ought not to have thrown myself into the power of such a man, and that I ought to take for my pains what had befallen me." She will not stand as public evidence against Lovelace; she will not expose herself in that way. She declares that her mind is still "untainted," her morals intact, and her "will unviolated" (VII, 232; IV, 186). The letter she writes is, then, the only public acknowledgement she will make.

Whether or not the letter creates a "spectacle"—to use Belford's term, when he attempts to dissuade Lovelace from pursuing his plan of seducing Clarissa—it always involves an acknowledgement. For that reason, too, it can be dangerous: by agreeing to correspond secretly with Lovelace from Harlowe Place, Clarissa acknowledged her attraction toward the rake. How dangerous acknowledgement can be, especially for a woman, is explained by Harriet Byron in *Sir Charles Grandison* when she writes to her family, "I know that he has no notion of the Love called *Platonic*. Nor have I: I think it, in general, a dangerous allowance; and with regard to our sex, a very unequal one; since, while the man has nothing to fear, the woman has everything from the privileges that may be claimed, in an *acknowledged* confidence" (II, 331–32). In love with Sir Charles, Harriet must face the question of how much, if at all, she should acknowledge her feelings. In an important sense, however, the moment of acknowledgement is the moment the pen meets the paper. If letter writing has "that advantage from sitting down to write . . . which prompt speech could not always have" (IV, 288;

II, 432), creating what Anna Howe calls the "witness on record" (IV, 85; II, 294) has its drawbacks also. Letters frequently serve as evidence, as when at Harlowe Place Clarissa hastens to put the letters away from herself, into the "secret place," lest they incriminate her. Lovelace uses the term "indict-ment" to Belford in a letter where sexual excitement runs high, and he de-scribes his intent to join surprise to intimidation in his invasion of Clarissa:

> I must add, that I have for some time been convinced, that I have done wrong, to scribble to thee so freely as I have done (and the more so, if I make the Lady legally mine); for has not every Letter I have written to thee, been a Bill of Indictment against myself? . . .
> I am so ready to accuse myself in my narrations; yet I have some-thing to say *for* myself *to* myself, as I go along. (IV, 382–84; II, 495–97)

The rake suggests, further, that the indictment points in two directions: that one is always creating a spectacle for oneself as well as for the corre-spondent; that writing to the fellow rake is an act of self-extension. Rich-ardson has structured some two-thirds of his novel around correspon-dences between two like individuals. He describes *Clarissa* as "a series of letters written principally in a double yet separate correspondence between two young ladies of virtue and honour . . . and between two gentlemen of free lives" (author's preface). According to the dynamic Richardson sets up here, when the positions of Clarissa and Lovelace change vis-à-vis each other, after the rape, each moves away psychologically from his/her correspondent.

Self-extension, the process whereby the individual letter writer may substitute self for addressee, is built into the epistolary endeavor.[20] François Jost has referred to the "*Ich-Roman*" (I-novel) as one in which the "I" is both subject and object;[21] in epistolary form we have the added dimension of the "I" as reader. The letter reveals a version of the self to the self as the writer sees "what he is living and what he is writing."[22] Harriet Byron in *Sir Charles Grandison* speaks of "undrawing the curtain" (on self), "putting off disguises," when she writes to her own family of her love for Sir Charles (I, p. 308). Clarissa, isolated from her family, is faced with some-thing more difficult. In her first letter to Anna after leaving Harlowe Place, she writes, "Here I must suspend my relation for a while: For now I am come to this sad period of it, my indiscretion stares me in the face; and my shame and my grief give me a compunction that is more poignant me-thinks than if I had a dagger in my heart" (II, 359; I, 485). What the heroine sees in her own letter brings "shame" and "grief." The act of writing the letter concretizes the event, which literally stares at the writer from the paper where it has taken on a separate existence. Here is the writer as "object as well as subject," and here is the pain of recognizing one's own guilt, the pain of acknowledgement. But Clarissa will write on because the creation of the visible image takes the form also of an exorcism of guilt. One writes to "disburden" oneself, as she tells Anna after she has gone off with the rake:

> And I must write on, altho' I were not to send it to anybody. You have often heard me own the advantages I have found from writing down everything of moment that befals me; and of all I *think*, and of all I *do*, that may be of future use to me. . . . [When] I set down what I *will* do, or what I *have* done, on this or that occasion; the resolution or action is before me either to be adhered to, withdrawn, or amended; and I have entered into *compact* with myself. (III, 221; II, 128)

To enter into a "compact" with the self necessitates the construction of an objectified "I," what Cynthia Wolff has called an alter ego. In her work on Richardson's characters seen against a background of Puritanism, Wolff has cogently demonstrated the relationship between Puritan diary keeping and the function of letter writing in both *Pamela* and *Clarissa*. The preoccupation with minutiae, with matters pertaining to sexuality, with the search for God's perordained plan in an individual life, the anxiety to ferret out hidden motivations—these are the characteristics of diaries and letter journals kept by individuals trying to find out where they stand in regard to membership in the body of the elect.[23] These are the characteristics of self examining self within the private place, room or letter.

If "putting off the disguise" and seeking out what Clarissa calls the "dangers within" ("[In the ages from sixteen to twenty-one] our dangers multiply, both from *within* and *without*" [III, 215; II, 124]) are also functions of letter writing, then the "double" created in the letter is far more than a visible mask.[24] Especially during the long trial period before the rape, the letters are written, as Clarissa has said, for the self; they record the shape of the inner life. The plot underlines the self-examining function of letter writing in the London sequence, because Lovelace prohibits Clarissa from sending out and receiving her letters; but in so doing, the rake sets up circumstances that in fact strengthen the victim's will. Clarissa is never separated from her letter in the way that the morally dead whore is separate from her mask or the inner house from its outer face. That bonding between self and letter is tantamount to moral wholeness. By the same token Richardson's exploration of the images of privacy—the room, the body, and the letter—is also a moral statement.

Clarissa's search for privacy in the brothel parallels the earlier attempt within Harlowe Place, but now Richardson compresses and interweaves the images of room, body, and letter, and the preservation of all three acquires greater significance as Lovelace increases his attacks from without. From the point in the London sequence where we see Clarissa mellowing toward the rake/seducer—"I am afraid to look back upon what I have written" (IV, 298; II, 439)—until her first letter after the rape (VI, 115; III, 321), Lovelace controls the letter space of the novel. Lovelace's dominance is perfectly appropriate to the brothel setting, for he belongs to the world of masquerade and corrupted fantasy that we have seen as characteristic of the whorehouse. This means, however, that Clarissa's chamber, her place of retirement, is no longer the active place it was in the Harlowe Place sequence or even in the earlier part of the London confinement. Rather, this room becomes, like its occupant, something acted upon, which Clarissa tries vainly to maintain free of Lovelace's invading presence. More exactly than at Harlowe Place the images are those of interiority: the moral battle is waged within.

Two letters from the brothel exemplify how Richardson sets up what I have called the images of privacy within the inner house. Letter III, no. 59 (II, no. 56), first of all, is the "to-the-moment" account of Clarissa's experiences soon after her arrival in the inner house of Mrs. Sinclair's establishment. The letter moves us through Clarissa's consciousness of her own experience of entrapment, even as it sets up spatial relationships that point toward Lovelace's ultimate control of the situation. In its essential structure it is similar to the letters we have already examined as written from Harlowe Place; but the situation is really quite different, too, for Clarissa is now "in the *world*" (as Anna will tell her in her next letter, III, 327; II, 200), and this letter, though apparently under her own control, is being written under circumstances that we know are not what Clarissa thinks they are. Much more than at Harlowe Place, Lovelace "pulls the strings."

Clarissa begins with an apparent brightness and confidence: "At length, my dearest Miss Howe, I am in London" (III, 315; II, 192). She expresses some slight concern at the mien of the "old gentlewoman" (Mrs. Sinclair) but passes it off. It is clear that she is feeling the effects of Lovelace's "genteel spirit." Suddenly, however, there is a break on the page, and when the text continues again, Lovelace himself has entered the picture: "Here I was broken in upon by Mr. Lovelace; introducing the widow leading in a kinswoman of hers to attend me, if I approved of her, till my Hannah should come" (III, 316; II, 193). Lovelace has entered her room, her letter, her consciousness, and with Lovelace, enter also the inevitable questions. Should she accept Dorcas (the supposed servant; actually Lovelace's hireling, another whore in disguise)? Dorcas cannot read—but Clarissa will easily forgive that, for an illiterate servant insures privacy for one's written correspondence—and she seems to have a "sly eye." Also, the "servant's" respectfulness "seems too much studied . . . for the London ease and freedom." But Clarissa accepts Dorcas, for how can she do otherwise? She has granted her first concession.

Having accepted Lovelace's spy as her servant, Clarissa attempts to assert her own selfhood through the familiar device of outlining her own space (III, 317; II, 193). Lovelace seems to be withdrawing but stops and asks at that moment for her company in the dining room. She sees he "has no mind to leave me, if he can help it" (III, 317; II, 194). She also sees and observes to Anna that "when once a woman embarks with this sex, there is no receding." They are still talking at the door (we are reminded of other doorway conversations, particularly at Harlowe Place), and though Clarissa wishes her intruder gone, to "recede" from Lovelace, spatially or otherwise, is not easy. To his pressing her to have supper with him in the dining room, however, she declares that she does not eat supper.

Clarissa does not actually report Lovelace's departure from the room. We are left to assume that fact, as we are left to assume that she will not eat supper with him that evening. We think, like Clarissa herself, that she has won this round. It seems mere trivia when she reports to Anna that she has been examining the books in her room—Stanhope's *Gospels*, Sharp's, Tillotson's, and South's *Sermons*, plays by Steele, Rowe, and Shakespeare, *Tatlers*, and *Spectators*—and that she has discovered "in the blank leaves of the Nelson and Bishop Gauden" Mrs. Sinclair's name; and in those of most of the others "either Sarah Martin, or Mary Horton, the names of the two Nieces" (III, 319; II, 195). The heroine makes no further comment; we are left only the editorial dots indicating a break.[25]

When the text again continues, we are surprised to discover that Clarissa has not won the supper argument after all: she has given Lovelace her company in the dining room and made the concession that sets the pattern for the greater concessions to come. The reason is quite obvious—the names in the religious books. By inscribing a whore's name in a "sacramental piece" Lovelace has allayed suspicion in his apprehensive victim. He invades not only her room but the blank pages of her book.

Richardson's setting up of the pattern of events in this letter is masterful;

each detail fits perfectly as he describes how skillfully Lovelace erects his trap. The rake has Clarissa to agree to two conditions: that she support his pretense to the ladies of the house that they are married, and that she allow him to spend the night in the house. His method is to have Clarissa think she is making a decision on what has in fact already been decided. The heroine is at first incensed that the tale he has told the ladies obliges her to appear what she is not (III, 322; II, 197), but she can do nothing when told that his motive was to avert further mischief from her brother's seeking them out. As to the other condition, once she has agreed to the first, the second follows naturally, for a husband would surely spend the night in the same house. Clarissa attempts to explain her position to Anna:

> I thought, notwithstanding my resolution above-mentioned, that it would seem too punctilious to deny him, under the circumstances he had mentioned:—Having, besides, no reason to think he would obey me; for he looked, as if he were determined to debate the matter with me. And now as I see no likelihood of a Reconciliation with my friends, and as I have actually received his addresses; I thought I would not quarrel with him, if I could help it, especially as he asked to stay but for one night, and could have done so without my knowing it; and you being of opinion, that the proud wretch, distrusting his own merits with me, or at least my regard for him, will probably bring me to some concessions in his favour—For all these reasons, I thought proper to yield *this* point: Yet I was so vexed with him on the *other*, that it was impossible for me to comply with that grace which a concession should be made with, or not made at all. (III, 323–24; II, 198)

The passage presents a linguistic description of the trap. Clarissa is hemmed in by the circumstances (Lovelace's having already told the people of the house they are married). Circumstances supersede resolutions, and yet Clarissa feels compelled to go back over the mental ground that has led to her concession on the important point. Hence there is a piling up of the "as" clauses, each one a bar in the mental prison, and the final grasping after an acceptable mode of behavior, one that pertains in a world where resolutions may indeed be kept. Clarissa is aware that concessions *should* be honorable and *should* merit "grace" in their compliance; but the concession here is only wrung out of the awful circumstances whose weight dominates the entire passage. The torturous syntax that conveys the breaking of a resolution undercuts the heroine's earlier statement on the efficacy of setting resolutions down on paper (III, 221; II, 128). In a

house controlled by Lovelace, one may not have power over one's own resolutions—or one's own written words. Lovelace's invasion is well under
way. Clarissa only underlines that fact when, after his withdrawal from the
room, she carefully inspects the "doors, windows, and wainscot, the dark
closet as well as the light one . . . [the] fastenings to the door, and to all the
windows" and ends her letter to Anna with the warning: "look carefully to
the Seals of my Letters, as I shall to those of yours. If I find him base in this
particular, I shall think him capable of any evil; and will fly him as my
worse enemy" (III, 326; II, 200). Locking up the room and locking up the
letter have become acts of grave importance.

Clarissa is still writing letters here, struggling to keep herself free of
Lovelace's power even as we witness her gradual defeat. The attack takes
on a specifically epistolary cast in Letter IV, no. 8 (II, no. 75), beginning
once again in Clarissa's hand, with the heroine telling her friend Anna that
she has no one else to "unbosom" herself to and that she cannot bear the
life she is living: "I am but a cypher, to give *him* significance and *myself*
pain" (IV, 40; II, 264). As if to emphasize Clarissa's loss of power, the editor interjects and effects a transition to Lovelace's pen. Lovelace appears to
take over the letter space (at least, editorially speaking), and it seems particularly fitting to find him telling Belford that he "must come at the correspondence" between the young women. The fears of Anna and Clarissa
are well founded. We approach here the point of the first physical struggle
between Clarissa and Lovelace over letters but note again how carefully
Richardson prepares for that confrontation through interlocking various
images of privacy. Lovelace fantasizes first about Clarissa's pockets in a
manner suggestive of how intimately her clothes are a part of her body
("my mind hankers after them, as the less mischievous attempt" [IV, 46; II,
268]); he then explains that he has instructed Dorcas to cultivate her lady's
favor and muses why Clarissa can be so suspicious since "no company [is]
ever admitted into his inner house" (IV, 47; II, 269), and then, having decided that the correspondence with Anna Howe must be keeping his victim
so apprehensive, he declares again, "I must, I must come at (the letters)."
Richardson's imagery doubles back on itself; the letter we are reading—
and that Lovelace has taken over in a textual sense—becomes in turn an
image for invasion on all fronts: Clarissa's clothing, her consciousness
("inner house"), and of course her correspondence.

The following letter (IV, no. 9; II, no. 76) gives us the actual encounter
in the dining room, as Lovelace tries to "come at" Clarissa's inner identity
by snatching at what John Dussinger (in discussing *Pamela*) has called the
"recorded identity."[26] Lovelace comes upon Clarissa busily reading her

correspondence and notices at her feet a letter dropped unseen. He dashes in with "an air of transport" and boldly clasps the intended victim—while she tries madly to stuff her papers "into her handkerchief" to connect them yet more intimately with her own person. A kind of dance ensues in which Lovelace tells Clarissa with great happiness that he has arranged a "charming house, entirely ready to receive her" and gives her a "more fervent kiss" than he has dared before; but at the same time he moves the letter farther from her with his foot (IV, 52; II, 272). Then, while Clarissa works herself into a "passion" over his "liberty" with the kiss, he whips up the letter into his "bosom." Clarissa, frightened of being "ravish'd" herself, is suddenly aware of the "ravish'd" paper and snatches it back. Lovelace continues:

> What was to be done on so palpable a detection?—I clasped her hand, which had hold of the ravished paper, between mine: O my beloved creature! said I, can you think I have not *some* curiosity? Is it possible you can be thus for ever employed; and I . . . not . . . burn with a desire to be admitted into so sweet a correspondence? (IV, 52–53; II, 272)

Lovelace cannot bear his position of being shut out of the correspondence because to be admitted into the correspondence is to be allowed visibility into the private space. In this instance, however, he can get at neither the letter nor its owner. Clarissa grabs her paper and flies to the door. When Lovelace puts himself between her and the door, Clarissa, using brute strength, pushes him away, shoots through the door, double locks and double bolts herself in—and "wafers her letters in two places" (IV, 48; II, 269).

The attack on private space that so closely allies Clarissa's letter to the preservation of the inner self is imaged too in the notion of the shrinking enclosure. The elaborate pattern of drawers and boxes functions throughout the novel to suggest what is intimately connected with self. We come to see the heroine's drawers as what Gaston Bachelard has called "veritable organs of the secret psychological life."[27] As Clarissa inhabits a room, or her own body, so does the letter lie in its box. In Harlowe Place we were also aware of these epistolary hiding places; but Clarissa gave up the keys to her family so that they could search her drawers and boxes because she felt it proper that they do so (and because she had already sent the letters to the other "secret place" in the wall). In Mrs. Sinclair's house, threatened from without and increasingly persecuted by Lovelace's plots, she is forced to seek smaller and more obscure hiding places. She must move her papers from the mahogany chest, which contained her *outer* clothing (IV, 47; II, 268–69), to a smaller "wainscot box, which held her linen, and which she put into the dark closet" (IV, 291; II, 434). As pressure increases, the letters are placed with her *underclothes* ("linen"), an act suggestive of still closer proximity between the letter and the body.

Lovelace's reactions to the box only point up more acutely the relationship of the woman and the letter. Referring to the thaw in Clarissa occasioned by his feigned illness, he crows to Belford:

> Mrs. Sinclair and the nymphs are all of the opinion that I am now so much a favourite, and have such a visible share in her confidence, and even in her affections, that I may do what I will, and plead for excuse violence of *passion*; which, they will have it, makes violence of *action* pardonable. . . .
>
> They again urge me, since it is so difficult to make *Night* my friend, to an attempt in the *Day*. They remind me that the situation of their house is such that no noises can be heard out of it. (IV, 346; II, 471)

This notion of employing violence to come at Clarissa's person parallels another use of violence in the preceding paragraph: "Dorcas, in our absence, tried to get at the wainscot box in the dark closet. But it cannot be done without violence" (IV, 345–46; II, 471). It will take violent measures to gain possession of either the box or the woman. Of course the reference to the box is not without sexual connection, but even more significantly the box is important for the *letters* it contains. Jean Rousset has written that the letter "records the shape of the inner life";[28] and it is, after all, the "inner life" that is at stake in Mrs. Sinclair's house. The movement within, seen literally in Clarissa's placing the letters with her underclothing in the dark closet, is soon conveyed through the text of the heroine's letters. Having been taken in by Lovelace's feigned illness and, more seriously, forced to realize that she is attracted by the "man of errors," she queries, "Has not my own heart deceived me?" (IV, 298; II, 438):

> Dissatisfied with myself, I am afraid to look back upon what I have written: and yet know not how to have done writing. I never was in such an odd frame of mind.

"What she has written" is another acknowledgement of self; the letter is an image of her own heart. Clarissa addresses Anna in this instance, but once again the written utterance is a revelation of self to the self.

Nowhere is the self-revelatory function of letter writing more strikingly revealed, however, than in the papers Clarissa writes just after the rape. These distracted fragments are not exactly letters at all; they have no addressee but have been strewn about by Clarissa in her half-drugged condition, picked up by the prostitutes, copied by them, read by Lovelace, and then sent to Belford. Most important, they are messages written—though in a demented state—by the self for the self and are all the more meaningful because in their fragmentation they represent also the broken body of the writer. They represent, in their chaotic form, self-acknowledgement. Hence we read in "Paper III": "And who was most to blame, I pray? The Brute, or the Lady? The Lady, surely!—For what *she* did, was *out* of nature, *out* of character, at least." And in "Paper IV": "How art thou now humbled in the dust, thou proud Clarissa Harlowe! Thou that never steppedst out of thy Father's house, but to be admired! Who wert wont to turn thine eye . . . to different objects at once as thou passedst, as if . . . to plume thyself upon the expected applauses of all that beheld thee" (V, 329; III, 206). These are truly private statements, and the elaborate epistolary mechanism that brings them to our eye underlines how great is Lovelace's encroachment upon Clarissa's privacy. Yet, though raped and in one sense broken, Clarissa still writes. That is the important point. Writing sustains existence and affirms existence; these papers are Clarissa, indicating that though the body has been invaded, the moral core has not been altered. Clarissa will survive this final test. Lovelace still has both the heroine and her letters confined at this point, but that Clarissa can emerge from this rape/"death" and recognize her own role in it is evidence that the inner being still lives. The error, she suggests, was pride—a moving beyond the proper limits of character, turning the eye outward "to different objects," courting applause; but the capacity to recognize the error comes, of course, from "turning the gaudy eye inward"—toward the inner house.

In many ways, reading *Clarissa* is like reading Joyce's *Ulysses*; there is the sheer enormity of the text and, even more important, the exacting attention the reader must give to it. Richardson was fully aware himself of the demands his novel made, and the Dutch theologian Stinstra with whom he corresponded was quite correct in cautioning that a reader of *Clarissa* must recognize the necessity of the "careful examination of all its parts."[29] It is the thesis of this study that the parts do fit, and out of the jigsaw that is the epistolary novel emerges a definite pattern.[30] Always we must be attending; we must be asking who is writing, what kind of letters, and where is the writer in relation to the subject and his text. It is the last question to which

I have chiefly addressed myself in these two chapters on Harlowe Place and Mrs. Sinclair's house, and it is the last question too that I feel is especially important as we examine Clarissa's release from the confinement of the inner house.

Because Richardson so skillfully expresses Clarissa's gradual loss of freedom in epistolary as well as purely physical matters, it should not be surprising that her first escape attempt (to Hampstead) ends in failure. Lovelace is still in control through the somewhat tedious Hampstead episodes, which may be seen as an overly lengthened *excursus* from Mrs. Sinclair's house. With the exception of the one letter Clarissa writes to Anna explaining that she has escaped, but her "terror is not yet over" and she will not set foot out of doors till she has direction from her friend (V, 56–57; III, 19)—and this is all undercut by the fact that Lovelace has already written a forged letter to Anna explaining that Clarissa is ill and warning Anna *not* to come to her aid—Lovelace writes all the Hampstead letters; and behind them sits the presence of Mrs. Sinclair's house, whither all his schemes are directed.

On the first night of being lured, through the aid of the masquerading whores, back to Mrs. Sinclair's house, Clarissa is raped. She suffers the symbolic death that presages her actual death in volume four. Lovelace's marvelously cryptic statement to Belford, "And now, Belford, I can go no farther. The affair is over. Clarissa lives" (V, 314; III, 196), is doubly ironic: he can truly go no farther; and Clarissa, though she will die, will also live. If Clarissa loses one self, her moral being still exists and impels her to assert her will and to attain the ultimate release as public, beatified saint. Like the letters she writes and which are an integral part of her existence in the inner house, Clarissa experiences a transition from private to public. "Once more have I escaped," she writes to Anna in her first real letter after the rape, but "alas! I, my *best self*, have *not* escaped! . . . And let me, at awful distance, revere my beloved Anna Howe, and in her reflect upon what her Clarissa Harlowe once was" (VI, 115; III, 321). What Clarissa refers to in this impassioned outpouring as the "loss of self" is really, within the movement of the whole novel, the birth of another, now fully asserted being. She is truly at an "awful distance" from her friend: her difficulty in reaching Anna attests to that distance, and later she will eschew Anna's down-to-earth advice to marry Lovelace despite the rape.[31] She is symbolically another order of being.

The rape of Clarissa Harlowe in Mrs. Sinclair's house is not, then, a predominantly sexual affair. It is an attack on private space that is in turn connected with inner being—the "productive interior" from whence the letter derives.[32] In the structure of the entire novel, the rape is the focal point in what I have called a transition from private to public: the letters change after the rape and are no longer imaged in the closed, interior, differentiated setting, for private space has been destroyed. In Clarissa's history, the rape is followed by the unbolting of the door, the flight down the passage to the outer house—and finally to release in death.

Although release itself is multidimensional in *Clarissa*, connected with the language of both sexual and spiritual passion, it is, first of all, a physical action through which the heroine moves from one place to another. In exploring the details of where Clarissa is, we examine also what she is. To this degree, attentive reading indicates that the unbolting of the door after the rape is connected with the total pattern of doors and locks that functions in the novel to emphasize the vital importance of maintaining privacy, and of writing letters. Hence, just after the climactic fire scene (where Lovelace has been able to burst in upon the heroine's chamber under the supposed conditions of "fire"), Clarissa, now apprised of Lovelace's motives, takes special care to lock herself in. "I thought I heard her coming to open the door," Lovelace reports to Belford; "but it was only to draw another bolt, to make it still the faster" (IV, 397; II, 506). The following accounts to Belford are punctuated with "Her chamber door has not yet opened" (V, 1; II, 507); "Three different times tapped I at the door; but had not answer" (V, 3; II, 509); "her door was fast" (IV, 397; II, 506). Lovelace is allowed sight of the heroine only through the keyhole, and what he sees there is a kind of medallion image, a spectacle in miniature of what Belford will paint in larger canvas in the second half of the novel: the view of Clarissa as suffering soul, "on her knees, at her bed's feet, her head and bosom on the bed, her arms extended . . . and in an agony she seemed to be, as if her heart would break" (V, 11; II, 514). The scene points in erotic as well as spiritual directions (the former supported by the juxtaposition with keyhole). Nevertheless, even Lovelace is moved to examine—however briefly—his own motives. What he has seen bespeaks a moral lesson also.

Locking up is a reiterated theme in the brothel episodes leading up to the rape, where Clarissa is ever in retreat, her letters placed in smaller, darker places, her private space shrinking. Something quite different happens after the rape. Before her second, and successful, flight from Mrs. Sinclair's house, Clarissa must unlock her door. There are three abortive attempts to leave the house after the rape, all of which are reported by Lovelace to Belford. The first is reported in Letter V, no. 39 (III, no. 36), when Clarissa sends via Dorcas a message to Lovelace requesting a meeting in the dining room, and when Dorcas is out of the way, she hastily attempts an exit. But the layout of Mrs. Sinclair's house proves her undoing: "Had she been in the fore-house and no passage to go thro' to get at the street door, she had certainly been gone," but Sally Martin hears the "rustle of silks" and steps between Clarissa and the door (V, 358; III, 226–27). Lovelace suggests, at Clarissa's insisting that she will go, a negotiation in the foreparlor, that is, the parlor of the outer house, fronting on the street. The heroine, still furious at being detained, throws up the window sash to jump out to the street, but prevented by the iron palings on the window, she can only call out for help. A crowd gathers, and Lovelace is forced to carry his unwilling prisoner back up to the dining room (their usual encountering place) in the inner house.

All Clarissa's energies are now focused upon gaining access to the world outside the double house. In a second attempt, she gets as far as unbolting the street door before she is found out and taken back to the inner house (V, 374; III, 238); in a third (after another furious session with Lovelace in which she has declared, "I am sick of thee MAN!" [IV, 37; III, 267]) she again gains the street window and is calling out for help, until forced back again by that frightening virago Mrs. Sinclair.

Certainly, on a psychological level, it is understandable that Clarissa is so anxious to leave Mrs. Sinclair's house after she has experienced the full extent of Lovelace's villainy; but Richardson's adroit fitting together of the parts of his novel conveys still broader implications. We are moving toward the last letter (VI, no. 13; III, no. 53) in which Lovelace has Clarissa as subject—confined in the house and in his own letter. We know, too, that Lovelace will lose his domination because Richardson has now identified Clarissa as a force bent on gaining freedom and an identity outside of the "vile house." The elaborate attention given the escape attempts and the final unbolting scene point up the significance of such a release: Clarissa must move out from the corrupted body of the bawd's house and into a new existence. That is why Lovelace's letter is such a *summa* creation, the climax of one of his most intricate contrivances, the "last trial" (VI, 58; III, 282)—and of course doomed to failure because it is after all only contrivance. His description to Belford focuses upon the unlocking of the door:

> Now, Belford, see us all sitting in judgment . . . And hear her *unbolt, unlock, unbar* the door; then, as it proved afterwards, put the key into the lock on the outside, lock the door, and put it in her pocket. . . . The Street-doors also doubly secured, and every shutter to the windows round the house fastened. (IV, 65; III, 287)

Lovelace thinks that because he has closed the house off entirely from the external world he will be able to control the inner space entirely; but Cla-

rissa's words inform him he is wrong: "I am a person, tho' thus vilely betrayed, of rank and fortune" (VI, 66; III, 288). All the energy of the sen-
tance rests on, "I am a person." Typically, the affirmation of self is seen
also in spatial terms: "I have gained this distance, and two steps nearer me,
and thou shalt see what I dare do" (Clarissa holds the penknife to her
breast and threatens death to herself if they approach). When, at the conclusion of the scene, she unlocks her chamber door, enters, and double
locks again, the act signals her victory. She has seen through Lovelace's
design (to frighten her through a trumped-up charge of bribing Dorcas),
and this time the play-maker can only retire to his own chamber and lock
himself in (VI, 72; III, 291). Lovelace's reign of power is over.

Clarissa's bolting herself in at the end of the penknife scene is only temporary, and though parallel to the bolting at the end of the earlier fire
scene, the differences are significant. Two of the rare epistolary exchanges
between Lovelace and Clarissa take place after the fire scene and the penknife scene respectively. In the former, however, both characters write, and
the letters are presented to us as copies included within Lovelace's letter to
Belford (V, no. 2; II, no. 128). Lovelace is still in control. In the second
instance, Lovelace writes to Clarissa, pleading with her to reconsider marriage (VI, nos. 15, 16; III, nos. 55, 56), but Clarissa does not answer. There
are no more enclosed letters. Lovelace is "shut out," unable to come at
Clarissa in either a physical or epistolary sense.

It is in an epistolary sense too that we have perhaps the most striking
indicator of the significance of Clarissa's movement out of the privacy of
the inner house after the rape. Letter VI, no. 25 (III, no. 65), giving the
details of Clarissa's final, successful, escape attempt, is written by Belford's
pen: Clarissa has found a public audience. Belford steps into the novel to
play the role of reporter of Clarissa's death in the room above the public
shop in the final volume—and to become the executor/editor of the heroine's letters.[33] In the epistolary framework, Belford is the vehicle for the
publication of the novel. As the plot develops, Belford arrives in London to
attend to Clarissa for Lovelace, who is called to the country to see his uncle
who is ill; but more significantly, Belford, representative of the world outside, arrives just in time to record for Lovelace Clarissa's attainment of
freedom outside the privacy of Mrs. Sinclair's house. Belford will, as fellow
rake Mowbray writes to Lovelace, tell us everything; he is "taking minutes
of examinations, accusations, and confessions, with the significant air of a
Middlesex Justice; and intends to write at large all particulars" (VI, 94–95;
III, 307). From Belford we can expect a different kind of letter. His first
report to Lovelace is that Clarissa has tricked Mabel, an inmate of the

house, into changing clothes; and in a whore's "gown and petticoat over her own, which was white damask," she has slipped out of the house (VI, 101; III, 311). After just one intervening letter in Lovelace's hand, Clarissa writes her first "free" letter to Anna Howe (VI, no. 27; III, no. 67).

The ultimate development of Clarissa's escape from confinement in Mrs. Sinclair's house is the confinement of the coffin and the burial vault of Harlowe Place, which we will examine in the account of the heroine's funeral in the following chapter. There, however, in Colonel Morden's epistolary reporting, Richardson achieves the creation of a paradox wherein what is confined and closed in the coffin is also the most open and public. Formerly private, differentiated places are opened as one great stage for public viewing. That Clarissa herself considers death a release from confinement in the body is clearly evident in her dying statements (typical, of course, of those in accounts of Christian death):[34] "never Bride was so ready as I am," she writes Mrs. Norton (VII, 406; IV, 303); and Mrs. Lovick and Mrs. Smith (fellow lodgers in the rooms above the glove shop) speak of the heroine's "late tranquillity and freedom from pain" as a "lightening." J. Paul Hunter has written in his work on Defoe and the tradition of spiritual biography that although the diary is a private form, the funeral sermon specialized in "moral exhortation."[35] Death becomes a public concern, the moral strength of the dead a public example. The release into death is also release into a more public identity. Cynthia Wolff has also argued this point in what she describes as the transition from "Puritan self-examiner" to "saint," and she attributes the inclusion of several hundred pages of postdeath text in *Clarissa* to Richardson's wish to confer a "public image" on his heroine.[36] Certainly the thesis I am presenting here sees such a transition as essential, but it would seem that it actually begins with the rape—which Clarissa herself refers to as a "death" and which, as her letter to Anna Howe indicates, she sees as the loss of her former identity (VI, 115; III, 321). It is after the rape that she is compelled to reach the external world and the public audience personified in Belford. What Clarissa does not see and Richardson does is that the flight down the passage from the inner house to the outer house and then to the street without signals not only escape from the "vile house" but a new birth. Paradoxically, the house as corrupted body, hiding behind its mask, is also the house as "productive interior." "Think not of me, my only friend, but as we were in time past," she writes to Anna; "And suppose me gone a great, great way off!" (VI, 348; III, 479).[37] She is on her way toward that moment of actual death when "God will soon *dissolve* [her] *substance; and bring* [her] *to the house appointed for all living*" (VI, 412; III, 523).

THE ROOM OPEN:

3

Public Image and "Affecting Scene"

> . . . the main purpose of a door is to admit.
>
> Edith Wharton,
> *The Decoration of Houses*

Like Samuel Richardson, Edith Wharton was particularly interested in the function of doors; although "no room can be satisfactory unless its openings are properly placed and proportioned," she writes, "it should be borne in mind of entrances in general that, while the main purpose of a door is to admit, its secondary purpose is to exclude."[1] An outer door in particular should proclaim itself an "effectual barrier."

Wharton's language is consistent with that of *Clarissa*; admission and exclusion, the poles of her discussion, are also the foci of the epistolary world. Social sign and ritual determine the assignment of both physical and textual space. We have already seen Clarissa's attempts at exclusion, warding off her invading sister Bella by retreating into the small private closet: closing her door, drawing the silk curtain over the window. We have seen too how the addressee is granted admission to consciousness and its recreation in the letter. Like a door, the "Honoured Sir" or "My Dear Brother" serves as an opening into the letter content even as it sets up the relationship between writer and addressee.[2] Who is admitted, who addressed, is essential to our knowing the circumstances of the letter writer, for even a confined heroine seeks out the intimate relationship of the confidante.

I return in this chapter to Harlowe Place because the transformation that Richardson effects in that house represents the larger structural and epistolary transformations in the novel. Following the rape of Clarissa and her flight down the narrow passage and out of the enclosed interior of Mrs. Sinclair's "vile house," a different kind of letter dominates the novel: a letter more particularly didactic in orientation, addressed to a broader audience, and relying heavily on visual detail.

Harlowe Place is, as we would expect, a different structure in this final sequence of the novel because another letter writer recreates it for us. Morden is the director, spectator, and reporter of the account he sends Belford; but he is not the central actor as Clarissa was in her Harlowe Place letters. His letter is attended with none of that epistolary apparatus that figures so importantly in the heroine's letters, because letter writing is no longer the highly self-conscious and self-preserving act it was under Clarissa's pen. It does not matter where Morden writes, for the definition of the letter as a private space is no longer operative, its connection with the enclosed writing chamber broken.

The colonel's letter is a public document, open in the same way as the funeral scene it describes. It is as if an outside audience is invited to look in with no apparent distinction of degree or relationship. Although the death of Clarissa had its most profound effect on the Harlowe family and is to this degree a private matter, it is also an occasion of public significance. Clarissa, who, unlike Pamela, could not be "tucked into a social structure," has now transcended all earthly chambers. She is now larger than life.[3] Fittingly, Morden himself takes on the identity of allegorical figure as he makes his first substantial appearance in the novel only to be present at the death of his sainted cousin. Robert M. Schmitz has correctly observed that Richardson's "scene painting" here—to borrow Belford's preface to his description of the death of Mrs. Sinclair: "O Lovelace! I have a scene to paint" (VIII, 53; IV, 379)—achieves a tableau effect: a staged lesson.[4]

Schmitz does not note, however, that Morden the death figure also takes on, in writing to Belford, the role of reporter that Belford has already established as the dominant mode of letter writing in this part of the novel. Morden's very distance—in miles and in relationship—from his addressee requires that he provide the carefully detailed account that also admits the wider, novel-reading, supposedly unaddressed, audience. Colonel Morden's description focuses upon the entrance of the coffin into the rooms of Harlowe Place—not upon invasion, a negative penetration into the interior, nor upon the exclusion that invasion necessitates. His account of the return of the heroine's coffin to the family house clearly underlines the significance of opening an enclosed place to public visibility. The closed room, and letter—self-creating spaces—yields to the stagelike open room or sequence of spaces. If architectural and epistolary space have already conflated in this novel to define privacy as self-space, Richardson's representation of the public requires the dramatist's power to render within publicly visualized stage-space the details of private and domestic experience. Clarissa's search for integrity of self, her search for the privacy of her own room and letters, is borne out in one sense in her attainment of the privacy of the grave; but, by the same token, the staged and ritualistic quality of her funeral, its being recounted by Morden, returns us to the epistolary paradox: a letter is not, cannot, be written ultimately for the self. The doors that once closed on the differentiated parts of the house and the private recording of experience are laid open; once private letters now compose in totality a public image.

In the architect's commentary appended to a 1720 house plan, James Gibbs explained that an octagon salon included in the plan could be "private or publick at pleasure because of the Passages of Communication betwixt the Hall and with-drawing Room."[5] Gibbs was referring to the fact that corridors on both the right and left sides of the octagon room enabled one to pass directly from the main entrance hall into the "withdrawing room." Such passages of communication allowed ready access to servants and at the same time more effectively shut out from their view the activities of the family of the house.[6] The inclusion of corridors, so loudly espoused by architects like Kerr in the nineteenth century, signals the increased delineation of space and personal privacy.

By preventing visibility into separate rooms, corridors also drastically alter our perception of the space of a house. They obliterate, for example, our sense of rooms as spaces connected such that we seem to move both through and within: perhaps toward the most intimate place, as at Ham House, Middlesex, where we proceed toward the major apartment, the queen's bedchamber, and then beyond to the small dressing room or closet, the place for the most intimate audiences, the locus of the writing desk. The notion of moving within when one goes from one room to another in the suite is frequently seen in contemporary commentators. We can look, for example, to that inveterate seventeenth-century traveler Celia Fiennes, who depicts the home of a relative near Southampton by explaining:

By the Servants Roome is a large back Staire that Leads to the Next Story . . . and in the Left hand they lead into a large Dineing

Roome—then a drawing Roome and next a bed Chamber which had a back doore to the Back Staires by the kitchen . . . *Within* the dineing room on the Left hand is a very Large bed chamber [and off the back kitchen stairs are] a Chamber, anty Roome, dressing roome, 2 Closets.[7]

The bed chamber within a dining room is in the direct line of access from the dining room. Even a grand Palladian house like Houghton Hall, built by Colen Campbell in 1722 for Sir Robert Walpole, contains a bedroom and cabinet opening off a dining room; and Houghton became a standard model for grand domestic design in the 1740s and 1750s.[8] On a much smaller scale, Mrs. Delaney, wife of Swift's friend, Dr. Delaney (whose sermons Richardson printed), wrote to her sister that in her new house in Ireland the bedchamber and closet were "on the left hand of the drawing room," and on the right were "a pretty square room, with a large dressing-room within."[9]

The effect of looking within, into an intimate space, is captured too in Dutch painting of the seventeenth century and in the eighteenth-century English conversation piece—both celebrations of the family within its domestic space. As Mario Praz has pointed out, the environment is depicted with an attention to detail "no less scrupulous than we find practised in the portrayal of the sitters, and thus gives to the picture a *Stimmung*, an intimate feeling." The family portrait, Praz continues, "developed simultaneously with the representation of interiors in the bourgeois Low Countries."[10] An 1855 watercolor entitled *Doorway to a Suite of Rooms at Old Burlington House, London* helps substantiate visually Praz's emphasis on the intimacy of interior space.[11] Burlington House was designed by the Earl of Burlington and Colen Campbell around 1730; and, as we would expect, in the watercolor depiction we look through a suite of rooms or, more exactly, a series of doorways. Kerr quite rightly emphasizes the publicity of the arrangement: when the doors are open, private spaces are made public before us.[12] In the present example, too, we see the figure of a woman just disappearing from view into the second room, perhaps attempting, like Clarissa, to escape. She moves into another frame within the frame. There is no bypassing corridor here, but rather a passageway through the rooms. The picture draws us in toward some private place, but paradoxically the only way in is through a series of revealed spaces. In our own century, John Summerson has criticized the Burlington design as containing essentially separate units worked into a "rigid inorganic whole";[13] but the anonymous creator of the watercolor I am using here emphasizes not separation or rigidity but communication through the open door: we are talking about doorways—not barriers. Each room is part of the sequential pattern in the same way that each of the letters comprising Richardson's novel is part of the total structure. It is only when letters—and rooms—are connected that the whole pattern emerges, that we see how the house expresses "all its riches within."[14]

In his letter, Morden represents in little Richardson's own achievement; the novelist's craft, like the letter writer's and the dramatist's consists ultimately not in bypassing private rooms but in opening them up, making them visible. If, when we return to Harlowe Place in the final volume of *Clarissa*, the inner world, the enclosed interior, has acquired the value of a sacred place and the heroine a public identity, such publicization has come about only because the individuated records of private experience are available to us: we have passed through the rooms, have read the letters. Harlowe Place, a house of differentiated, separate rooms in the early pages of the novel, must be viewed finally as a structure of intercommunicating rooms. In the epistolary house of fiction, the parts are contiguous and, as Clarissa would say, "communicating."

Ritual, as Colonel Morden's epistolary account demonstrates, also demands the interconnected spatial arrangement typical of the large eighteenth-century house. It is the ritualistic character of life itself that so clearly emerges in Mark Girouard's *Life in the English Country House.*[15] As John Cornforth and John Fowler concluded too in their earlier attempt to deal with how individuals in past times lived in their houses, by the late seventeenth century most large houses contained a great apartment (state bedroom or chamber of state) "preceded by one, two, or even three rooms that served as a Presence Chamber, a Drawing Room and an Ante-Room and followed by a dressing room and closet"; throughout the century there had developed a stronger emphasis upon the "processional character of the sequence of rooms," each element in the pattern acquiring value according to where it was and who was allowed access to it.[16] As the result in part of French influences, the dressing room (*cabinet*) was the most intimate of the rooms and usually had one or more closets opening from it. As at Ham House and in the much smaller house of Mrs. Delaney the most imtimate room is also the deepest within. That references within eighteenth-century letters, as well as inventories of houses of the period, indicate that a woman's dressing room was often her writing place attests to the concept of writing itself as intimate activity. Clarissa was not alone in her predilection for the closet.

The notion that particular spaces are valued according to who may enter, and the sense that as we move toward an interior we proceed also toward the most intimate and significant space, is of particular interest in Morden's description of Clarissa's return to the family seat. Let us look in some detail at Letters VIII, nos. 20–24 (IV, nos. 139–43). Here we find Morden reporting as fully as possible to Belford the grief and guilt of the Harlowes over their treatment of the unfortunate Clarissa. "Who could behold such a scene, who could recollect it in order to describe it (as minutely as you wished me to relate this unhappy family were affected on this sad occasion)?" Morden asks (VII, 72; IV, 392). Belford wants to have every minute detail, and the colonel uses "scene" as an exact counterpart of Belford's preceding letter to Lovelace (VII, no. 19; IV, no. 128). A scene must give us every detail as the reformed rake has amply shown in his description of the hideous death of Mrs. Sinclair ("O Lovelace! I have a scene to paint" [VIII, 53; IV, 379]), and Richardson wants this juxtaposition of the two examples, one of corruption, the other of saintliness.

Both Belford and Morden are self-conscious narrators; but the latter, citing various locations of Harlowe Place, is clearly concerned with the spatial ordering of his scene. He takes into account all those parts of the estate that Clarissa has already outlined (particularly in the gate scene, II, 303; I, 446–47), though with the important difference that he moves from the outside toward the interior, his description taking the same direction as the coffin itself: "When we were within five miles of Harlowe-Place, I put on a hard-gallop. I ordered the herse to proceed more slowly still, the cross-road we were in being rough; and having more time before us than I wanted; for I wished not the herse to be in till near dusk" (VIII, 70; IV, 391). Morden has planned his scene carefully then; he has chosen his own position and even the proper time for the arrival of the hearse, which he himself precedes. He does not tell us exactly why he wishes to arrive first; perhaps it is to prepare the family, or perhaps—and I think this more likely—he wishes to be outside of the procession itself in order to describe it from the viewpoint of an audience.

The colonel is more than narrator: he presents himself as both director and audience of the proceedings. He needs the distance that comes from arriving first, entering the house, and only then describing the arrival of the hearse. The distancing, in turn, directs our attention toward the described object within a total scene. Clarissa's narratives from Harlowe Place also revealed a keen eye for visual effect, of course, but the heroine could never distance herself from her scene. When Morden makes a special point of the arrival of the hearse at the "outward gate," he directs us to witness a public spectacle at which he is also spectator: "at least fifty of the neighboring men, women, and children, and some of good appearance" gather about the coffin, which takes its route into the house:

> the corpse was thus borne, with the most solemn respect, into the hall, and placed for the present upon two stools there. The plates, and emblems, and inscription, set everyone gazing upon it. . . . They wished to be permitted a sight of the corpse; but rather mentioned this as their *wish* than as their *hope.* . . .
> The servants of the family then got about the coffin. (VIII, 77; IV, 396)

Note that the coffin rests in this instance in the hall, the more public part of the house, really the entrance passage. The group that gathers around it is not identified directly as the Harlowe family; they are not even servants, who are named specifically as the second ring of observers but would have to be identified as the neighboring people, tenants perhaps, but in any case a more public audience. When Morden mentions the Harlowe servants, he is approaching the inner ring of family members: the audience becomes more private, or more intimate.

The closer one comes to the Harlowe family as audience, however, the further must the coffin be moved into the interior of the house, the parlor, which now asserts its connection with the familial zone of the house:[17]

> But when the cropse was carried into the lesser parlour, adjoining to the hall, which she used to call *her* parlour, and put upon a table in the middle of the room, and the Father and Mother, the two Uncles, her Aunt Hervey, and her Sister came in, joining her Brother and me, with trembling feet, and eager woe, the scene was still more affecting. (VIII, 77–78; IV, 396)

The shrinking audience, now reduced to family members, the movement toward the interior, all underline the privateness of the "affecting scene"; but in this same parlor, from which we have seen Clarissa so often attempting to extricate herself, now rests the coffin that asserts the public value of all that transpires here.

The term "affecting scene" implies an audience that will be drawn in also. Certainly Morden does not remain only an outsider. He tells Belford even at the outset of his account, "In vain, Sir, have I endeavoured to compose myself to rest. You wished me to be very particular and I cannot help it. This melancholy subject fills my whole mind" (VIII, 75; IV, 394). The statement is quite different from that which opens the letter: "According to my promise, I send you an account of matters here" (VIII, 69; IV, 390). The businesslike reporter gives way to the affected audience. And yet Colonel Morden can still stand back and refer to the painting of the scene or ask for a review of his narrative; the scene does not lose its spectacle aspect. There is a frozen quality too in the colonel's description of the funeral ritual. His scene painting, like Belford's in the preceding account of Mrs. Sinclair's death throes ("what a spectacle presented itself to my eyes! . . . Behold her then, spreading the whole tumbled bed with her huge quaggy carcase . . . her bellows-shaped and various coloured breasts ascending by turns to her chin" [VIII, 57; IV, 382]), presents pictures that are directed to the audience/reader as object lessons.[18]

In the funeral account, however, the gradual movement toward an interior, with doors opening one after the other to admit the coffin, conveys the sense too that we are seeing pictures within pictures. We follow the coffin as it moves into the house; where it stops we stop and gaze about; when it moves from hall to parlor we move within also. Each place where the coffin rests is then endowed with a special value; the place functions not only as a mnemonic device for Morden, who was so anxious to omit no detail in his account, but is seen also in relation to all the spaces forming the route of the coffin.[19] Movement toward the interior, paired with the spectacle quality of the entire scene, results in a blending of the private and public: the significance of the enclosed coffin radiates out in ever widening circles.

The tendency to transform private experience into affecting lesson, a private (domestic) space into a public stage, is hardly unique to Richardson. It seems particularly fitting, for example, that Richardson approached Hogarth about doing the frontispiece for the second edition of *Pamela*;[20] for in the domestic scene as portrayed by Hogarth in his conversation pieces the depiction of the family and its habitat usually contains elements of the dramatic. To both Richardson and Hogarth, the room must be more than what Edith Wharton was to call a "small world by itself."[21] The entirely enclosed room is a prison. Ronald Paulson has suggestively demonstrated the conflation of room, prison, and stage in Hogarth's imagination, a contention borne out clearly, for example, in the 1728 painting, *The Beggar's Opera*;[22] and it was perhaps to free the denizens of private enclosure that Hogarth conceived of them also as "representations on the stage." "I have endeavoured to treat my subjects as a dramatic writer," wrote Hogarth; "my picture is my stage, and men and women my players, who by means of certain actions and gestures are to exhibit a dumb show."[23] In *The Cholmondeley Family* (1732), the example cited by Praz in his work on the conversation piece, the cupid figure on the left of the picture draws a curtain suggestive of a stage curtain; and behind the cavorting young boys on the right we look deep into a room hung with paintings and resembling an inner stage.[24]

Both Hogarth and Richardson then transform the room into an element in a larger picture. It is as if the painted flats on the eighteenth-century stage move aside to reveal the total perspective that is as important to the epistolary novelist as to the dramatist.[25] Exposure, a traditionally epistolary notion, should be regarded first as a visual phenomenon. If perception, affect, and morality form the indissoluble knot upon which sentimental art depends, it is not surprising that Richardson, no less than the dramatist, guides the perception of his readers. Such guidance is particularly marked in the final sequence recounting Clarissa's death where tableaux and the framing of moral lessons on an interior stage recall both the techniques of contemporary stagecraft and the efforts of the novelist to force readers to perceive the total sequence of scenes and of letters.[26]

The use of the inner stage in Restoration and post-Restoration theater has been the subject of some dispute among theater historians who disagree as to whether the inner stage was primarily a "scenic" or an "acting area."[27] It is clear, however, that scenes were quickly created by sliding panels into grooves in the floor of the stage, and hence the term "scene opens" refers to sliding the panels apart to discover what lies behind. Scene changes took place in full view of the audience, and the actors often did not leave the stage at the end of a scene.[28] In *Changeable Scenery*, Richard Southern explores in detail how one act of Aphra Behn's *Sir Patient Fancy* may actually have been staged.[29] For example, the garden "draws off" to disclose Lady Fancy's antechamber, which in turn "draws off" to disclose a bedchamber; that is to say, the grooves in which the painted panels were placed, were arranged in rows so that the bedroom scene was placed behind the antechamber, the antechamber behind the garden, and so on. Obviously, the spaces between the panels would have to be deep enough to accommodate the actors and whatever furniture might be used. Because of these factors, and because the limited size of the theater would make it possible that actors be heard even from within the scene, one theater historian has proposed that particularly in tragedy there was an increased tendency to use the area within the scene as an acting area.[30]

Although we do not know the exact depth of either the forestage or the area behind the proscenium in the Restoration, we may still conclude then that the scene is composed of a series of side wings spaced along each side of the area and backed at the deepest point by a back shutter, usually painted in perspective and capable of being closed completely across the scene area. In discussing the function of the long street scene in *Sir Patient Fancy*, Southern explains that on occasion a scene can open up, "occupying the space of both stages, its deeper parts penetrating into the recess at the back," and in this case the scene is called a *lungo*, "long" scene.[31]

Such descriptions of the stage help us visualize Colonel Morden's description of Clarissa's coffin as it penetrates the interior of Harlowe Place: doors open and scenes are created. At the point when Morden has just completed his account of the placing of the coffin within the parlor and before he goes on with the funeral itself (closing of Letter VIII, no. 20; IV, no. 139) he tells Belford: "Indeed, I am altogether indisposed for rest, as I mentioned before. So can do nothing but write. I have also more melancholy scenes to paint. My pen, if I may so say, is untired." In the spatial terms I am using here, Morden is more than halfway toward the burial vault. He announces a hiatus necessitated only by postal expediency and is anxious to continue the painting of melancholy scenes: the final farewell to the heroine from family members, Anna Howe, and friends. He is anxious to get on with his journey within. Critics such as Alan McKillop and Ira Konigsberg have already noted the similarity in plot and characterization between Richardson and Restoration and post-Restoration dramatists but have not paid much attention to the larger question of how such drama sought its effect visually upon the stage.[32] Morden's casting himself as spectator as well as director of a scene reminds us that the epistolary reader is also both learner and spectator; and the lesson, like that of the dramatists I will discuss later, depends on a stage that may be viewed as a sequential pattern of spaces opening up even as they lead the eye within.

Charles Gildon, who was to bring out two miscellanies, including the well-known *Post-Boy Robb'd of His Mail*, produced in 1701 a play entitled *Love's Victim: or, The Queen of Wales.*[33] In the preface to the play, calling Otway his master, Gildon states that the end of tragedy is the "moving of Terror and Compassion"; the play should "look into Man and study the motions of the soul, and the nature of the Passions." In language close to that he employs in his epistolary works, Gildon states that his is the "language of the Heart" as affected by the "natural sentiments of the Passions." To this degree he draws "incidents and sentiments" from Euripides but transfers them to "Persons of our owne Clime . . . who therefore cou'd differ from us only in things, that depend meerly on Customes and Religion." Gildon places great importance, then, on the audience's identifying itself with the characters of the play; the ancient poets, he says, used "domestic fables," and as the manners of the characters were similar to those of the audience, "their Examples were more moving and instructive."

If Gildon's avowed aim is to depict the state of the heart for the edification of an audience, it is particularly important to ask what the audience did see. Gildon's stage directions are unusually detailed for a play of the period:

> The Inside of a Magnificent Temple the whole Extent of the Stage: at the farther End of which a stately Altar, on it the Statue of Mercury; beneath that a Couch. The Curtain rises with terrible Claps of Thunder, and Guinoen is discover'd sitting an a melancholly Posture . . . ; on the Front of Stage Dummacus and a Druid.

The action of the play takes place either within the temple, a sacred place where the heroine is safe from her persecutors, or within the grove in front, which we would assume to be the area before the proscenium arch. Like Clarissa, Guinoen (supposedly an eighth-century queen) is a paragon of virtue, and like Richardson's heroine, her preservation is connected with the interior of the sacred temple. In Gildon's play, however, the temple functions also as a framework for the public example of virtue. The play opens with an "affecting Scene": Guinoen sits in a "melancholy Posture" while "on the Front of the Stage" the character Dummacus remarks to a Druid, "See yonder, where she sits all drown'd in Tears" (I, i). Following the latter's speech, the heroine "rises and comes forward."

The placing of the virtuous heroine within the part of the scene referred to literally as the "scene" establishes her identity at the outset as the "Phoenix of her Sex." At the end of the play, after Guinoen has been undone through the evil of the King and Queen of Bayonne, has been poisoned and suffered a grim death, the chief druid remarks to the victim's son:

> Thy Mother might have longer life enjoy'd
> But ne'r cou'd with such Glory have expir'd.
> The Phoenix of her Sex.

The chief druid directs our attention to the scene and asserts its public value. The technique is similar to that employed by Richardson through Belford and Morden. As Morden leads us through the rooms of Harlowe

Place, we are always aware that we are being led, that Morden is a kind of presentor, that we do not sit entirely as the "fourth wall" associated with naturalistic theater.[34]

This is not to deny that sentimental drama approximates a level of life-likeness. As Beaumarchais was to argue in *Essai sur le genre dramatique sérieux*, the spectator may take the most sympathetic interest in persons on the same social standing as himself, persons with whom he can identify; hence, what Arnold Hauser calls a "bourgeois fondness for the intimate, the direct, and the homely" renders to the stage the character of a self-contained microcosm readily recognizable by the audience.[35] "We ne'er can pity what we ne'er can Share," wrote Nicholas Rowe in the prologue to *The Fair Penitent* (1703),[36] and since "one of the main Designs of Tragedy is . . . to excite . . . generous Pity in the greatest Minds,"

> Therefore an humble Theme our Author chose,
> A melancholy Tale of private woe:
> No princes here lost Royalty bemoan,
> But you shall meet with Sorrows like your own.

Still, even though Rowe uses "private" to denote persons of no public identity, domestic intimacy is not finally at issue here. The creation of the affecting scene—its very affect—requires the exposure of all the details, sharing them through an act of admission to the interior space. The so-called lifelike scene is transformed into the larger than ordinary life.

Recognition is key to this art. Diderot, a vigorous enunciator of bourgeois drama and one of Richardson's warmest continental admirers, explained in "Eloge de Richardson" that the author of *Clarissa* enables us to see what was not evident to us in everyday life. "The sounds of passions have often struck your ears," writes Diderot, but the purpose of art is to show you the "fugitive circumstance" that has escaped your notice. The novel allows us to hear the "noise of the day which makes the silence of the night more moving."[37] The concealment of the fictitious nature of what is presented thus emphasizes the power of the "multitude of small things" to produce the illusion of a real world. In an epistolary novel, this is tantamount to the multitude of all the letters (what "sacrilege" if any be missing, laments Diderot in *Eloge*, p. 218); in the dramatic presentation, details may be identified and valued according to the physical stage space in which they occur.

In *The Fair Penitent*, Rowe uses interior stage space as a means of sharing "private Woe" by freezing it in a scene. Lothario, having seduced Calista and set in motion the tragic chain of events, meets his end in the fourth act; the stage directions of the first scene in the fifth act then read:

> Scene is a Room hung with Black; on one side Lothario's
> Body on a Bier; on the other, a Table, with a Scull and
> other Bones, a Book, and a Lamp on it.
> Calista is discover'd on a Couch in Black; her Hair
> Hanging loose and disorder'd: after Musick and a Song,
> she rises and *comes forward*. (italics mine)

We have already seen in this play four major settings: a garden, a hall, a street, and an apartment (in that order). The "Room hung with Black" may have used the same flat as the apartment but, in any case, would have to have used the interior part of the stage. Calista is also "discover'd" on a couch, and the normal place for stage furniture would be the inner stage. Calista herself, in black garments and with her "loose and disorder'd" hair, functions as part of the scene so long as she is still within the interior. Note, however, what happens when she comes forward and speaks:

> 'Tis well: these solemn Sounds, this Pomp of Horror,
> Are fit to feed the Frenzy in my Soul.
>
> . . . .
>
> Now think, thou curst Calista, now behold
> The Desolation, Horror, Blood and Ruin,
> Thy Crimes and fatal Folly spread around. (V, i)

Calista detaches herself from the scene and now regards it as a "Pomp of Horror." Private woe has been publicly ritualized; Calista, like Morden, is a spectator as well as a participant, observing the scene as an object in the moral lesson. We are reminded of Morden's distancing of himself from the funeral cortege and his question, "Who could behold such a scene [and not be affected]?" In the stage version of the affecting scene, however, where we see Calista as both part of and removed from the scene, the point is made visually that the character is fully aware of her own role in the "Desolation, Horror, Blood and Ruin." What the audience sees is an enactment of Adam Smith's later dictum that we should "examine our own past conduct as we imagine an impartial spectator would examine it";[38] the individual must be both spectator and agent. That is to say, the audience of Rowe's play sees upon the stage a character seeing.

Charles Johnson's *Caelia* (1733) resembles in both plot and characterization Richardson's *Clarissa*;[39] but, just as important, Johnson's staging of "mournful sights" also suggests Morden's dramatic presentation of events in the letter to Belford. Seeing tragedy in a state of decline, Johnson wrote in the dedicatory note to *The Force of Friendship* (1710) that "expiring tragedy" can hope for "Countenance" only from those spirits

> who are pleas'd with the Distress of a well wrought Scene, who with the utmost Indulgence of their Reason, behold the Conduct of our Passions of the Stage, and with a generous Sympathy feel alternately Joy and Pain, when Virtue either conquers, or in contending with adverse Fate.[40]

In all Johnson's tragedies characters look toward "mournful sights." The stage directions for the final scene in *The Tragedy of Medea* (1731) point out that the servants should "repose" Creusa on a couch. Creon enters, begins his speech with "Yet, ere I die, let me behold my Child . . . Oh, sadly moving object," and ends with "There, there she lies, speechless and pale Creusa." Since the heroine on the couch would have to be located toward the interior of the stage, we have the familiar pattern of what I have called the framed picture, the visual example from which the audience is to draw the moral lesson. Perhaps the most striking example occurs, however, in Johnson's charming comedy, *The Country Lasses: Or, the Custom of the Manor* (1715).[41] The play is concerned with teaching, learning, and loving; the plot involves the romantic relationships of two couples, Flora and Heartwell, Aura and Modely, country maidens and city swains. Having rejected in true Pamela fashion Heartwell's proposals that she become his mistress, Flora readily succeeds in reforming her lover ("Oh thou hast touch'd my Soul; I *feel* thy Words, a conscious Pain stabs thro' my Heart, and covers me with Shame," says he). Heartwell and Flora marry despite the apparent lack of marriage portion on the bride's part. Modely the rake, however, is more difficult to save. "I love the whole Sex," he says in terms that Richardson's Lovelace might later have used; and Aura's father, Freehold the Farmer, tells him, "You have broke every Social Virtue, and yet Imprudently imagine you are in the Character of a Gentleman." The play must then focus upon the testing of Heartwell and the instruction of Modely in the ways of the "character of a Gentleman."

Teaching takes the form of play, but more important in the present discussion, play upon the inner stage. The stage directions read: "The flat Scene opens, and Flora and two Women Servants appear drest very genteely. Servants with Candles before them, they move down towards Heartwell." Heartwell, the spectator, stands forward on the stage. Meanwhile, Aura has already set in progress the testing of Modely by dressing as a boy, engaging Modely in a supposed duel, and pretending to be killed; now her attention is centered on ascertaining whether her new husband has married her for herself. She is dressed for a role in the play that is called *Custom of the Manor* and explains that she must perform also for the lord of the manor, the right of "first night's lodgings." Heartwell is driven to distraction by this notion, until he is finally informed that Aura is indeed herself the mistress of the manor, and he must now be lord. She has tested Heartwell because she had to know that he has married her for herself, not for fortune.[42] The revelation to Heartwell is followed by the trial of Modely, who also repents, offers marriage to Flora, and is given a sentence of a two-year trial period before such marriage may take place.

In domestic drama as exemplified in playwrights like Charles Johnson and George Lillo (*George Barnwell*, written in 1731), characters are reformed by what they see, the scene taking place on the inner stage, and what they feel as a result of that scene. Teaching and showing are inextricably bound for characters within and audiences outside the play. Johnson questions in the "advertisement to the reader" in *Caelia*: "How many Families have suffer'd irreparable Injuries of this sort [when a daughter runs off with a rake]?"[43] Hoping his scenes shall have an effect upon the "Morals of our Youth" and prove a "Caution to the Young and Innocent of the Fair Sex," Lillo exploits in both *Caelia* and the more famous *Barnwell* the prison scene in the final act.[44] Richardson may have been thinking of the latter in his own description, through Belford's pen, of Clarissa in Letter VI, no. 66 (III, no. 106). The stage direction in *Caelia* says merely "Room poorly furnish'd" (act V), but a kind of prison is intended. To Meanwell and Lovemore's plea for entry the keeper replies, "I will not expose her (Caelia)," but the father and faithful family friend press, and the "Scene opens"; "Caelia is discovered in her Chamber" declaring her own penitence. To be discovered is also to be exposed as part of the affecting scene. Meanwell's final speech, "Blush, blush, ye libertines," then directs the attention of the entire audience toward the framed image of the room and its occupants.

The directive to the audience is perhaps even more specific in *Barnwell*, which, according to Theophilus Cibber, "Spoke so much to the heart" that even "gay persons" pulled out their handkerchiefs.[45] Consider the scene in the fifth act where we see the morally corrupted but now contrite Barnwell reading in his dungeon room. His trusty, upright friend Thorowgood enters before the proscenium arch, indicates Barnwell from the audience's perspective, and commands us to "*There see* the bitter fruits of passion's detested reign." We look once again within the stage to witness the moral example. "Sir," says the Keeper, "There's the prisoner." It is a "dismal scene," made all the more so by our seeing, further within the confines of the stage, the "place of execution. The gallows and Ladder . . . a crowd of spectators." Johnson, Lillo, and Richardson (through Belford and Morden) all lead the eye toward an inner frame;[46] and at the same time, all make an appeal to audience that renders the interior picture a public experience. The place within is no longer private. It belongs not to the consciousness of one individual but to the wide community of believers.

The flat opens to reveal the scene within; the door opens to make the once private room visible. With Colonel Morden, emissary of death itself, we penetrate the rooms of Harlowe Place and witness the affecting scene. Morden's description of his own role suggests an opening too: "When the unhappy mourners were all retired," he writes, "I directed the lid of the coffin to be unscrewed, and caused some fresh aromatics and flowers to be put into it" (VIII, 80; IV, 398). When the lid is replaced, as it must be according to Clarissa's posthumous directive, we do not think of closure as we once saw it in this novel. To return to the dramatic analogy, in the theater of the final volume of *Clarissa* Morden and Belford are the presenters of the action to the audience. If, however, we were to see Clarissa's pre-rape letters enacted on the stage, we would need two frames. In the first we would see the heroine writing; in the second we would see the heroine again, this time experiencing all the conflicts that mark her story. But we can only look into the second, interior, frame through the first, which is really a filtering consciousness. Anna Howe, in the first frame, perhaps to the side, looks in also. These characters are seemingly oblivious of us; it all seems so real; we are, in Belford's terms, "affected." The interior room, the private place in Harlowe Place and in Mrs. Sinclair's house, is like the inner frame of this stage of ours: to look into that room is to discover the private.

As soon as Clarissa Harlowe stops writing from Mrs. Sinclair's house, and as soon as her own private space is broken by the invading Lovelace, the inner frame becomes dark. When Clarissa flies down the corridor and into the public street, the inner stage is permanently obliterated as a separate entity. More exactly, it becomes one with the forestage—one space upon which the audience will soon see Belford's scenes depicted. Certainly it may be argued that physical space actually shrinks in the course of Morden's description of the funeral of Clarissa; yet the burial vault is still described as a "very spacious one" (VIII, 97; IV, 409), and a former admirer of Clarissa murmurs, "In that little space . . . is included all human excellence!" The ritualistic force of Morden's description depends on this: the universal value of "human excellence." Through the letters, we have all shared the story of such excellence as it suffered its "private woe." We have all seen, through her own epistolary productiveness, Clarissa's transformation into the totally visible or public. The coffin containing the body of the heroine now has the same publicness as the book containing her letters. Let us turn, then, to the letters for an examination of how the transformation from private to public is particularly fitting to the epistolary mode of the history of Clarissa Harlowe.

2

Letters

OPENERS | 4

Arrangers, Collectors, Teachers

[Eighteenth-century townhouses] . . .
expressed all their richness within.

The Georgian Society Records of
Eighteenth-Century Domestic Architecture

Quite appropriately Thomas Forde prefaced his 1660 volume of familiar letters entitled *Foenestra in Pectore* with the statement that letters are the "best Casements, whereby men disclose themselves."[1] A century earlier, the epistolarian Justus Lipsius had taken the commonly held Renaissance notion even further when he pointed out in *Institutio Epistolica* that in letters "our feelings and almost our very thoughts *are exposed* as if engraved on a votive tablet."[2] The heart is the secret, private place; the letter, "window into the heart," is both the vehicle of exposure and exposure itself.

Forde and Lipsius are talking, of course, about individuated letters and the individuated writer/addressee relationship. Samuel Richardson uses exposure in yet another way when he asserts in the preface to his epistolary manual *Familiar Letters*, a work concerned with the proper forms of conduct as well as of letter writing, that he will "expose the empty *Flourishes*, and incoherent *Rhapsodies*, by which *shallow Heads*, and designing *Hearts* endeavour to exalt their Mistresses into goddesses, in hopes of having it in their Power to sink them into the Characters of the *Most Credulous* and Foolish of their Sex."[3] To communicate a didactic message is to expose the documentary evidence within a changed context. The same principle applies if we are to document good behavior: in both instances, just as sequences of rooms or stage-spaces may be opened up to allow visibility and

79

the negation of differentiation and enclosure, so is exposure within the single letter transformed when it becomes exposed doubly through inclusion in an entire collection. At that point, the so-called private purpose of the letter writer yields to the larger, public intent of the collector—manual writer, miscellanist, or novelist. Privacy, defined as the degree to which an individual controls exposure of self, is, must be, sacrificed.

The question of private and public is also, then, one of parts and wholes. Clarissa's interior drama is projected not only onto external space—as Georges Gusdorf describes the autobiographical endeavor[4]—but onto the external spaces of the book. Looking into the heart, like opening a letter or even a sack full of letters, is tantamount to participation in the transformation of private space into public form. Hence my assertions on the opening or visualization of space are specifically related to the world of epistolary discourse and render a particularly epistolary application to Roman Jakobson's formulation of the metaphoric and metonymic poles in narrative. Jakobson sees the predominance of metonymy underlying and predetermining what he calls the "realistic trend" in narrative. "Following the path of contiguous relationships," he writes, "the realist author metonymically digresses from the plot to the atmosphere and from the characters to the setting in space and time. He is fond of synecdochic details."[5] Whereas the "principle of similarity underlies poetry," according to Jakobson (hence the predominance of metaphor in poetry), "Prose, on the contrary, is forwarded essentially by contiguity."[6] My own reading of *Clarissa*, Jakobson to the contrary, also depends on perceptions of similarity in prose fiction; and I will argue that we must ultimately reexamine the referential function that Jakobson attributes to the language of realism ("Poetry is focused upon the sign, and pragmatical prose primarily upon the referent," p. 73). Yet, the concept of contiguity, connoting spatial relationship, is particularly useful to the epistolary critic: in epistolary fiction, contiguity applies not only to the content of the discourse but to the placement of texts themselves. Who reads what, when, and in what context—questions of placement—are essential to the definition of epistolary exposure. What is really at stake in *Clarissa* is the distinction between the "authentick letter" and "feign'd story."[7] This distinction, as I hope to demonstrate here and in the following chapter, is a matter of context and contiguity.

If, as epistolary rhetoric suggests, an individuated letter represents an acknowledgement of the "real," Clarissa's attempts throughout the first two-thirds of the novel to maintain intact her room, body, consciousness, and of course her written documents, may also be viewed as a struggle to protect the authenticity of individually written letters. Like door and walls, salutation and subscription represent barriers that we, outside readers, cannot pass with impunity. Clarissa's eschewal of premeditation, the planning of sequential moments and texts, is also a denial of storytelling. Richardson thus turns to formal ends and gives new force to the old epistolary claim of authenticity: the validity of the letter as the faithful record and real document.[8] From authenticity itself derived not only moral value but verisimilitude and credibility. For example, when Thomas Brown and Charles Gildon published in 1697 *Familiar Letters: Written by the Right Honourable John Late Earl of Rochester, and several other Persons of Honour and Quality*, they were careful to point out that most of the letters (which Robert Adams Day has called "conscious literary productions") were written "upon private occasions . . . with no intention to be ever made publick."[9] Within the text appears an advertisement promising a second volume and asking if any gentlemen would be "willing to oblige the Publick" with any letters of Rochester, the Duke of Buckingham, or of Sir George Ethredge. The reader is to be enticed into reading what was ostensibly intended to be "conceal'd." What is private is more true.

The authenticity of documents written "upon private occasions" bespeaks the closeness of language to its referent that Jakobson has associated with the realism of prose. This is particularly true in letters that contain specific details, particularly topographical; we read a real text and see a real picture. While authenticity and realism are not interchangeable terms (rather, the former is an element within the latter), they may be at least interdependent. For example, in her *Apology*, a work that Richardson certainly knew, Teresia Constantia Phillips, a lady of dubious reputation, used supposedly "authentick copies" of letters to stand as evidence and explanation of her own conduct.[10] Charles Walker, in his *Authentick Memoirs of the Life, Intrigues, and Adventures of Sally Salisbury* (1723), includes identifiable London localities to buttress the credibility of his epistolary production.[11] Sally, a prostitute, pleads passion as excuse for her rather colorful career; but the narrator disputes her explanation and offers as evidence letters from Sally's former admirers explaining how they have been bilked by the infamous lady. Each separate piece of evidence is written by a particular character, each recounting a particular incident. Along the way we are told that Sally goes to Kensington to convalesce after an attack of veneral disease, then takes lodgings in Villiers Street and so on.

Letters serve as another kind of documentary evidence, however, in Defoe's *The Storm*, which purports to be a collection of epistolary accounts of the ravages of a storm on November 26, 1703.[12] Defoe says in the preface of the work that the storm is a lesson to mankind from God, that the letters "keep close to the Truth," and that the "Plainness and Honesty of the Story will plead for the Meanness of the Stile." Once again, the specificity of epistolary reporters, from highly educated clerics to mean farmers, supports the credibility of the whole, which is further strengthened when writers mention that they have been solicited to send in their accounts by an advertisement appearing in the gazette. Finally a plethora of documentary detail, including data on barometric readings and a listing of naval losses on the fateful night, serves to convince readers that this is the "real thing," these documents truly "authentick."

What Defoe calls "keeping close to the truth" really means a denial of fictionalizing and form, the preservation of specificity. Individuated letters capture not only the "sentiments of the Heart which are not to be imitated in a Feign'd Story," as Hughes asserts, but individuated moments: time recorded in letters is supposedly synonymous with the natural ordering of clock time. So says too the anonymous author of *Love's Posie*, an epistolary fiction published in 1686, when he or she points out that the letters are arranged in "natural order according to how they were sent to me."[13] Processes of anticipation and retrospection, forming connections, apprehending—that is, processes of novel reading—seemingly have no place here.[14] What is separate and isolated is more real—Heloise in her convent cell, Clarissa in her enclosed rooms, a letter separated from a complete text.

The readability of isolated texts is, however, fraught with limitations. "Facts," writes one epistolary character, Jane Austen's Mrs. Johnson in *Lady Susan*, "are such horrid things";[15] but facts and the order of truths to which they refer are, in both *Lady Susan* and *Clarissa*, not readily attainable in individual letters. That intext addressees in epistolary fictions are so often duped, deceived, even seduced, by individual letters, casts doubt on the value of authenticity and on the capacity of the private, encapsulated word to convey truth to an individual addressee. Epistolary victims of deception are not so much inadequate as incomplete readers.

Hence the function of Belford, that rather pedestrian everyman, is crucial in *Clarissa*. Just as Belford assumes an active role in the novel when he records Clarissa's escape from the confinement of Mrs. Sinclair's house and "write[s] at large all particulars" (IV, 94–95; III, 307), so does he, acting as the novelist's own surrogate, effect the double exposure by making all the letters available to a larger audience. He is the opener/collector who corrects and completes our reading, becoming literally an opener after the heroine's death. "We went together . . . into the deceased' chamber," he writes Lovelace; "I unlocked the drawer, in which . . . she had deposited her papers" (VIII, 14; IV, 353).

Belford's role is hardly unique in epistolary fictions. In mailbag miscellanies such as Charles Gildon's *The Post-Boy Robb'd of his Mail: Or, The Pacquet Broke Open* (1706), which I will discuss in some detail later, or in the earlier *Love's Posie*, we find a similar transition from the enclosed to the open. Timander, the major character in *Love's Posie*, hands over his correspondence with the beloved Iris to a frame correspondent, Lady D., explaining, "Tho I had resolv'd to conceal them from all the rest of the World, you constrain me now to put'em forth to the open view."[16] Timander is thus the opener/collector of his own correspondence; he wants to tell his story with "exactness" (p. 15) to Lady D., whose role as outside "static" addressee corresponds to our own.[17] As one who wants to know, Lady D. provides the broader context in which the whole sequence of letters is to be read. Though her connection with a didactic function is tenuous in *Love's Posie*, her role prefigures that of other correspondents in eighteenth-century epistolary fictions: those friends and confidantes in works such as Thomas Brown's *Lindamira* (1713), Mary Hearne's *The Lover's Week* (1718), and of course Fanny Burney's *Evelina* (1778), who also act as openers, helping young—letter-writing—persons in learning the ways of the world and emerging within it.[18]

Belford's role is doubly public, of course, because his is the most rhetorical voice in the novel, even as he goes about his collecting and opening tasks. He is preeminently, however, the executor, mediating between the heroine and her public, disposing not only of Clarissa's worldly goods but, most important, of her letters. He will see that the story is told, completing the work that Clarissa herself has begun. After the rape, from her rented lodgings, the heroine too is an arranger, sending off a "large packet" to Miss Howe and referring to transcriptions that Belford has made from Lovelace's letters: "I subjoin a list of the Papers or Letters I shall enclose. You must return them all when perused," she writes (VII, 111; IV, 103). For the heroine now thinks in terms of a future audience: "If it shall be found, that I have not acted unworthy of your Love . . . that will be a happiness to both on reflection," she tells Miss Howe; "Let any one, who knows my Story, collect his [Lovelace's] character from his behaviour to *me*" (VII, 42–43; IV, 58). But, aware of imminent death, Clarissa must entrust the story to other hands, those of Belford, whom she views as the "*only* person possessed of materials that will enable him to do my character justice":

> "It will be an honour to my Memory, with all those who shall know, that I was so well satisfied of my Innocence that, having not

time to write my own Story, I could entrust it to the relation which the destroyer of my fame and fortunes has given of it. . . .

"And who knows, but that Mr. Belford, who already, from a principle of humanity, is touched at my misfortunes, when he comes to revolve the whole Story, placed before him in one strong light; and when he shall have the Catastrophe likewise before him; and shall become in a manner, interested in it: Who knows but that, *from a still higher principle*, he may so regulate his future actions as to find his own reward." (VII, 74; IV, 79)

Belford is thus entrusted with the letters and the story they tell when collected; Belford, the reformed rake, is the proper choice not only because he is available to moral instruction, but because he has already read all the letters, including Lovelace's, in the original, individuated, context. Now he reminds us that double exposure, the process of opening, means double reading: both individual letters and a "whole story placed before him."

The way to moral reformation lies through the rereading, the reforming, of letter texts. To this degree, Belford must reverse Clarissa's earlier acts of enclosure or sealing of self: "I told you in mine of Monday last that she had the night before sealed up with three black seals a parcel inscribed, *As soon as I am certainly dead, this to be broke open by Mr. Belford.* I broke it open accordingly" (VIII, 14; IV, 353). In breaking open the letter, Belford represents the function of novelist and novel, changing the so-called authentic utterance by placing it within a larger structure.

The importance of the editor/arranger in bringing about this ironic transformation is, as we shall see, a given in epistolary miscellanies and even in the manuals; and the more enclosed the writing and reading space, or the more the letter is viewed as being a document, the greater is the irony when it is exposed at large. Editing and arranging are much less significant, however, in those early epistolary fictions where the reading and writing of texts and a tension between authenticity and art are not at issue. Texts are of little significance, for example, in early courtship tales and romances that simply incorporate letters as the *sermones in absentem*.[19] In a work like Lord Berner's *The Castel of Love* [1549?], the narrator is a postal go-between, and the text labeled "letter" is more accurately dialogue. The narrator in this instance is a kind of opener only in the sense that he knows the secrets that pass between the lovers and makes them known to us; his editorial functions, however, are limited: "The words and letter of Lereano finished, In stead of words, my eyes were filled with great weeping. . . . I wrote a superscription upon the letter in case Lauerola should be in doubt whence it came."[20] Fictions like *The Castell of Love* or its near contemporary, Aeneas Sylvius Piccolomini's *The Goodli History of the most noble and beautiful Ladye Lucres and her lover Eurialus* (1550), use letters within a first-person narrative to represent the enamored speech of the absent lovers. Such letters may function as concrete documents, as when Lucres speaks of her letters as moistened with her tears—but the emphasis rests on the speech contained within them. There is none of that elaborate epistolary apparatus connected with the procurement of writing materials and the difficulty of delivery that figures in both *Pamela* and *Clarissa* to focus our attention on the letter as private document and writing as an individual act.

Where the privacy of the letter is not a concern neither is the question of exposure—which is to say, neither is the question of audience. In *Clarissa*, by contrast, where intrigue and seduction are functions of the epistolary exchange, reader identification is crucial.[21] The novel provides ample evidence of what happens if the wrong reader obtains the letter, for example, when Lovelace reads—even edits—the letter Anna Howe has written the beleaguered heroine. The rake prefaces the enclosure of Anna's letter with his own comment to Belford: "Thou wilt see the margin of this cursed letter crowded with indices (*). I put them to mark the places which call for vengeance upon the vixen writer, or which require animadversion. Return thou it to me the moment thou hast perused it. Read it here, and avoid trembling for me if thou canst" (V, 30–31; III, 1). Of key importance for the plot of the novel because it reveals to Clarissa the danger of her position and the true tenor of Lovelace's motives toward her, the letter Anna has written never reaches its addressee and becomes instead a document within the correspondence of Lovelace and Belford. With this letter, Lovelace asks Belford to share his own experience ("avoid trembling"). For Belford and for us each one of Anna's warning statements becomes laden with irony: an irony that is doubled when we consider that we, Richardson's readers, are also unintended readers of Lovelace's own letters.

Epistolary fiction depends on the pretense that the reader is the unintended audience, that there has been some mistake in the communication process, that the writer is doing something he doesn't know he is doing. In discussing *Gulliver's Travels*, Robert Scholes and Robert Kellogg have pointed to the "ironic gap" between "what Gulliver thinks he is doing and what we know he is doing"; to this degree, Swift and his reader are "in collusion."[22] The more the writing of a letter is seen as a private act, the wider is that gap. The more *Clarissa* emphasizes the closed-up room in which the letter is created, the more ironic it is that we are after all seeing into that room. We are, as Walter Ong has stated in an article on audience, the "snoopers."[23] Clarissa herself remains confined and isolated however. Neither the intended (private) nor unintended (public) audience can preserve her at this point, because preservation depends on letter writing, letter reading—and letter collecting.

It is a concern with language itself—how it orders our lives, our relationships, and our fictions—that we find in epistolary manuals and miscellanies. I will not be the first to state Richardson's debt to the letter-writing manuals and miscellanies or to point out that the plethora of domestic detail in his novels finds its counterpart in epistolary guides that functioned also as codifications of domestic conduct.[24] I would go beyond other commentators, however, in suggesting that the manual or formularies—and to lesser degree the miscellanies—provided not only the subjects for future fictions but demanded readers for whom the realistic detail of individuated texts would serve also the purpose of a broader context: readers who would participate in the process of double exposure and view the whole as well as the separate parts.

We must of course begin with details, for the isolation of detail may itself be seen as a hallmark of epistolary fiction. Richardson's own *Pamela II* may be read as a conduct manual as well as an epistolary novel; in both, readers are urged to remember that the world they read of is a real place, in fact, their own place. Miss Darnford, in *Pamela II*, urges Pamela, now Mrs. B., to relate all the "*steadier* Parts of Life."[25] It is as if the process of accretion, piling up the parts, spells out the reality of the milieu described: as if words correspond exactly to objects and situations.

Ostensibly, the readers of manuals share a real-world context, a cultural code encompassing interpersonal and interfamilial relationships. The manuals set forth the forms for both good letter writing and good living; the two are not really separate. In her valuable work on the manuals, Katherine Hornbeak pointed to their growing adherence to domestic matters relating to middle-class life.[26] In one sample letter from J. Hill's *The Young Secretary's Guide* (1696) a young man asks his parents to send him clothes: "I send this letter as an humble Suiter . . . to entreat you to procure me those necessary Cloathes and Books";[27] another son seeks reconciliation with his family: "I doe beseeche you sir, that at the last, you will receive . . . to your common and ordinary liking, the most disgraced of all your children";[28] in yet another sample, a young daughter pleads to return to her parents for whom she is so homesick.[29] The letters in the formularies sound like what Barbara Herrnstein-Smith has called "natural discourse," an event that may be described in relation to an actual context in which it occurred.[30] As supposed slices of life, cameo views of domestic affairs, their very incompleteness as story underlines their authenticity.

Although we do not find out what happened next (was the young man, for example, taken back into the bosom of his family?), Hornbeak was nonetheless correct in asserting that the manuals were more than blank forms, that they carried within them the kernel of fiction.[31] The appeal of these works may well rest in their realism and in the sense they convey that their language is referential to particular persons and situations. Language appears as a closed system, seemingly fitting to the ever narrowing world of the closed domesticated family and the notion of the individual heart as a private place.[32] The closet, study, cabinet, pocket—these enclosed loci all reinforce the definition of the epistolary document as a private space shared by writer and assigned reader. As William Fulwood wrote in *The Enimie of Idlenesse* (published initially in 1568 but enjoying popularity well into the seventeenth century), the letter

blabbeth not about the hid
and secret of our mynde
to any one, save unto him
to whom we have assignde.[33]

But the assigning takes on a particular spatial orientation too when the editor of *The Secretarie's Studie* (1652) says, "It is impossible that these Epistles breathe their passions in your Closets and Studies, and you not . . . feel them in your bosoms."[34] In this case, even the unassigned responds to the document; an example of particular personalization or privatization within the family group is seen when a "letter of concell from a Brother to his Sister upon her going from the country to the Court" (from *A President for Young Pen-Men, or The Letter Writer*, 1615) receives this reply: "My most loving Brother, I most kindly take your most loving Letter, which I will lay up for your sake and mine owne good, not in my pocket nor my cabinet, but in the inward chest of my heart." Once again, the enclosed writing or hiding place is equated with the inward chest of the heart itself.

To break into the heart or private text wherein two persons share a spatial and linguistic context is to read the letter within a changed context. When the author of *The Wits Academy* (1677) says his letters will be found helpful to the "inexpert to imitate, and pleasant to those of better Judgment," he refers really to two pleasures:[35] looking in, in the manner of the voyeur, at a so-called real letter and situation; and at the same time reading doubly and knowing that the language is not in fact enclosed or referential in the way intended by the individual letter writer. Nicholas Breton's *A Poste with a Packet of Mad Letters* (1633) is a case in point. Considered as an epistolary instructor by Hornbeak, the work is called by Robert Adams

Day the first example of epistolary fiction totally in letters.[36] The problem of classifying *A Poste* arises particularly because Breton's letter samples stand out so strongly as individuated documents created by individual voices. Although the letters are not always placed or dated and are only signed with initials, specificity dominates. No letter is *only* an epistolary example. If a supposed young man named Robert writes, "Margerie, I have received your snappish Letter whereby I see you are more angry, than I thought you would have beene for a misword or two, but I hope to mend what is amisse," then Robert and Margerie are individual characters who create themselves before our eyes in their letters.[37] Despite editorial intrusion through the title of the letter ("Robert to Margerie his sweetheart"), the characters sound real. They are involved in a real human relationship, and we are pleased and charmed when Margerie answers, "I thought you were misused to write to me as you did: but friends are nere so farre out, but they may be as far in againe" (p. 38). At the same time, of course, we realize how "farre out" we, readers of Breton's book, really are from the enclosed epistolary relationship.

Angel Day's manual *The English Secretorie* (1586), subtitled *Wherein is contayned, A Perfect Method, for the inditing of all manner of Epistles and familiar Letters,* clearly states its didactic function, setting forth its letter samples with marginal notations of classical rhetorical divisions. If, however, we look at one of Day's letters like the "example Disswasorie, wherein a man of wealth sufficient, is dissuaded from the marriage of his daughter, to the riches of an older wealthie Miser," we have only to remove the rhetorical marginalia and the label, "Example Disswasorie," and we have something quite similar to Breton. Ostensibly, Day is not interested in telling stories, but certainly a story in miniature is suggested here, where the situation might be one created by Eliza Haywood (who published a miscellany in the 1730s) or Samuel Richardson. Here is the old marriage-for-property question, presented with all the stops pulled out. The writer admonishes the wealthy father to avoid proceeding in

> an Action so unhonest, an intendment so vile, a matter so much impugning nature, as that the verye earth, or hell it selfe, could not belch out against the fayre Virgine, so huge and so intollerable a mischiefe, to matche I saye, the matchlesse favour of soe young and dainty a piece, to the filthy tawnie deformed and unseemely hue, of so wretched and ill favoured a creature . . . whose toes are swolne with the gowt, and legges consumed with the dropsie, whose leane carkase beareth no apparence but of olde scarres.[38]

The argument depends on the concrete details it heaps up, and the writer seems so swept up in his epithets—"swolne" and gouty toes and dropsical limbs—that we wonder how much control Day's rhetorical terms, *distributio* and *hiperbole*, really provide.[39] The writer seeks to deter the wealthy father from his course by creating a horrific image of the future son-in-law. Although the grasping parent is not appealed to on the grounds of his daughter's feelings about such a spouse, a sentimental tale may be seen in embryo in the letter; and it is as if to restrain such a tendency that the epistolary instructor summarizes the letter's arguments under the appropriate rubrics and removes from it the specific data of place, date, and signature that would allow the document to stand on its own as a qua letter.

For the example cannot ultimately stand on its own. If its realism derives from our sense of a private textual space where words correspond to real-life situations shared by writer and reader, the manual, in its completeness, stresses broader referents. Typically, a manual such as Angel Day's or J. Hill's contains a preface explaining the nature of the familiar letter and setting forth instructions on how to use the manual. Both Day and Hill label epistolary examples according to category: "Letters of Advice," "Letters of Recommendation," and so on, Hill taking particular note of his audience when he states that he has arranged his book by pedagogical principle: he will begin with examples suitable to younger people of both sexes and "by degrees (rise) to matters of such Moment as may be of universal Concernment."[40]

If the notion of "universal Concernment"—or universal audience— contrasts strikingly to the careful assigning of a letter to a specified addressee, so, as we would expect, do the manuals stress the ordering function of language beyond the strictly personal. Angel Day declares that he provides letter models in his book because "nothing . . . in the common use and conversation of men deserveth more praise, than that which is well ordered, and according to the time place and presence usually appointed and discreetly furnished" (p. 4). A manual is after all a book about language and the act of written expression within both a private and social context; it depends on the use of general rubrics—time, place, and presence—even if it defines the individuated letter as "the intent and meaning of one man, immediately to passe and be directed to an other, and for the certaine respects thereof, [it] is termed the messenger and familiar speeche of the absent."[41] We are reminded too of Richardson's own directive (in the preface to *Familiar Letters*) that he will instruct the "*Forms* requisite to be observed on the most important Occasions" in order to "mend the Heart, and improve the Understanding." Forms of using written languages are tantamount to forms of moral and social behavior.

Public forms in the epistolary world, like the private, may be also expressed in spatial terms. Words become the yardsticks of human relationships: "Give me leave to tell you, that though you shut me out of the Sanctum Sanctorum of your Friendship, nor will admit me into the inner Court of your Familiars, you shall not exclude me from the outward Court of your acquaintance."[42] Letter writers, as the manuals indicate, also assign space. Not only the selection of phrase, but its place on the paper helps define the relationship that has occasioned the writing of the letter. To one's equals, Fulwood advises, one should place the subscription in the middle of the sheet. J. Hill, some hundred years after Fulwood, explains that the subscription "ought to express in some measure the Quality of the Person, by an owning Superiority in him to whom the Letter is directed, or a Power and Authority in him who writes it over him to whom it is written"; thus, to a person of quality, the writer must leave a good distance between the body of the letter and the subscription.[43] As Richardson's Pamela would learn in the next century, space on paper bespeaks both private and social space.

If writing a novel in letters allowed Richardson to make readers sense they were listening to—or reading—real people, if letters enabled the novelist to tap sources of natural discourse, they also helped make possible a work that is about the capacity of language to fulfill both private and public needs. It is the consciousness of the fluidity of language, its capacity for transformation from the narrow to broadly referential, from closed to open, that Ian Watt fails to account for in his discussion of the language of formal realism. Certainly the novel—and we would add, the letter samples of the formularies—"allow a more immediate imitation of individual experience set in its temporal and spatial environment" than other literary forms;[44] but language is not a "purely referential medium" in *Clarissa* or in epistolary collections. In establishing the decorum of the individuated letter as dependent on time, place, and presence, Angel Day pointed to the content of letter language as a fluid entity coterminous with the other two counters in the communication triad.[45] Even here, words do not "correspond to objects" but are always qualified by the context of the reading and the identification of the reader. To this degree, language that appears encapsulated in letters is in fact always subject to the ironic transformation resulting from changing that context. In conceiving of language as a one-to-one referential medium in *Clarissa*, perhaps Watt was responding to that very avoidance of literariness that marks so much epistolary rhetoric: the letter viewed as the window into the heart, a real picture of its creator. I would argue rather, however, that what one sixteenth-century epistolarian called the "pleasure of perusal" is the reader's conscious participation in the transformation of language from private to public, from referent to sign.[46]

If we turn from the manuals to mail-bag miscellanies, we find borne out in the fiction the opener figure who effects the double reading called for by this transformation of individuated letter documents. The post-bag "robbers" in such works as Breton's *A Poste* or Charles Gildon's *The Post-Boy Robb'd of his Mail* draw us in to the individuated letter and supposed real-life situation and at the same time remind us that we are standing outside the epistolary correspondence in a position that may be more ambiguous than that of epistolary learner.

In both Breton and Gildon, the collection of letters we are reading seemingly derives from a robbery and subsequent invasion of a mailbag wherein individual letters reach not their intended addressees, but ourselves, readers of the book. Reader identification is in fact a key issue in these miscellanies since no one letter is only a letter or only an epistolary sample. Breton apparently wants it both ways, intentionally creating an ambiguity between private and public. The editorial voice in *A Poste* focuses attention on the opening and arranging of letters, even as it emphasizes the closed, or private, nature of the epistolary relationship. Breton's reader is involved in the fiction of looking into a private space. If he were playing the part only of epistolary instructor, Breton would be able to assign us, unintended readers, the role of would-be letter writers; but he intentionally leaves open what part of the audience is to play—except perhaps that of people who like to read other people's mail. He tells us in the preface that the postman dropped a "Packet of Idle Papers, the superscription whereof being onely to him that finds it, being my fortune to light upon it." He goes on to explain that he then "fell to opening . . . the inclosure," in which, he says, "I found divers Letters written, to whom, or from whom I could not learne" (section entitled "To the Reader"). Ambiguity dominates here; the letters are "idle papers," the writer and reader supposedly unknown.

That is, private documents remain ambiguous, or unreadable, until they are no longer private; the particular interest of mailbag miscellanies lies in their literal depiction of the invasion that transforms the individuated letter text. We too become invaders, looking into the broken mail sack whose contents—the matter at hand, the terms of the epistolary relationship— cannot be fully known to us; rather we must place the letters within a broader, perhaps didactic, frame of reference provided by the whole text.

The reader's role is more accurately, then, to read actively, placing individual documents into a completed whole. In this sense, the rifled mailbag motif looks toward not only later epistolary narratives but even non-epistolary sentimental fictions: Henry Mackenzie's *Man of Feeling*, for example, a novel in ostensible "fragments," renouncing literariness even as it forces readers to complete the narrative by filling in the missing parts.[47]

The role of the robber editors is to help in the act of completion. *The Post-Boy* elaborates on a situation similar to that so briefly described in Breton. A group of young men robs the postboy and reads the contents of the mailbag; but unlike Breton, the principal narrator recounts the events of the exploit as well as the contents of the robbed letters to a frame correspondent whose identity remains vague ("Sir"). The so-called robbers comment upon each letter as they read it to one another, enclosing this commentary in the whole packet sent off to the frame correspondent. The robbers are intermediary characters, then, who as openers intercede between letter writers and unintended readers.

Though in crude form, the robbers suggest the work of the epistolary novelist as well as his fictive creations. They are both openers and arrangers. In underlining the irony of addressee substitution, the mailbag miscellanies anticipate the stock situation of the epistolary novel, the openers of the postboy's bag of private letters the precursors of the editorial figure or, as in the case of Belford, literary executor. But in invading the private space of the mail sack and the letters it contains, the robbers play Lovelace's role as well as Belford's. As we have already seen in *Clarissa*, opening and arranging are interdependent acts: Belford's function is posited on Lovelace's. Although the rake's committing the rape is, on its own, a highly destructive act—what he himself calls "unnatural"—Belford's entrance into the novel as epistolary reporter and his collecting of individual letters depend on that rape. Similarly, Lovelace's domination of the novel's space occurs between that of Clarissa and that of Belford: he is in this sense a bridge between the private and the public, just as Gildon's robbers are.

As in *Clarissa*, too, Gildon extols the value of the private: the letter's authenticity as document and as the sincere expression of the heart. The sacred character of the mail sack whose contents dominate *The Post-Boy* is imaged in the sacred character of the heart itself. Gildon, to a degree that presages Samuel Richardson, is interested in the value of interiority; like Richardson, he too seeks evidence of man's moral nature within the internal place. Letters, he says, represent "pulling off the Mask in a Corner of the Room," for "we are apt to write that in a Letter to a Friend, which we would not have all the World know."[48] The book itself is similarly described as an interior space: we are told in the preface that the author wishes not to "delay the Visitors in the Porch too long," but rather we must enter into the structure of the volume in order to experience the private and "secret villanies" of the human heart. And if the heart and the document in which it finds expression are individuated spaces, so too is language defined according to the individual voice; we are to be convinced that we are being given here a sincere view of the heart because we will not see in the letters "the Stile of an Etheridge, or a Dryden, a Temple, or a Lock; nor the Wit of Wycherly. For here as in Comedy, Jerry shou'd not speak like Manly, but everyone in the Dialect, and Language fitting his Character" (p. 3). Like Breton, but unlike the usual epistolary manual writer, Gildon announces himself as interested in individual speakers (writers). "Stile" is also a gauge of authenticity.[49]

Yet Gildon counters the private with the public function of the work as a whole. In the language of exposure that also foreshadows that of Richardson, he states that the design of his book to "lay open the secret Rogueries and Villanies of Mankind"; his aim is "Amusement, not altogether unentertaining, since it gives a view of the various Manners, Follies, and Vices of the Active Part of Mankind" (p. 6). If letters depict the state within, they also look without, presenting what an earlier epistolarian, Margaret Cavendish, called "scenes": "The truth is, they [the letters] are rather Scenes than Letters to Express the Humors of Mankind, and the Actions of Man's Life."[50] Although disavowing the influence of Etherege, Dryden, or Wycherley, Gildon, himself a writer of drama, is nonetheless interested in the transformation of private, authentic, letter into public, viewable form.

A quasi-moral tone, didacticism as the identifiable raison d'être of the epistolary exposure, is underlined through the frame correspondent, who bears a tutorial relationship to the young robbers. The principal narrator refers to the fact that this person has advised him to assume a "Sedate and thoughtful Life," but the "lighter Sallies of Youth" have proved too pleasant, and hence, he says, "I will by sending you a Relation of one of our Frolicks, convince you, that we make a better use of our Extravagences, than you do image" (p. 3). The young men are engaged in a study of mankind; the "frolick" is aimed at perception into the human heart. "Mankind walks in a Mist, and cannot be seen at a little Distance; you must keep close to it," the writer explains. In breaking into the mailbag, the young men have found evidence of the "Janus creature man" (any honest letters they have taken care to send on to their proper addressees). With their postal haul, they repair to a "Summer-House in the Middle of the Garden" to open their several packets. Hence it is within a retirement setting that these students of man's nature go about their work, a site for contemplation and discussion among friends, a place that contrasts strikingly with the hustle and bustle of the London scene, whose precisely named streets and neighborhoods have figured so prominently in the description of the robberies. We do not know the actual location of the summer house in the garden, just as we do not know the exact identity of "Sir." Such ambiguity, together with the lack of epistolary documentation marking the frame letter, once again illustrates the difference between the frame correspondence with its more didactic and hence public function and the private, carefully documented and specifically addressed letters within the mailbag.

Certainly it is a long way from Gildon's mailbag miscellany to the epistolary art of Richardson; yet the themes of exposing, opening, broadening—and transforming the letter language from its originally referential, or authentic, function—are central to both. In both, readers experience a transition from reference to rhetoric, the latter comprehending the former. The "air of probability" of Richardson's novel demands that letters be read as individuated documents. And at the same time, for the novelist who has resolved upon a particular method, with an "end in view," the authentic depiction of the heart must be countered against the formal rhetorical needs of the book. Images of opening function so effectively in Richardson, then, because they suggest the physical, spiritual, and *epistolary* dimensions of the novel. In Elizabeth Rowe's *Friendship in Death in Twenty Letters from the Dead to the Living* (1733), by contrast, moral message dominates over the individuality of the writer; a heavy-handed moralism results, as we sense that a public voice is only masquerading as the private. A "Young Woman who died in a Convent in Florence" explains how she preferred death in the cloister rather than seduction, and then the "Chrystal Gates Open'd a spacious Entrance, and the blest Inmates received me to their Mansions."[51] But how much more effective, how much more concrete the letters and the situation, when Belford says, "I broke [the packet] open accordingly." For Belford reminds us that letters are the issue here: the writing, reading, and exchanging of letters. If editors (or even robbers) as openers help balance the major dichotomies of the epistolary work, providing readers with a whole text that is more than, or different from, the sum of its parts, the dynamic of epistolary exchange is also part of the opening process. The relationships that exist between individual writers and readers, and the function of epistolary confidants and learners, provide the subject of the following chapter.

OPENERS | 5

Correspondents

Reception rooms are arranged in pairs.

A. E. Richardson
and H. Donaldson Eberlin,
*The Smaller English House of the
Later Renaissance, 1660–1830*

In view of the epistolary exposure of Clarissa that we have already witnessed, both at her own hands and at those of Richardson, Clarissa's careful directions regarding the treatment of her body after death can seem only ironic. "I will not, on any account, [permit] that it be opened," she writes; "I have already given verbal directions, that after I am dead . . . I may be put into my coffin as soon as possible: It is my desire that I may not be unnecessarily exposed to the view of anybody" (VIII, 106–7; IV, 416). Clarissa apparently desires her body closed to view because the physical body is of little importance at this point in her history. At the same time, however, the body of the book sits before us, spelling out the exposure, and the transformation, of the letters that compose it.

As I have suggested in the preceding chapter, the work itself, and the new context it provides in which the letters are to be read, is the ultimate opener. The point here is that epistolary arrangement varies in importance according to the kind of letters written: the more that writers connect themselves to the letters they write to their confidants and the more the writing represents phenomenological process, the more necessary is that double exposure that I have noted in chapter 4. For letter writers like Clarissa, knowing the self is predicated upon telling (writing) about that self. Richardson's mastery of the "to-the-moment" technique allowed him to create letter writers who attempt to break down the time gap between acting and writing, hence to negate the insurmountable duality of teller and actor;[1] but the more enclosed such correspondences, the more cut off from an outside world, the more necessary is the opening device. No less ambiguous than the "idle papers" found by Breton's narrator, an isolated letter is not readable by the unaddressed reader; neither is a correspondence wherein writer and addressee share a context to the degree that little needs to be written (taken to an extreme it will be seen that total sharing or enclosure in the correspondence would terminate the epistolary process altogether: there would be nothing to write, nothing to know). The very vulnerability of such correspondences indicates their lack of reliability or readability to the larger audience. That distance that epistolary opener figures place between letter texts and readers of the book is essential to our achieving the total view. For, once again, reliability comes about not only through authenticity—epistolary rhetoric to the contrary—but rather, through inclusion in a total context. Reliability can only emerge gradually as we proceed through the novel; it depends on authenticity initially—and certainly Richardson provides ample evidence of the importance of documents as documents—but transcends it.

It is not enough to speak of the letters that comprise *Clarissa*. We must ask, rather, what kinds of letters. The identification of the addressee, and the writer/reader dynamic, is, as the formularies have already told us, an integral element in answering that question. Lovelace and Clarissa, however, begin with themselves and their own inextricable connection to the letters they write. Lovelace tells Belford that his "heart . . . has communicated its tremors to [his] fingers," that his words will "expose" him to Belford's contempt (VI, 40; III, 269); Clarissa worries about the sincerity of her letters to Anna, remarking, "I can but write according to the shape he [Lovelace] assumes at the time. Don't think *me* the changeable person . . . if I seem to contradict" (III, 154; II, 82). She fears too that the desperation of her situation will make her guilty of evasions and "little affectations" in her letters. Writing to the moment is an attempt on Richardson's part to catch the image of the heart with as exact a stroke as possible. "Withdraw, fond heart, from my pen," writes Harriet Byron in *Grandison*; "Can the *dearest* friend allow for the acknowledgement of impulses so fervent, and which, writing to the moment . . . the moment only can justify revealing?" (III, 104). Clarissa, writing ostensibly to allay, not stimulate, passion, acknowledges, "Were I rapidly to pursue my narration, without thinking, without reflecting, I believe I should hardly be able to keep in my right mind: Since vehemence and passion would then be always uppermost; but while I *think* as I write, I cool, and my hurry of spirits is allayed" (II, 217; I, 387). Clarissa sees the letter as the keeping of the account, the documentary evidence, akin even to the will or testament.[2] She thinks here of letter writing as placing a distance between her self and her passion or suffering.

That logic is a fateful error, of course, as Lovelace well knows. His own writing is always a reflection of his passion, writing to the moment a device to keep himself at the pitch of tension; he writes to Belford shortly before the fire scene and his first planned attack upon Clarissa: "So near to execution my Plot; so near springing my Mine; all agreed upon between the women and me; or I believe thou hadst overthrown me. I have time for a few lines preparative to what is to happen in an hour or two; and I love to write to the *moment*" (IV, 385; II, 498). And after Clarissa has fled for the first time for Mrs. Sinclair's house and Lovelace's power, the rake admits:

> Yet I must write, or I shall go distracted. Little less have I been these two hours; dispatching messengers to every Stage; to every Inn; to every waggon or Coach, whether flying or creeping.
>
> . . . .
>
> But for this scribbling vein, or I should still run mad. (V, 16, 28; II, 518, 525)

Lovelace really mocks Clarissa's own faith in the distance and reflection asserted in letter writing when he tells her during one of their more mellow periods:

> I proceeded, therefore—That I loved Familiar letter-writing . . . above all the species of writing: It was writing from the heart (without the fetters prescribed by method or study), as the very word *Correspondence* implied. Not the heart only; the *soul* was in it. Nothing of body, when friend writes to friend; the mind impelling sovereignly the vassal-fingers. It was, in short, friendship recorded. (IV, 286; II, 431)

Lovelace's statement on familiar letter writing, despite its reference to the "fetters" of epistolary "method or study," recalls the language of the letter-writing manual. "Friendship recorded" attests to the dual nature of the epistolary correspondence: the letter has decorum if its content and "stile" are suitable to both reader and writer. But clearly, Lovelace's own letter writing is much more *self*-centered. His strange dream of the "stolen pen" (V, 240–42; III, 145–47) is testimony to his pride in his own literary creation, his own consciousness. In a work that is dominated by the notion of invasion, Lovelace dreams that Clarissa has penetrated his consciousness and has made him write as she would have done in regard to his vile schemes; a note of contrition is evident in his remarks to Belford:

"As I hope to live, I am sorry . . . that I have been such a foolish plotter . . . I hate compulsion in all forms; and cannot bear, even to be *compelled* to be the wretch my choice has made me! . . .

"Upon my soul, Jack, it is a very foolish thing for a man of spirit to have brought himself to such a height of iniquity, that he must proceed, and cannot help himself."

But, a moment later he states:

> Thus far had my *conscience* written with my pen; and see what a recreant she had made me!—I seized her by the throat—*There!*— *There*, said I, thou vile impertinent! . . . Had I not given thee thy death's wound, thou wouldest have robbed me of all my joys. . . . Adieu, to thee, O thou inflexible and, till now, unconquerable bosom intruder.

He has dealt her the "death's wound" because "she was a thief, an imposter, as well as a tormenter. She had stolen my pen."

That Richardson should choose the strange phantasmagorical realm of dream in order to expose Lovelace's consciousness is not so unusual. We have already witnessed Clarissa's dream of being stabbed through the heart by the demon lover (II, 283; I, 433), and the rake's reference to dealing the "death's wound" recalls the interweaving of sex with violence.[3] Clarissa's sexual fears and Lovelace's sexual aspirations may be seen fully crystalized in dreams, which, expressed in letters, become in turn part of the reality of the novel. But the obvious sexual imagery of Lovelace's dream also holds a specifically epistolary significance. The "death's wound" is clearly a sexual death (in her will Clarissa expresses her concern lest Lovelace view "*her dead,* whom he Once before saw in a manner dead" [VIII, 107; IV, 416]), but so also is the power of the invading phallus suggestive of the pen that invades the space of the letter paper. In taking over Lovelace's "pen"—according to the terms of the dream—Clarissa has only reversed the normal action of the novel. She has taken on Lovelace's role and has invaded the physical space of *his* letter.

Typically in *Clarissa* the invasion of the letter (which we see in the text before us) is mirrored in the invasion of both the body and the consciousness of the writer; but ultimately, of course, it is Richardson himself who penetrates the private worlds and private beings of the characters of his novel: he shows us their letters. Even more important, he plays off the letters one against the other. A pattern of refraction and reflection appears. Richardson adopts, through Belford, the stance of arranger of letters, each letter becoming a building block or piece in a large mosaic.[4] Writing of Henry James, Raymond Williams has pointed out that though James eliminated moralizing from the novel, he did not exclude morality, for "any knowing, any showing, any *presentation*—to take the exact word for James—is moral inevitably. The selection and the placing are the judgments."[5] To consider the "selection and placing" in *Clarissa* is to consider also how the dynamic of epistolary exchange effects a disclosure: a letter writer, to letter reader, and to Richardson's reader.

The dynamic within the epistolary exchange may vary enormously according to the individual example; for we are really asking what roles the addressee may play. In an important sense, however, the letter reader always performs a public function. That the letter exists at all presupposes its writer's faith in a public, or shared language. The notion of sharing is seen in Emile Benveniste's statement that in epistolary exchange the "*you* cannot be thought of outside of the situation set up by *I*."[6] If, then, the *you*, transformed into an *I*, writes a letter in reply, he or she must do so within the context established by the received utterance. The addressee is allowed—even forced—to share the situation set up by the initial letter writer. He or she is the stimulus because of whom the writer ostensibly recorded all the details comprising the letter, and as the individual who wants to know, he or she puts together all the details (or pieces) received.

The letter must reach its proper addressee, first, because no other reader can read it (or put it together) in the same way as the epistolary confidant. Anna Howe alludes to the importance of audience when she tells Clarissa that although Mrs. Howe wishes to be privy to the correspondence of the young women, Anna does not desire such an extra audience; as she explains:

> My mother *might* see all that passes between us, did I not know, that it would cramp your spirit, and restrain the freedom of your pen, as it would also the freedom of mine; And were she not moreover so firmly attached to the contrary side, that inferences, consequences, strained deductions, censure and constructions the most partial, would forever be hawled in to teaze me, and would perpetually subject us to the necessity of debating and canvassing. (III, 210; II, 121)

An onlooker, especially one whose own attitudes will conflict with those of the correspondents, will spoil the freedom of the letter. As an unsympathetic reader, it is implied, Mrs. Howe will turn the letter into something different from Clarissa's original intent. Audiences determine performances.

The relationship between the correspondents is a special one. Anna quite rightly points out to Clarissa early in the novel that the heroine has granted a significant gain to Lovelace in agreeing to a private correspondence. "I know he has nothing to boast of from *what* you have written," Anna tells Clarissa; "But is not his inducing you to receive his Letters, and to answer them, a great point gained? By your insisting that he should keep his correspondence private, it appears that there is *one secret* which you do not wish the world should know; And *he* is master of the secret!" (I, 66; I, 45). To involve oneself in a private correspondence is to commit oneself to what Raymond Williams has called the "secret sharing." The epistolary novel is above all things the work of "secret sharing."[7] In the preface of *Foenestra in Pectore*, Thomas Forde wrote that "Friends mingle souls, and make mutual discoveries of, and *to* one another,"[8] but if the pen, like the pulse, "discovers our inward condition," it does so according to the context established in the epistolary exchange. Brown was still thinking of mutual relationship when he "edited" *Familiar Letters: Written by the Right Honourable John late Earl Rochester* (coauthored with Charles Gildon, 1697). Here, a "letter of Courtship to a Woman of Quality" reads:

> To express the grateful sence of the Obligation I have to you, Cannot be effectually done, unless I had *your* Pen. If you observe my stile, you will have reason to conclude I have not received your ingenious Letter of yesterday, which shou'd have been a precedent to me, and a rule to write by.[9]

The very self-conscious writer of this letter is concerned that his own creation is not appropriate to the "stile" of what he has received. To that degree a role has been forced upon him; whatever he uncovers of himself will be dictated by the received epistle and the writer's judgment of the reader's expectations.

When we deal with epistolary exchanges, then, avid writers must also be avid readers. That attention to text that Richardson demanded of his readers is a reflection of the attention his characters pay the texts of the letters they read and write. We are reminded of Diderot's fantasy of finding the letters of Pamela or Clarissa; having read them, he says, "with what anxiety [*empressement*] did I arrange them by order."[10] And what sacrilege if any line be omitted. Richardson's own real-world correspondence with Lady Bradshaigh provides a superb example of careful textual analysis. Here we see Richardson and one of his favorite correspondents carefully numbering paragraphs so that they miss no detail in responding to one another's letters; phrases dance back and forth like Ping-Pong balls, read, analyzed, played upon, returned—and of course savored.[11] Nothing is really let go, for as Mrs. Carter had said, no detail is ever too trivial for the familiar letter.[12] The detail is important because it belongs jointly to the participants in the epistolary game.

John Carroll suggests in his preface to Richardson's *Selected Letters* that the novelist's correspondents may have encouraged the plethora of detail in the novels; reacting to created characters as if they were living persons, the correspondents wanted to know more and more of the private lives of these fictional beings.[13] I would argue further that letter writing itself encourages the seeking after trivial detail. We have seen how even the early letter-writing manual isolates the activities of an ordinary life, emphasizes separately each facet of an individual's social existence by outlining a specific rule. So also is Richardson a seeker after detail. He tells Miss Mulso, "I only want a description of the room you all generally sit in, then shall I have in view [your own countenance and that of your family]."[14] To Lady Bradshaigh he writes of his desire to "stimulate ladies, to shew what they are able to do."[15] The response of Mrs. Scudamore, another correspondent, to the stimulation was quite typical: "What encouragement do you my dear Sir give to my trite Pen! you, not only give a sanction to my running on about my Boy, but for every material circumstance that may occur; this sure is very indulgent to me, since it can only relate to me, and mine."[16] Even the product of the "trite pen" is significant to Richardson, the investigator of private places; he reminds us of Miss Darnford, Pamela's correspondent/student in *Pamela II*, who describes herself as a "diligent Observor of the Conduct of People in the marry'd Life to each other." Miss Darnford wants not only the "rapturous Scenes" (!), but the "steadier Parts of life"; she wants to know, for example, how Mr. B. behaves in his wife's "Retirements."[17]

Miss Darnford's—and Richardson's—desire to penetrate private places suggests the enthusiasm with which earlier epistolary editors invaded the contents of the private mailbag for public (didactic) purpose. *Pamela II* is really a conduct manual in epistolary form with Miss Darnford as correspondent playing the role of student seeker-of-evidence. Her function is an important one: she is, as Lady Bradshaigh observed in another context, a "sting" that "draws the honey."[18] She is a stimulus for release because she is one who wants to know. So too is Richardson an observer, though with the important difference that he is more actively a teacher, turning the details outward. Through his surrogate Belford, he places the reader in the place of learner, hence emphasizing the didactic function of the whole work.[19]

Richardson teaches in both his personal correspondence and his fictions. For him and his circle of correspondents the fictional world may even intrude upon the real.[20] Miss Westcomb, one of the novelist's young woman correspondents (later, Mrs. Scudamore), was not pleased by such intrusion, of course, when Richardson sent her pages from *Sir Charles Grandison* in lieu of a personal letter; when she complained, however, Richardson argued for the importance of the reading context, asking whether the letters intended for the novel, "having been seen by very few, might be said to be written only to those few." "When they are laid before the World," he goes on, "then they are written to that World."[21]

Lady Bradshaigh seems much more accepting of fictional intrusion, her responses to Richardson's "stimulation" simulating those of a Pamela or Clarissa. Explaining the apparent incoherency of her own letters, Lady Bradshaigh says, "I write just as I was affected at the time, now thinking *one* way, now another."[22] Note how Lady Bradshaigh casts herself as a Richardsonian heroine in this comment, again "to the moment":

> Here it is, just brought me, another letter from you. Now for an end of Suspence at least. What ails me? I cannot open. Lord, how I tremble. What an unconscious rising in My throat? . . . I cannot go on. . . . I was forced to lie down, very griev'd for a moment by a flood of tears. . . . I was not without some hopes of further reliefe from your letter, but at last! I am but more confirm'd in what I dreaded [her advice has not been taken: Clementina will not marry Sir Charles Grandison].[23]

In her letter, Lady Bradshaigh moves through time. She transforms an actual past into present ("Here it is. . . . I cannot go on"); and a moment closer to the presence of the writing moment is described as past: "I was forced to lie down." Then she moves still further past ("I was not without some hopes"), until finally she comes back to the present writing: "I am but more confirm'd." Time is a fluid medium here, seemingly contrasting to the day-to-day quality of the actual letter, which began on February 22 and ended on February 27, 1754. The letter becomes a performance throughout which Lady Bradshaigh recognizes the existence of her absent audience. Implying her control over the audience, she ends the long letter: "It is therefore high time to release you."

The release *of* the audience terminates the process of release of details *to* the audience. It is by now a commonplace of epistolary criticism that the letter writer must have a reader/receiver.[24] Nathalie Sarraute's discussion of the importance of receiving in the dialogue of the modern novel seems particularly appropriate to eighteenth-century epistolary form. Words, she explains, move outward like "protective capsules," records of "interior movements," reaching out to another individual, hopefully to be "protected" there from "exterior dangers."[25] In epistolary exchange, however, where we deal always with written words, literally recorded detail, the role of the receiving audience is particularly significant: the receiver reads, responds—even collects—letters. The letter is a concrete entity, exerting a force of its own within the exterior world. For Richardson, the letter's existence in the exterior, public realm verifies the value of private experience. The epistolary receiver, acting as an agent in the publicizing process, is never, then, what Anna Howe calls a mere "Stander-by" (I, 72; I, 49). "I shall run mad—with what heart can people write when they believe their letters will never be received?" asked Lady Mary Wortley Montagu;[26] and Clarissa, who tells Anna that she would write regardless of the presence of a reader, admits that "it would be more inspiriting to have some end in view in what I write, some friend to please; besides merely seeking to gratify my passion for scribbling" (III, 221; II, 128). The end is the reader who partakes in the transformation of scribbling into public form.

Clarissa's need for the "end in view," or addressee, bespeaks an active receiver who helps maintain the epistolary action through which all must ultimately be made known: to writer, addressee, and novel reader. More exactly, the epistolary dynamic must be translated into the novel space, thus complicating and qualifying the question of where, or when, the knowing occurs; arrangement itself takes on particular importance, and the epistolary showing so often leaves us suspended in a partial knowing. Our perceptions derive from the kaleidoscopic configuration wherein disjunctions in writing, receiving/reading, and novel-reading time function to break apart any single letter as letter. For epistolary characters and for ourselves the reading of any one letter alters what we thought we understood: the bits in the kaleidoscope now form another pattern, this one no less tenuous than the last. Clarissa's questions in Letter II, no. 43 (I, no. 88), where she agonizes over the decision whether to leave her father's house with Lovelace, the questions and exclamations, "What am I about to do!," or "What to do I know not" (II, 314; I, 454), reverberate in an apparent vacuum. They hang suspended, awaiting answer or resolution. Clarissa has not yet received Anna's letter of advice (which Richardson has just shown his novel readers as Letter II, no. 42; I, no. 87). She deals alone with the cajolery of Lovelace's "ecstatic letter."

There is an answer of course, at least, an answer for the questions of this present: Letter II, no. 44 (I, no. 89), written "in answer to" Letter II, no. 42

(I, no. 87). More exactly, there is an answer to a letter. Saturday night (the writing time of II, no. 43, I, no. 88) gives way to Sunday morning. Clarissa has not read Anna's letter with its counsel that if she elopes with Lovelace she must marry as soon as possible; and the heroine's tone differs markedly from that of her preceding letter. The anxious questioner gives way to the reader of a letter text ("But now I come to the two points in your letter which most sensibly concern me: thus you put them"). Anna has pointed out that Clarissa could do worse than marry Lovelace, and we have seen in Letter II, no. 43 (I, no. 88) Clarissa herself quoting Lovelace's promises in a manner suggesting that she does not reject them outright. But actually seeing on the page of Anna's letter the question of marriage, the heroine is convinced of the rashness of the plan. Hence her response: "The manner of putting your questions abundantly convinces me that I ought not, in *your* opinion, to *attempt* it. You no doubt *intend* that I shall *so* take it; and I thank you for the equally polite and forcible conviction" (II, 318; I, 457). Clarissa admits that she had "begun to waver" in her last letter, but Anna's letter has now "absolutely determined" her not to go off. Through reading, an at least momentary resolution has been achieved—for Clarissa and for us.

Such discontinuity and partial resolution is a function of the distance between writer and addressee. The closer the addressee and the more active a role he or she plays in the epistolary knowing, the greater is our sense of the inadequacy of any single letter text. This is not to deny that written narrative always presupposes a certain distance between writer and reader;[27] but if the correspondent receives the minute recordings of a self in the process of writing, then reading recreates that self and reinforces the intimacy between two individuals. If, on the other hand, the addressee receives an objectified account or description, the letter may be said to assert distance between its writer and reader. The point seems obvious, but we cannot say in *Clarissa*, for example, that Anna is *always* a mere reader, always an advice giver, or always a reflector.[28] Description for the sake of description tends to distance its reader. In Angel Day's "letter Descriptive wherein is particularly described, an auntient Citie by laying downe the severall parts thereof," the "severall parts" of the city dominate the writer's interest.[29] Although a brief exordium expresses the "friendship betweene both parties" (writer and addressee), the exact identity of the audience is really irrelevant. Something similar occurs in Gildon's *The Post-Boy Robb'd*, where the role of the frame correspondent appears to fade out as the narrator becomes caught up in the details of his robbery story as a story.

To the degree that letters deal in scenes, so do correspondents play a passive role. For example, though the *Letters from a Lady at Paris to a Lady at Avignon* (1716) purport to emanate "more from the Heart than the Head," they in fact "open new Scenes of Gallantry among the most considerable Personages in France."[30] The epistolary exchange turns out to be a tandem gossip column with little apparent connection between the two ends of the correspondence. Scenes, as we have seen in the Belford letters, are not intended to be private. The notion of opening is irrelevant in this context to the opening of the heart or a private place; and there is, as we would expect, none of that epistolary apparatus which emphasizes the transformation of private into public visibility.

Similarly, "scene" is the term Margaret Cavendish uses to describe her *Sociable Letters*, pointing out that she has not chosen to write in the form of a play because she has already written twenty plays and besides: "I saw the Variety of Forms did please the Readers best, and that lastly they would be more taken with the Brevity of Letters, than the Formality of Scenes, and whole Playes."[31] Margaret Cavendish says that her two correspondents, "two ladies, living at some Short Distance from each other," express in their letters their "Tye in Friendship" and "Discourse by Letters, as they would do if they were Personally together"; but once again, the letters, bearing no detail as to place, date, or even exact name, seem focused upon a much more impersonal audience. The writer is not really personally involved with the scene described and appears to use the epistolary friendship only as the stimulus for delivering moral observations: "Thus you say see many of our Sex are made Saints, though they be Sinners, but they are Sainted for their Beauty, not for their Piety, for their outward Form, not for their inward Grace," writes Cavendish (p. 15). The writer's observation upon one Sir F. O., who married his servant, may be of particular interest to students of *Pamela*: "I am sorry Sir F. O. hath Undervalued himself so much below his Birth and Wealth, as to Marry his Kitchinmaid, but it was a sign he had an Hungry Appetite, or that he lived a Solitary Life . . . or he hath tried her Virtue, and so Married her for Chastity" (p. 88). But the tendency to moralize—the writer here has little hope of happiness for the mismatched pair—for a generalized audience places Cavendish much closer to the Renaissance instructive letter than to that which properly became an element in the novel.

The novel is concerned rather with the contents of the heart, the letter as a text that expresses the writer's recreation of experience; it depends too on an interested reader who will also be drawn into the experience described in the letter. The difference between Margaret Cavendish and Samuel Richardson is the difference between the scene and what Anna Howe calls an "affecting narrative." When Madame Du Noyer says that descriptions of places and things "relieve the Mind by changing the Scene, and varying the Objects of its Pleasure," she is thinking of the epistolary description in the same way as Angel Day had done two centuries before. For the scene to be affective in the sense intended by Anna Howe, readers must be interested in writers; and confidants, as letter readers and exchangers, are more than learners. As Clarissa's confidante, Anna Howe becomes, for example, an extension of the writer herself.

The more the writer is conscious of him or herself as the writer of a letter, the more active and the less distanced the audience is. Amaryllis, in Mary Hearne's *The Lover's Week* (1718), is seduced by a Lovelace-like rake; yet she does not write a confession based upon close introspection and examination into individual experience, as Clarissa does: she consciously tells a story.[32] Distance between writer and addressee is maintained throughout. Similarly, Lovelace expresses his sense of his own role as epistolary audience when he complains to Belford that the latter has written him a letter of moral exhortation: "A confounded *long* one! tho' not a *narrative* one" (IV, 374; II, 490). The rake wishes to maintain the distance of the narrative audience; he voices his strong disinclination to become the object of Belford's moralizing. Belford's letter, in behalf of Clarissa, has faced its addressee directly, like Angel Day's "Disswasorie" example: "O Lovelace, Lovelace, how many dreadful Stories could this horrid woman [Mrs. Sinclair] tell the Sex! And shall that of a Clarissa swell the guilty List?" (IV, 372; II, 489).

Lovelace himself is keenly aware of the kinds of letters people write and where writer and reader stand in relation to each other. After Clarissa's final, successful escape from Mrs. Sinclair's house, the rake writes Belford a long letter spewing forth his anger and frustration in half-fantastical accounts of Clarissa and her fate: a "confession," he calls it, written "for the sake of humouring [his] conscience" (VI 112; III, 318). Near the close of this letter, evaluating his own creation, Lovelace writes:

> This, thro' [*sic*] written in character, is a very long Letter, considering it is not a narrative one, or a journal of proceedings, like most of my former; for such will unavoidably and naturally, as I may say, run into length. But I have so used myself to write a great deal of late, that I know not how to help it. (VI, 113; III, 320).

Again, Lovelace distinguishes between narrative and confession, the latter serving mainly the self but attempting to draw in the reader too. He speaks of wanting to "show the sincerity of my contrition" (VI, 112, III, 319). To show the reader is to show the self also. In stating that his letter is not narrative, Lovelace indicates that he does not conceive here of a distanced audience. To this letter Belford will not respond as he has on a previous (narrative) occasion: "Thou, Lovelace, hast been long the *Entertainer*; I the *Entertained*" (III, 264; II, 157).

Belford is no longer the entertained because at this point in the novel he plays a much more active role; at the moment of Lovelace's writing his "confession," Belford is in London himself and has in the preceding letter given the rake the long narrative account of Clarissa's escape to freedom. Lovelace, in the country attending his uncle, is in fact removed from the events that compose the narrative (as the narrative audience must be). His letter, written from confinement and thus suggestive of Clarissa's own, is, then, also an enforced "disburdening" ("I know not how to help it," he has said) of the individual to whom action other than epistolary is impossible.

When Richardson experimented with character and situation in *Familiar Letters*, by contrast, he concerned himself mainly with narrative letters in which the entertained addressee stands at some distance from the writer entertainer. For example, the young woman who writes in "A facetious young Lady to her Aunt, ridiculing her serious Love," is a variation on the witty young woman who appears in earlier epistolary works— Berina in Mrs. Davys's *Familiar Love-Letters Betwixt a Gentleman and a Lady* (1725)[33] or the young Iris in *Love's Posie*—who was to make her reappearance as Anna Howe and Charlotte Grandison. Describing the visit of her would-be suitor, the "facetious" lady writes:

> After he had pretty well rubbed Heat into his Hands, he stood up with his Back to the Fire, and with his Hand behind him, held up his Coat, that he might be warm all over; and looking about him, asked with the Tranquillity of a Man a Twelve-month married, and just come off a Journey, How all Friends did in the Country? I said, I hoped, very well; but would be glad to warm my Fingers. Cry Mercy, Madam!—And then he shuffled a little further from the Fire, and after two or three hems, and a long Pause [he went on to talk about sermons].[34]

The answer from the aunt, however, is hardly what the young woman is expecting. "I am sorry," writes the older woman, "that a Woman of Virtue and Morals, as you are, should treat so ludicrously a serious and pious Frame of Mind, in an Age, wherein good Examples are so rare" (p. 115). The aunt's answer asserts the force of Richardson's prefatorial statement that he will expose "shallow Heads." The young writer's letter does not meet with its expected response because the lively description has only, in the aunt's terms, betrayed weakened virtue. What was for the writer (and is, for us) the pleasure of detail is, for the moral guide, grounds for remonstrance; and the response turns the letter into something its supposed writer never intended. Hence, in the manner typical of the writer of the epistolary miscellany, Richardson, we may say, has it both ways: he diverts even as he turns that diversion to didactic ends.

Lovelace's narrative letters to Belford and the moralizing responses function similarly to the "facetious young Lady" exchange. Belford turns the rake's accounts into what are, for the unintended reader, exposures of the evil heart. Something different happens, however, when Clarissa writes to Anna Howe a description of her undesired suitor, Solmes:

> The man stalked in. His usual walk is by pauses, as if (from the same vacuity of thought which made Dryden's Clown whistle) he was telling his steps: And first paid his clumsy respects to my Mother; then to my Sister; next to me, as if I were already his Wife, and therefore to be last in his notice; and sitting down by me, told us in general what weather it was. Very cold he made it; but I was warm enough. (I, 153–54; I, 105)

Like the young lady, Clarissa also catches visual detail: Solmes's stalking gait, his clumsiness, his strained attempt at conversation, and, like the gentleman in the *Familiar Letters*, his appearance of taking a relationship for granted. But the confidante, Anna, responds in a way unlike that of the moralizing aunt. When Clarissa receives an answer to this description and to her narrative relating to her family's behavior she is surprised by her friend's vehemence. "I would be in my own mansion," writes Anna; "I would shut my gates against them; and bid them go, and be company for each other" (I, 182; I, 125). Clarissa in turn admits then in her next letter: "[When] I come (upon reflection) to see by *your* severity what I have given occasion for, I cannot help condemning myself" (I, 193; I, 132). Like the facetious young lady, Clarissa has received a somewhat unexpected response to her description; but within the novel, and notably not within the manual, the letter in reply allows the original letter writer to recognize what in herself she has not seen before. The entertained party is a reflector, a source of self-knowledge to the writer.

More exactly, Anna's letter serves as a concretization of what Clarissa calls "latent inclinations" ("I know not my own heart, if I have any of that *latent* or unowned *inclination*, which you would impute to *any other but me*" [II, 315; I, 455]). In responding to what she has read, consciously or unconsciously, the confidante brings to the surface the implications of the letter she has received, even expressing those same confused latent inclinations toward Lovelace that Clarissa herself experiences but cannot explain in her own written words. In the brothel sequence, after Clarissa has reported Lovelace's latest "encroachment," the physical struggle over the letter, Anna responds vehemently, "I hate the man—Most heartily do I hate him, for his teazing ways. The very reading of your account of them teazes me almost as much as they can you" (IV, 61; II, 278). . . . "Let your Anna Howe obey the call of that friendship which has united us as one soul, and endeavour to give you consolation" (IV, 63; II, 279). Anna gives, however, more than consolation. Although claiming that "the man is really a villain, my dear," we find her suggesting what are in fact the same tactics that Lovelace has contemplated with Belford just two letters preceding: Anna writes, "I wish you could come at some of his letters. Surely a man of his negligent character cannot be always guarded. . . . Let him be called upon at a short warning, when he is writing, or when he has papers lying about, and so surprise him into negligence." That Anna is indeed "teazed" by the rake, as she has had him described to her by Clarissa, is seen further when she, like Lovelace, equates invading a letter with invading a person:

> Such enquiries [looking into other people's letters], I know, are of the same nature with those we make at an Inn in travelling, when we look into every corner and closet for fear of a villain; yet should be frightened out of our wits, were we to find one. But 'tis better to detect such a one when awake and up, than to be attacked by him when in bed and asleep. (IV, 62; II, 279)

Granted the confidante spends most of her letter bolstering the spirits of the beleaguered heroine, but her fantasies of postal and sexual invasion demonstrate more than passive reading: "It was therefore to be some *man*, or some *worse spirit in the shape of one*, that, formed on purpose, was to be sent to invade you." That Clarissa's trial should be expressed in terms so obviously sexual is of course an appropriate reaction to the account of the struggle over the letter, which is in turn a struggle over control of the heroine's person. Anna is even surprised at her own eloquence, which, on re-reading, she finds superior to her usual style. "Warm imaginations are not without a mixture of enthusiasm," she concludes (IV, 67; II, 282). Through the epistolary dynamic we have seen, however, that if Anna's imagination is warm, it is because Clarissa's own is warm in the telling.

Anna has been invited to share as completely as possible in the experience of the enclosed room. This means that the linguistic cues signaling the invitation are supposedly not intended for an audience at large—contrast, for example, Belford's "I will give thee an account of a Scene" (VI, 270; III, 425)—but rather, take the form of statement of subjective reaction to experience. In a useful article on Richardson's style as a record of "movements within," A. R. Humphreys has found in the syntax of both *Pamela* and *Clarissa* what he calls an alternation between subjectivity and objectivity.[35] In *Pamela*, he cites instances of an "elliptical counterplay of action and comment" and concludes that, in the letter, form, action, thought, and speech both direct and indirect can all be treated as simultaneous unity: there is a blending of "reported speech and internal monologue."[36] Since we do not have epistolary responses in the major portion of *Pamela* and only one letter from Pamela's parents during the period of Pamela's confinement at the Lincolnshire estate, it is mainly to *Clarissa* that I wish to apply Humphrey's thesis. I am, like Richardson, interested in correspondence; and as Clarissa tells Anna Howe, "That is not a *Correspondence* where Letters are not answered" (III, 153; II, 82).

Humphrey's notion of the merging of the subjectivity and objectivity of movement from the fact of mind to interpretation of fact must first be qualified: there are no freestanding facts in epistolary form; every fact or event is the product of the mind's recreation. In Rousset's dualistic terms, events belong to the I/actor as opposed to the I/writer, though the one creates the other. Certainly, however, Richardson's heroines not only write as close to the moment as possible but also, like the writers in *Familiar Letters*, recreate dialogue that comes close to *appearing* like events taking place in the present moment. The absence of "he saids" or "she saids" suggests the absence of recording presence. Such dramalike dialogue, which Clarissa uses in Letter I, no. 17 (both editions), for example, renders an apparently unified objective picture of the I/actor. Let us look at an extended passage from that letter for an examination of movements from objectivity to subjectivity and note at what points the writer demonstrates what we might call audience awareness. The subject of the letter is once again the proposed marriage of Clarissa with the "odious Solmes," and Clarissa is reporting her latest encounter with her mother. She writes to Anna:

> I wept.
> I have made enquiry already after a housekeeper. I would have your good Norton; but I suppose you will yourself wish to have the worthy woman with you. If you desire it, that shall be agreed upon for you.
> But, why, dearest madam, why am I, the *youngest*, to be precipitated into a State, that I am very far from wishing to enter with anybody?

You are going to question me, I suppose, why your Sister is not thought of for Mr. Solmes?

I hope, Madam, it will not displease you if I were?

I might refer you for an answer to your *Father*. —Mr. Solmes has reasons for preferring *you*—

And I have reasons, Madam, for disliking *him*. And why am I—

This quickness upon me, interrupted my Mother, is not to be borne! I am gone, and your Father comes, if *I* can do no good with you.

O Madam, I would rather die, than—

She put her hand to my mouth—No peremptoriness, Clary Harlowe: Once you declare yourself inflexible, I have done.

I wept for vexation. This is all, all, my Brother's doings—His grasping views—

No reflections upon your Brother: He has entirely the honour of the family at heart.

I would no more dishonour my family, Madam, than my Brother would.

I believe it: But I hope you will allow your Father, and Me, and your Uncles, to judge what will do it honour, what dishonour.

I then offered to live single; never to marry at all; or never but with their full approbation. (I, 114–15; I, 78).

There are in this passage only four instances of the narrator's even obliquely addressing the audience: "I wept," "interrupted my mother," "I wept for vexation," and "I then offered to live single." Note how suddenly "vexation" is followed by, "This is all, all my brother's doings" and how such rapid transition causes confusion as to whether Clarissa as narrator addresses her reader (as a continuation of "I wept") or her mother. The statement is an example of that telescoping of subjective statement and objective response to which Humphreys has referred. Only Clarissa's mother's response—"No reflections upon your brother"—informs us that the accusation of the brother has taken place within the dialogue. Clarissa moves in an instant from recorder of detail ("I wept") from a later vantage point in time to participant in the dialogue that is now being recorded. She is playing two roles at once.

As the dialogue continues, Clarissa's interruptions become more prevalent and more prolonged:

O my dear, how my Mother's condescension distressed me at the time!—Infinitely more distressed me, than rigour could have done. But she *knew*, she was to be sure *aware*, that she was put upon a harsh, upon an *unreasonable* service, let me say, or she would not, she could not, have had so much patience with me.

Let me tell you then, proceeded she, that all lies in a small compass, as your father said. . . . You know your father has made it a point; and did he ever give up one he thought he had a right to carry?

Too true, thought I to myself! And now my Brother has engaged my Father, his fine scheme will *walk alone*, without needing his leading strings; and it is become my *Father's will* that I oppose; not my Brother's grasping views.

I was silent. To say the truth, I was just then *sullenly* silent. My heart was too big. I thought it was hard to be thus given up by my mother. (I, 117–18; I, 80–81)

Clarissa now records less of the dialogue and more of her own reactions to it: "how my mother's condescension distressed me," "Too true thought I to myself," or "My heart was too big."[37] The heroine retreats from the dialogue, falls into silence, her very distance from her mother seen in the latter's misunderstanding of that silence: "I see, my dear, said she, that you are convinced," Clarissa reports to Anna. As Clarissa increases the distance between herself and her mother, however, she decreases that between herself and her audience/correspondent. Every interruption of the dialogue, whether a simple "proceeded she" or a statement of internal distress, represents an acknowledgment of the reader's presence. Finally, there is the direct address to the correspondent: "Did not this seem to border upon *cruelty*, my dear, in so indulgent a Mother?" (I, 118; I, 81). The narrator's question is really gratuitous; she herself has created the scene so that cruelty is demonstrated within it. The writer always controls the audience, her subjective reactions to the reported dialogue serving as a link between herself and her correspondent. With each statement, writer invites reader to share the distress, or, in the terms I am using here, to share the private space of consciousness.

In the subjective letter the addressee is invited also to share a temporal world created by the writer. The telescoping of time within Clarissa's epistolary accounting to Anna is particularly marked in another example of encounter, this time between the heroine and Lovelace (III, no. 25; II, no. 22). Having by now placed herself under the rake's power, even to a degree to which she herself is not yet fully aware, Clarissa quotes to the length of a full paragraph Lovelace's protestations of love, then summarizes:

These were his words as near as I can remember them; for his behaviour was so strangely wild and fervent, that I was perfectly

frighted. I thought he would have devoured my hand. I wished myself a thousand miles distant from him.

I told him, I by no means approved of his violent temper; he was
too boisterous a man for my liking. I saw *now*, by the conversation
that had passed, what was his boasted regard to my *Injunctions*. (III,
152; II, 81)

In this instance, Clarissa initially distances the event from the time of writing to the correspondent: "These were his words as near as I can remember them." The *now* of "I saw *now*," however, belongs to another point in
the past, a midpoint presumably after the conversation with Lovelace but
before the writing time; and it is apparently that *now* that has determined
the writer's frame of mind: Clarissa wants to tell Anna what she has perceived. But still, that is not enough either; another summing up is required,
another viewing of the events, this time even closer to, perhaps commensurate with, the point of writing: "But on recollecting all that passed, I
plainly see, that he means not, if he can help it, to leave me to the liberty of
refusing him." She plainly sees now the awesome fact—as she apparently
did not at the first remembrance of his words—because the act of writing
down the recollection has effected a new level of awareness. The phrase
"Yet you see," which begins the next paragraph, underlines the force of
Clarissa's new perception that Lovelace is gradually cutting off her own
options, but does so through turning that insight outward to the addressee:
the *you* cannot see unless the *I* has plainly seen also.

The letter of subjective interpretation may lead its addressee freely
through frames of time and space because its only context is the state of
mind that creates it. In the novel, unlike the manual or miscellany, there are
few labels to limit the context and guide our reading. This is an important
point if we are considering the differences between letters asserting a public role within a manual or miscellany and those like Clarissa's that serve to
describe a process of individual self-awareness within a novel. For example, in Eliza Haywood's *Love-Letters on All Occasions Lately Passed Between
Persons of Distinction* (1730), each letter is given a title that may characterize
its writer ("The repenting Aristus to the too cruel but most adorable Pan-
thea"); or the circumstance of the writing ("from Elismonda on having
fail'd to meet [Theano]"; or from the same "on hearing he [Theano] had
not been at the Place appointed").[38] In Clarissa's pre-rape letters, on the
other hand, subjective interpretation, called into play through the process
of writing, encloses and interacts with what is reported; the mind of the
writer actively creates the context in which the letter is to be understood.

Visual evidence or so-called objective fact—"his [Lovelace's] behaviour was so strangely wild and fervent"—is linked causally to the narrator's reaction: "I thought he would have devoured my hand. I wished myself a thousand miles distant from him." Even if, as in Letter III, no. 25 (II, no. 22), Clarissa begins with an apparently freestanding statement of fact— "Mr. Lovelace has seen divers apartments at Windsor, but not one, he says, that he thought fit for me" (III, 142; II, 74)—she will end: "O my dear, how uneasy to us are our reflections upon every doubtful occurrence, when we know we have been prevailed upon to do a wrong thing!" (III, 144; II, 75). Again, the subjective summation dominates, calling upon the distant addressee to witness her statement of mind.

Letter III, no. 25 (II, no. 22), is written in two parts, "Saturday Evening" and "Sunday Morning." The "Sunday Morning" section, which includes the passage quoted above ("These were his words"), begins: "Ah! this man, my dear! . . . he is such a wild, such an ungovernable creature (*He reformed!*) that I am half afraid of him" (III, 144; II, 75). The dialogue to follow will clearly be an exposition of Lovelave's "wildness" and "ungovernable nature," ending, as we have seen, with Clarissa's conclusion that the rake will not readily accord her the liberty to refuse him (III, 152–53; II, 81). The uneasiness of Saturday evening has given way to outright anxiety following the encounter on Sunday morning. In a profound sense, Clarissa's letter is an image of the heart and mind. The subjective state is the filtering lens, a window through which all events in the inner house must be viewed. To this degree, the so-called objective world in *Clarissa* is inseparable from the subjective.

As the epistolary formularies also made clear, in any communication triad of addresser, message, addressee, the verbal structure of the written message depends on which element in the triad receives the greatest emphasis. What gives particular force to Clarissa's expressive letters, dominated as they are by the writer, is that Richardson contrasts them with Belford's much more rhetorical or referential epistles. My purpose here has been to identify the broad characteristics of Clarissa's letters before the rape: that they are written in a confined space, that even dominated by the subjective state of the writer, they assert the presence of an actively reading confidante who receives the details and stands as reflected image of the writer herself. The internal state of the writer is crucial in this letter, the private space of the epistolary setting signaling the dominance of the creating consciousness. With its connections to the literature of spiritual consciousness, such a letter is, on its own, a sacred article.

Yet, the force of my own argument here is that the sacred letter is not enough. To complete our discussion of the correspondent as opener is to examine also those letters that do not require the opener in the same sense: public letters where the intended reader is the learner or character in need of advice or reformation. The letter serves here as moral exhortation, its efficacy depending on the relationship not between reader and writer but rather between reader and letter content qua content. The epistolary setting is no longer important, and it is irrelevant to speak of the blending of objective and subjective because the letter is focused on an objective rendering of event.

I have discussed in chapter 3 the relationship between the open letter and the visual picture as it appears on the stage in sentimental drama. In the present context, I wish to emphasize that the intended reader is still an epistolary opener—that is, he or she provides the raison d'être of the letter's being written—but no longer opens the consciousness of the writer, because the details the writer recounts are already distanced from his consciousness. In a letter such as VI, no. 65 (III, no. 105), for example, as in Angel Day's "Example Disswasorie," all the details are focused on the reformation of the rake. Written by Belford after he has replaced Lovelace in London, this letter runs to nineteen pages and is the first instance in the novel of Belford's assuming a major letter-writing role. Together with its companion, Letter VI, no. 66 (III, no. 106), it describes Clarissa's arrest, incarceration, and persecution by the whores on a trumped-up charge intended to return her to Lovelace's power and it precedes Belford's arranging for Clarissa to be reinstated in her lodgings above the glove-maker's shop in Letter VI, no. 68 (III, no. 108).

If we look to Belford's leter for the establishment of context, we will see that at the outset the letter is turned toward its reader: "What a cursed piece of work hast thou made of it, with the most excellent of women," writes Belford to Lovelace. "Thou only, who are the author of her calamities, shouldst have attended her in her prison. . . . This last act, however unintended by thee, yet a consequence of thy general orders, and too likely to be thought agreeable to thee . . . has finished thy barbarous work" (VI, 270, III, 425). Of the first six paragraphs of the letter, five address Lovelace directly, establishing him as the author of the scene that is to follow. Furthermore, the narrative account is prefaced by, "*Little knows the public what villanies are committed by vile wretches in these abominable houses, upon innocent creatures drawn into their spheres.*" Belford seemingly invites a public to look in at his scene also.

Like Clarissa in her early letters, Belford also uses dialogue in his letter;

but unlike the heroine, he can report in dialogue the "shocking particulars" of Clarissa's arrest only as he has heard them from the whores at Mrs. Sinclair's house. These are not particulars of the self. He himself realizes the difference between such secondhand reporting and the real thing when he remarks, "I will give thee an account of a Scene that wants but her [Clarissa's] affecting pen to represent it justly; and it would wring all the black blood out of thy callous heart" (VI, 270; III, 425); but he carries on, like the affecting pen, with the dialogue between Clarissa and the arresting officers, only sparsely sprinkling his account with "he saids" or "she saids."

Since Belford is reporting a dialogue in which he himself held no part, he is always distanced from it, and there can be none of that telescoping of objective and subjective that we saw functioning under the truly affecting pen. The visual detail provided in the course of the scene ("A crowd had before begun to gather") as well as the "said she's" when they do appear, are all of a piece with the actual words spoken. They do not bespeak audience awareness in any special way, because the *whole* scene is turned toward an audience. Neither is there any question as to whom the writer addresses, for Belford faces Lovelace directly: "*The divine Clarissa, Lovelace—reduced to rejoice for a cup of cold water! By* whom *reduced!*" (VI, 277; III, 430).

In the same way that Colonel Morden distances himself from the funeral scene, Belford casts himself as a spectator, to this degree aligning himself with the addressee. Before turning to Lovelace directly at the conclusion of the first segment of the letter, he remarks, "Here I must rest." It is not so much the effort of writing, but rather, the effect of the narrative itself. Similarly, the second section of the narrative is concluded: *Pause here a moment, Lovelace! and reflect—I must*" (VI, 279; III, 431). We are reminded that Belford has been a rake, too, and hence most suitably exhorts Lovelace now to think on the evil he has perpetrated:

> If thou thinkest this reflection uncharacteristic from a companion and friend of thine, imaginest thou that I profited nothing by my long attendance on my Uncle in his dying state. . . . And could I have another such instance *as this*, to bring all these reflections home to me? (VI, 284; III, 435)

In a work that concerns itself with letters and learning, Belford is a learner, death part of his lesson. His role it is to preside at three death scenes: that of his uncle, of Belton (a fellow rake), and finally of the "divine Clarissa."

Ultimately, Belford evolves into the totally reformed individual worthy to execute the will of the heroine.

There is nothing new in itself in the kind of letter that Belford writes. His exhortation to Lovelace sounds, for example, like that of Lyly's Euphues to his friend Philautus: "Thou wilt must Philautus to heere Euphues to preach . . . yet wil I exhort thee as a friende, I would I might compell thee as a Father."[39] What is unique in *Clarissa* is Richardson's structuring his work so that the public force of Belford's letter—like that of Morden's funeral account—depends ultimately on the private letters that precede it. Clarissa herself has seen this of course. "May my story be a warning to all," she has written (VII, 365; IV, 275); and if Lovelace wants his letters back from Belford in order to keep them secret (VI, 251; III, 413), Clarissa is concerned to have hers for their public value (VII, 110–11; IV, 103). Similarly, her reference to death as that "last closing *scene*" (VI, 205; III, 381; italics mine) again underlines her sense of her life as rendered public and visible. Finally, Clarissa, Belford-like, writes Anna Howe advice on the advisability of accepting Mr. Hickman as husband. Hers might be the language of the conduct manual.[40] The agony of private consciousness is no longer reflected in Clarissa's letter. "Our *views* must now be different," Clarissa writes her friend. About to suffer (or, in her terms, enjoy) the final release, the heroine no longer needs her confidential correspondent.

FROM SOLITARY TO SOCIAL || 6

These . . . private things, walling us in,
have . . . public endings.

Weldon Kees

Clarissa is a great work of epistolary fiction because it draws on two separate but complementary streams of epistolary tradition: the solitary and the social.[1] The solitary needs her confidante, we have seen, as a vehicle of release, a stimulus to the self and a receiver of the letter that embodies that self. To this degree, the attempt on the part of the letter writer to bridge the gap between herself and her audience expresses a conscious awareness also of the self as the center of experience: the movement outward to the external other is held in tension by the creating center. When the dynamic is broken, however, the social function, always latent in the letter, asserts itself anew; "private things" indeed have "public endings." Privately written letters are realized in public form.

To authenticate the private and render it ultimately an instrument in the moral teaching of individuals available to the lesson may be seen as a central concern of sentimental literature and its introspective forebears, secular and spiritual. A language of release characterizes the Ovidian love letter as well as the spiritual diary:[2] the release of emotion, of experience, of self; the release that in *Clarissa* is seen as tantamount to transcendence. The higher authority for which the heroine yearns in her arduous journey back to her father's house and the structure of Christian pilgrimage that dominates the broad pattern of the novel underline termination in what Richardson called the "consummating perfection."[3] When letter-writing friends

118

like Lady Bradshaigh complained of Clarissa's dying, the novelist reminded them that they had not read the novel adequately. If they did not see that the death of "divine Clarissa" represents a consummating perfection, they had missed the analogous "perfection" of the heroine in the form that is the novel.

In *Clarissa*, unlike the Ovidian letter and its descendants, however, the language of release denotes not only emotional, imaginative, even spiritual, process but also an awareness that experience is authenticated ultimately in a complete story. Stories belong to the world—a world of details, issues, relationships, the world of the formularies and conduct books that also explored the use of so-called private documents to frame public lessons. From the stuff of individuated moments Richardson rendered the realism that Ian Watt has so well explored. But it is the fusion of the transcendent and the mundane that so strikes us in *Clarissa*, Richardson's effecting the process wherein release to a more spiritual realm is incumbent upon release in a series of day-to-day documents. He made the myth of Christian redemption real—no less than his own created character Belford makes the real records of that suffering available in the novel; or Pamela, the first heroine, having moved beyond her own "contrivances" or imaginative acts, delivers herself through her own letters.

As if to follow the pattern of Clarissa's own story and complete the circle at its beginning, I begin this final chapter with a return to the solitary and the writing closet as locus of subjective, imaginative experience. Here is Lady Mary Wortley Montagu explaining in a letter to a friend, "Excuse my dullness and be so good never to open a Letter of mine in one of those minutes when you are entirely alone."[4] And here is the notion of the letter as play or performance: Lady Mary will avoid the "plain Spitalfields style," she says, for it is more "diverting" to create scenes within the letter: indeed, she goes on, it is a "cheat so pleasing that I can't helpe [*sic*] indulging it" (I, p. 9).

The pleasure of the cheat is also that of creating and controlling an audience. "I believe I am the only body who thinks the better of people for being absent. My Fancy represents to me only what is pleasing in them," explains Lady Mary (I, p. 34). In a similar vein, Mrs. Carter, whose "Ode to Wisdom" Clarissa quotes, apparently enjoys the "long telescope" in which she gazes to catch an "imperfect sight" of her addressee. Such a telescope allows no very distinct outline; it leaves room for the play of imagination, and one may, as the Countess of Pomfret said, fly to the correspondent in an escape from a perhaps unpleasant reality.[5] There is apparent comfort in the one-to-one epistolary relationship. Mrs. Carter writes to her friend Elizabeth Montagu expressing her pleasure that the latter found time to write a letter despite the presence of many friends: "that might pretend to a right of excluding me . . . from your thoughts. . . . But still I longed to have you tête-à-tête in your dressing-room talking from your heart, talking to me."[6] So too Richardson expresses to his correspondent the Reverend Mr. Skelton another variation on the theme of "only to me": "Let me beg of you to suppose me on the dreary spot with you," writes Richardson; "and as then you will have no other person near you that will be tolerably conversable, I shall hope to have you all to myself."[7]

Having the audience to oneself is really controlling the vision of the addressee. A double vision, recalling the dichotomy of the I who experiences and the I who writes, is evident when Mrs. Carter gives her friend an account of a particular landscape and remarks: "You would have been charmed . . . I saw and thought for you as well as myself."[8] Mrs. Carter writes here a letter that Angel Day would have classified as descriptive, but unlike Day's examples, she attempts to lessen the gap between self and addressee by expanding her own experience to take in the correspondent. The degree to which the writer may succeed in this process is seen from the letter reader's point of view when the Countess of Hertford remarks that the Countess of Pomfret's accounts of her European travels enable her both to see the foreign scenes rendered in the letters and to feel the "satisfaction you enjoy while you are observing."[9] The notion of experiencing doubly is emphasized more strongly in a particularly moving correspondence between Mary Granville Delaney and her sister, when Mrs. Delaney points out: "I am sure were the art of writing unknown my loss would be infinitely greater than yours. . . . How happy I am to have my thoughts correspond so exactly to yours."[10] The words could be those of Clarissa to Anna Howe: "I should *indeed* deserve censure, if I kept any secret of my heart from you" (IV, 299; II, 439). Or Anna to Clarissa: "I cannot separate myself from you; althou' I give a double instance of my vanity in joining myself with you in this particular assertion [that we know "what is the rightest to be done"] (III, 292; II, 177). In the same letter where Anna expresses that she, like Clarissa, is also teased by Lovelace, she implores her friend: "Let your Anna Howe obey the call of that friendship which has united us as one soul, and endeavour to give you consolation" (IV, 63; II, 279). Finally, after the rape when Clarissa feels her "awful distance" from her correspondent, she sees in Anna her own former self; "You shall be my subject," she writes, "as you have long, long been my only pleasure" (VI, 115; III, 321). Is not the self really the subject of the letter, and in addressing the still whole, virginal Anna, does Clarissa not attempt to assert her own wholeness (despite having been broken by the rape)? The writer and addressee are seen as two sides of a split personality: one soul.

It is as if through such splitting that writer and addressee play out the dichotomous roles that Adam Smith called "I, the examiner and judge" and "I, the person whose conduct is examined into and judged."[11] The result is the "lively and affecting" letter (VII, 77; IV, 81), record of the mind in motion. Mrs. Carter seems to lament the lack of a pen to note every mental movement when she says,

> When I endeavour to think every thought is clouded by confusion, and sinks in languor. Under such circumstances one cannot help reflecting with transport on a machine so constituted as to answer every motion of the directing mind. But such an advantage would be a dangerous temptation in our present state.[12]

Mrs. Carter's ideal, like that of Samuel Richardson, is to capture in entirety the elusive present immediately as it is perceived; but, like the novelist, she cannot in fact create a "machine" that will truly "answer every motion of the directing mind." She can only write letters—an activity that seems however to have its own therapeutic effects: "I have writ myself into contentment," Mrs. Carter ends her epistle.

Process is the characteristic that Northrop Frye particularly notes when he attempts to define the "Age of Sensibility."[13] Frye, in his well-known essay, counters process and "fragmentary utterance" against product and totality, pointing out that when a reader achieves the sense of literature as aesthetic product then also is there detachment from the work. Clearly, in the examples I am citing here, such detachment is not sought; rather—and I am using Frye's terms—pity and fear become states of mind without objects, moods common to both the work of art and to the reader that bind them together psychologically.

Frye does not emphasize, however, how important is the breaking of such binding in epistolary literature, a breaking that throughout this study I have read as central to the emergence of the epistolary novel. Anna Howe, the confidential correspondent, is the heroine's life line beyond the confining walls, and she actively attempts to free the beloved friend; but Anna must fail because, as confidante, she is herself too closely bound into the letter written in confinement. In reading Clarissa's letters as she receives them—perhaps even delayed or forged by Lovelace—she is witness only to isolated moments of experience, individuated process. Release for

Clarissa must take, as we have seen, other forms. The language of subjective process must yield to the power of the complete text.

Language on its own will not do; that is why the sentimentalist's language so often seems inadequate. One critic (Edward Copeland) has gone as far as to assert that "sentimentalists are trapped by words in an attempt to present essentially nonverbal experiences" (consider Mrs. Rowe's statement that the "pomp of language fails");[14] but to argue, as Copeland does, that *Clarissa* demonstrates the "same undeviating, simple-minded descriptive orientation of *Fanny Hill*" is surely to misread Richardson's epistolary effort. Copeland isolates *Clarissa* both from other process literature and from its own novelistic structure. He fails to see that Richardson was interested in both process and arranged products: with writers and with readers.

Pamela is a case in point. Although my purpose here is not to discuss Richardson's first heroine in the same detail as his second, we nonetheless find in Pamela, a diarist and letter writer, a particularly useful example of the language of release turned to the purposes of both subjective process and epistolary product. The servant girl's connections to the spiritual diarist and autobiographer have already been noted by critics: her preoccupation with detail, her search for preordained pattern and reassurance of her own spiritual state.[15] But as a confined writer, Pamela also presents dichotomies similar to those of Clarissa and other monologic narrators—fragment or part versus whole, isolation versus social integration.

Pamela begins as an isolate. Having resisted her master Mr. B.'s temptations to seduction, the servant girl has been duped and imprisoned by him in the Lincolnshire house. The letters to her parents, as letters, must now cease, and Pamela writes: "It is Grief to me to write, and not to be able to send to you what I write; but now it is all the Diversion I have, and if God will favour my Escape with my Innocence . . . with what pleasure shall I read [of these Prospects] afterwards!"[16] Despite the loss of her external addressee, Pamela tells us she will not stop writing; she will become a journal keeper and her own audience. She lives at this point in the novel in an enclosed circle, her own isolation imaging that of the individuated moments, or pieces, of her story.[17] If, in Frank Kermode's terms, "ending presupposes form," there is in this part of *Pamela* little "sense of an ending," little suggestion of form.[18] The future is a conditional. Spatial and temporal isolation mark the diary keeper who "writes to know what he is when not writing, but . . . can do so only in writing."[19] There is then only the writing, language on its own: "it is all the diversion I have," says Pamela.

For Richardson's heroines, as for spiritual diarists contemporary with them, spatial and temporal confinement may even be requisite to the business of knowing and writing. Mrs. Housman, a diarist of the mid-eighteenth century, records: "I think I was afraid of losing that little Sense I had upon my Spirit after the church service. So soon as conveniently I could, I retired, to breathe out a few Desires, and to beg spiritual Protection."[20] Or, even more strongly:

> I made all the haste I could to retire, that I might give myself Liberty; and I think I never had more sensible Impressions made upon me.
> I enter'd my Chamber, and I hope, with a Desire to enter into my Heart, that I might get some farther acquaintance with myself, my State in the general, and particularly what it hath been this Week and Day past. (p. 2)

For Mrs. Housman, seeking out the moment alone underlines the self-consciousness of the introspective act, and the capacity to gain "acquaintance" with oneself. The Quaker autobiographer Elizabeth Stirredge records that even as a child she would seek out the "privatest place" she could; later, still dissatisfied with her own spiritual condition, she would "mourn" unto herself and read her Scripture "alone in private."[21]

Elizabeth Stirredge explains that after meetings were over, "I separated myself from my Company, and Travelled alone two Miles and the Lord opened the eyes of my Understanding" (p. 15). Another Quaker, Mary Penington, in *A Brief Account of my Exercises from my Childhood*, describes again and again the search for salvation within the privacy of solitude. "I shut the door, and in great distress of mind flung myself on the bed and cried out aloud, Lord what is prayer?"[22]

"Deliverance," the diarists demonstrate, is posited on enclosure. Thus Pamela too seeks within the private room both to know and to transcend self. Having explained to her parents her desperate attempt to escape from the confinement of the Lincolnshire estate, and how, the attempt failing, she has just barely escaped the temptation to drown herself in the pond, Pamela goes on: "But yet, I will add, that tho' I should have prais'd God for my Deliverance, had I been freed from my wicked Keepers, and my designing Master, yet I have more abundant Reason to praise Him, that I have been delivered from a worse Enemy, *myself*" (I, 237; I, 152). We are reminded of Mrs. Housman's notion of "Liberty" or "enlargement," the sense of communion with God that is also a release from self. Begging to be released from the "monster self," the Methodist Mrs. Johnson cries through the pages of her diary: "O my dearest Lord, unlock, unhinge, and open wide my heart, expand and stretch it out that it may receive of thine immensity."[23] Images of opening, breaking, and piercing are typical of the spiritual diary, particularly among the Methodists contemporary with Richardson. Mrs. Johnson writes: "O come Lord Jesus, and break down this barrier; empty, strip, weaken, and impoverish me, let me become nothing, that thou mayst fill me with thy most adorable self" (p. 36).

But the fusion of the erotic with the spiritual in Mrs. Johnson's language is hardly unique to Methodism. Elizabeth Rowe similarly provides in *Devout Exercises of the Heart* (1738) a blending of the spiritual and the physical.[24] Mrs. Rowe's editor points out that the exercises will be seen to "speak the Language of holy Passion" and are the "Dictates of her Heart." As with the letter writer, the private utterance is to be believed in because it is private: Mrs. Rowe's meditations are the "aspirations of a devout Soul in her holy Retirements, when she had no Design to present the Publick with them" (p. xxi). Thus the devout lady addresses God as the "Centre of all my Passions"; like Mrs. Johnson, she asserts the importance of breaking: "O, let me break thro' all these Separations and see and confess the great, the governing Cause. Let no Appearance of created things, however Specious, hide thee from my view."[25] Although the force of Mrs. Rowe's holy passion seems even stronger in the "Devout Soliloquies," published the following year in *Miscellaneous Works* ("I must be satisfy'd, these longings quench'd. These infinite desires must find an object"),[26] the editor of *The Devout Exercises* nonetheless senses the need to temper Mrs. Rowe's effusions. He points out in no uncertain terms that the "Language of Rapture addressed to God" is *not* "but a new Track given to the Flow of the softer Powers after the Disappointment of some meaner Love"; that Mrs. Rowe does not pour out her pleas for Divine Love "owing to the Want of a proper Object and Opportunity to fix those tender Passions." We are not then to view Mrs. Rowe as a sexually frustrated spinster, for she has, he says, a husband and a happy marriage.[27] The so-called private meditations, not written for public viewing but indicating rather the "state of mind under various circumstances" represent a "seeking after an absent God": "I search thee in the Temple," writes Mrs. Rowe, "where thou hast often met me . . . I search thee in my secret Retirements . . . I pine and languish but thou fliest me."[28]

Even for Mrs. Rowe, however, the subjectivity of the private effusion yields at the moment of death to deliverance in yet another form. As readers of *Clarissa* well know, death is a "public ending," confirming the pattern of the life, establishing its exemplary character. The familiar terms of "transport" or "enlargement" that Mrs. Rowe used in describing a vision of death (to the Countess of Hertford) are, after all, *too* familiar;[29] but appended to spiritual diaries, such language does serve to enlarge a total text. Just as in *Clarissa* the letters written by the heroine in her anguish are followed by those in which Belford paints scenes, so, for example, in Mrs. Housman's diary the subject's own entries are followed by the "Account of the Frame and dying Expressions of Mrs. Housman . . . drawn up by her servant." The transition from individuated experience to instruction for the good of the whole is emphasized when the eyewitness states his hope that the words of the dying woman "may be of Use to myself and many others."[30] Such a structure is fully commensurate with the assertions of Cynthia Wolff and J. Paul Hunter that the "tortured isolation" of earthly experience is finally contrasted with the "joyful community of the Elect after death," and in the funeral sermon, for example, the individual is frequently characterized in social terms.[31] With the aid of the witness or editor, then, the individual believer is released to the community of believers.

Such enlargement in a text is posited, of course, on the notion that first-person documents derive their authenticity from the quality of the individual's experience. For example, the editor of the Quaker Joan Vokin's *God's Mighty Power Magnified as Manifested and Revealed in His Faithful Handmaid Joan Vokins*, goes as far as to assert that the "papers and epistles here collected together were written as given forth" by the "Will and hidden Wisdom of God." The reader is urged to note that the "following papers are not exactly placed, as to the Dates, which the Reader is desired to pass by."[32] In language suggestive of sentimental literature, an ordering of texts, chronological or otherwise, is eschewed as countering their authenticity. Created through the "will and hidden Wisdom of God," the texts derive from no merely human motivation. Vokins herself writes in her prefacelike "Epistle to Friends" that on November 3, 1669, while gravely ill, she felt "powerful Life . . . spring up in [her] heart, causing [her] to write" (p. 1); now, distanced herself from the experience, she proposes to use such "Life"—recreated in her journal—to stir up to the faith other members of the Friends community.

In spiritual monologic prose, the writer's stance as both private and public figure prefigures the assumption of sentimental literature that so-called privately motivated language fulfills public needs also.[33] Mere presentation of the text within a larger context effects its transformation for those writers who view the accounting of self as coterminous with an accounting of one's own historical and social epoch. In his manual on diary keeping (*The Journal or Diary of a Thankful Christian*), for example, the seventeenth-century Puritan John Beadle instructed his readers to divide their diaries in two parts: one for "Nationall" and "publick" matters, the other for "Personall, and more private concerns."[34] Again, placement is all.

By contrast, epistolary solitaries like those of Ovid's *Heroides*, never succeeding in moving beyond confinement in self, remain imprisoned in individuated texts. To late seventeenth-century and early eighteenth-century readers that very confinement may have been part of the appeal: the success of the Ovidian love letter and its descendents attests to a taste for self-analysis, the recounting of emotional detail, and the subordination of narrative to the expression of apparently unpremeditated thought put down to paper just as it came to mind.[35] Each separate letter in the *Heroides* tells its own story, or kernel of story, the events of a love affair experienced by the writer and her response to these events. Each individuated letter text represents an individual consciousness and the isolation of the present moment from a continuum of time; and even if, as the Renaissance epistolarian Lipsius was to point out, letter writing sets forth clearly to the self "even those things which are deeper and closed off by walls,"[36] it is confinement itself that particularly marks the Ovidian letter. In an English version in which Dryden and Pope are included as translators (*Epistles: With His Amours Translated into English Verse by the Most Eminent Hands*), Hermione complains to Erestes (from whom she has been stolen away by Pyrrhus) on the confinement of fate: "But how shou'd I this fatal Woe escape? / All our whole Race was subject to a Rape."[37] The writer is actually confined in the sense that no action is open to her—except to write the letter: "my numm'd Hand unequal Letters makes," Ariadne tells Theseus (p. 44). Distance is insurmountable, whether in the physical or social sense. Sappho locates herself in a "melancholy grotto" and in the grief of unfulfilled passion writes to her lover, "In spite of absence, I thy Love enjoy" (p. 3); and Aphra Behn paraphrases an epistle from Ormione to Paris:

such distance sits 'twixt thee and me.
Whilst thou a Prince, and I am Sheperdess,
My raging Passion can have no Redress. (p. 76)

Powerlessness is also joined to innocence. A nymph writes that hers is a "Heart unpractis'd in Love's mystic Pow'res; / For I am soft, and young as *April* Flow'rs" (p. 78). Now, with "wounded Heart," the writer presents a landscape that has validity only as a setting for past "deere stol'n Delights" and depicts herself as a figure of despair with "dishevl'd Hair" and garments torn in frenzy and aggravation (p. 83). If it is justifiably argued that nothing really happens in the Ovidian letter, that is because nothing *can* happen in the realm of physical action. The writer's description of her own emotions, as she writes, is the only action.

The Ovidian love-letter tradition found its most important expression for our period in 1678, when Roger L'Estrange translated the *Five Love-Letters from a Nun to a Cavalier* (hereafter, *Portuguese Letters*). A work that purported to be the genuine letters of one Marianna Alcoforado to Noel Bouton, Comte de Chamily and St. Leger, the *Portuguese Letters* have been called the "greatest single influence of the century" on subsequent epistolary fictions; it was such a success that it had appeared in ten editions by 1740.[38] The Nun is hardly to be considered the direct antecedent of Pamela or Clarissa, but as the solitary letter writer, she provides us with another epistolary example of presentness and privacy, helping us evaluate the notion of confinement and release in Richardson's first two novels. Like her forebears in Ovid, the Nun writes letters that provide little sense of a tale unfolding in time; the present moment is dominant, the what-is-happening. The moment must be caught, not as it is subsumed in a story, but as it is captured in the very act of writing. The Nun does refer to time past or even documents past—"Your last letter gave me such a Passion of the Heart, as it would have forc'd its way through my Breast and follow'd you," she says in Letter I[39]—and she even looks back to a year previous when she observes: "Yes, 'tis now a clear Case, that your whole address to me was only an Artificial Disguise" (p. 1); but the important word is *now*. The past is only to be interpreted in terms of the present; the effects of reading a past letter reverberate in the present writing. Similarly, allusions to agents outside of the self and the present letter remain vague. A brother has apparently granted the Nun the opportunity of writing (p. 8), and she refers to a lieutenant who has brought her some word of the chevalier (p. 20). In Letter IV, however, even the significance of the officer who is mentioned several times as waiting to take the Nun's letter is subordinated to the function of the letter itself: the officer grows impatient, but, says the Nun, "Alas! I have not the Heart to give the letter over. When I write to you, methinks I speak to you; and our Letters bring us nearer together" (p. 28). The officer who waits to take the letter away for delivery is an emissary from the outside world where the letter will ostensibly precipitate some form of action on the part of the lover/addressee; however, as we saw in the Ovidian translations, action aimed at releasing the writer but emanating from an outside agent is, in fact, not really to be hoped for: "I do not

know what 'tis I write for. Perhaps you'll pity me; but what good will that
do me?", the Nun asks (p. 17). Later, in another letter, she concludes that
she writes to "divert and entertain" herself (p. 30).

The Nun's letter is written, then, for the self; letters remain enclosed,
even individuated. The so-called answers from the Comte, present in the
English 1714 edition, were not part of the original text; and appended as
they are in one grouping, they are not really answers in the sense of the
epistolary dialogue between, for example, Clarissa and Anna Howe, or
even the exchanges of the formularies: the addressee is not really an
opener. The Nun's letters form, rather, pieces in an extended monologue.
Whatever insights she comes to—and the tone of fifth and final letter differs markedly from that of the preceding—are not readily explicable from
our reading of all the letters. The Nun alludes in Letter V to a received
letter—by whose "impertinent Professions, and most ridiculous Civili-
ties," she has found that her own epistles have been read in an unconcerned
manner—but since the letter is not provided in the sequence, outside readers can evaluate neither the Nun's interpretation nor her subsequent
change of heart. It is simply stated: "You will find, I hope, by the different
Air and Stile of this Letter, from all my Former, that I have chang'd my
Thoughts" (p. 31). Certainly we who have read the sequence of letters perceive the difference here, but we do not share with the Nun the process
through which she arrived at her final realization that she has been caught
in "licentious Idolatry." No threads have been provided with which to anticipate such an ending; it is as if individuated letters have passed, separately, into a void. Events do not follow one another, to be apprehended in
a temporal pattern, and there is no epistolary intrigue to underline the importance of letter texts *qua* texts—or the importance of the right reading of
them. That scholars for some generations accepted the collection as histor-
ically real only points again to the absence of form as we find it in
Richardson.[40]

The Nun's location within the confining walls of the convent, while underlining the individuation and enclosure of the letters she writes, also
posits an imagination confined against the intrusions of the world. In the
convent, nothing hinders one from being "perpetually intent upon one's
own passion," the Nun writes her lover; "the World . . . offers diversions"
not possible here (p. 11). She laments that she has had no letter from the
chevalier, that she is cut off from that world beyond the walls and is left to
enjoy only in reflection "those Delights that were so ravishing in their En-
joyment" (p. 7). The power of memory is all-important: the writer keeps
before her the picture of the beloved (as indeed, so did Lady Bradshaigh

keep before her the picture of her dear correspondent Samuel Richard-son)—the loved one to whom she has "deliver'd [herself] wholly up" (p. 29).

In citing what he calls the "Heloise motif" as an organizing pattern for the eighteenth-century novel and noting its first popular use within epis-tolary form, David Anderson points out that eighteenth-century heroines tend to decry "cruel reality" in favor of their own make-believe epistolary world; life itself, according to Anderson, is seen as the "vile seducer," and hence the juxtaposition of religion and love in the deserted and confined nun figure signals escape from the real world.[41] The point is well taken: in *The Portuguese Letters*, imagination spells not so much transformation as es-cape. The Nun's famous counterpart Heloise suggests something similar when she writes:

> The tears of Women shut up in a melancholy Place, and devoted to Penitence, are not to be spar'd. . . . We are much fonder of the Pic-tures of those we love when they are at a great Distance, that [*sic*] when they are near to us. It seems to me as if the farther they are removed, their Pictures grow the more finish'd and acquire a greater Resemblance; at least our Imagination, which perpetually figures them to us by the Desire we have seeing them again, makes us think so. . . . [If a picture has such an effect] what cannot Letters inspire? They have soule, they can speak, they have in them all the Force which expresses the Transports of the Heart.[42]

The woman shut up emphasizes her own distance from the addressee as the imagination circles back on itself. In the more secularized context of Eliza Haywood's *Love-Letters on All Occasions*, Theano similarly posits to his love Elismonda the value of imagination; separated from his beloved and writing from the country—though not, of course, from the physical confinement of the Nun or Heloise—he worries "how soon may ever vary-ing Imagination shift the Scene, and represent you, repentant of the Fa-vours you have so profusely showr'd upon me."[43] Mrs. Haywood argues in the more moralistic *Female Spectator* that imagination is the "assemblage or association of Ideas which convinces us we have a Soul [and] the Captive in his Dungeon may [thus] enjoy all the Sweets of Liberty," but such flights may prove dangerous too: those addicted to solitude must not "suffer their Fancy to fix itself on such things as can be no advantage," warns Mrs. Haywood.[44]

The external addressee—and by extension, a public audience—may provide a necessary anchor in the real world, a counterweight to fancy. *The*

Letters of Abelard and Heloise, for example, take the reader's role more firmly into account. The collection begins with the didactic voice of Abelard recounting, Belford-like, to his friend the story of his life. Abelard decries the cruelty and immorality of mankind; his is the letter of moral exhortation that, though addressed to one individual, seemingly takes in the larger audience. The audience's role is even more strongly asserted, however, when Abelard's letter falls by mistake into Heloise's hands, for what has been ostensibly intended by the writer as the stimulus to live the moral life becomes, for Heloise, the reawakening of passion. It would appear that the addressee determines the epistolary performance. Divorced from the total context of a book, the "speaking picture" can speak in different ways according to the identity of its reader. Despite the editor's eschewal of the "feign'd story" (the brush with which he tars *The Portuguese Letters*), the participation of the reader in the text *Abelard and Heloise* points toward an awareness of form (and story) that goes considerably beyond that of L'Estrange's work.

Epistolary process and product are thus separated in *Abelard and Heloise*, the language of release—which "horrifies" Heloise in its applicability to both physical and spiritual passion—now reminding us too that we are reading released letters. Though drawn with considerably more complexity by Samuel Richardson, this is, of course, the lesson of *Pamela*: release is not wholly meaningful until the letter reaches its proper audience. It is the audience that puts together the pieces—or epistolary products—that re-create Pamela within the tale. Although Belford helps publicize Clarissa for her wider audience, Pamela relies, at least initially, solely on her own letters, which ultimately transform isolated moments, the writer's enclosure within both time and space, into history. Her own early allusion to reading her letters "afterwards" (I, 149; i, 96) at least suggests a time when the pattern will be visible, the form clear. Though much later, that time does come when the erstwhile servant girl, well on her way to achieving a social identity as Mrs. B., can point to specific localities of the estate and view them not as isolated loci of suffering and to-the-moment reporting but as scenes in a "moving tale." Mr. B. reads and is reformed by Pamela's letter/journal by the same pond where the heroine herself has achieved her own deliverance from temptation. "Why this, my Girl," says Mr. B., "is a very moving Tale": to which Pamela, driving home the lesson, responds: "You may see, Sir . . . what I ventur'd, rather than be ruin'd; and you will be so good as hence to judge of the Sincerity of my Profession, that my Honesty is dearer to me than my Life" (I, 329; I, 213). Still later, Pamela walks over the estate with her father, "every Scene of it, that had before been so dreadful to me! The Fish-pond, the Back-door, and every Place: O what reason

had we for Thankfulness and Gratitude" (II, 81; I, 268). If Pamela the servant girl has no "room of her own" in the first third of the novel,[45] after her
"Deliverance" and union with Mr. B., she has, in a sense, the whole estate:
every room and every part of the park acquires value according to its place
in Pamela's story. Like time, space is subsumed within the tale, and the
rooms now convey the "what-happened-there" of the story rather than the
"what-is-happening-here" of the solitary's search for deliverance within
the act of writing.

As the action of the novel clearly demonstrates, Pamela finds enlargement, first in writing, then in being read. In *Pamela*, even more than in
Clarissa however, escape from the private individuated self, the first important step toward the new identity, is seen also as escape from the solitary's
necessary reliance upon imagination. That Pamela's epistolary documents
in the period of confinement are connected with contrivance underlines
their function as individuated texts and playing spaces of the self-conscious
imagination. Incarcerated at the Lincolnshire estate, but before Mr. B.'s
own arrival there, Pamela has "contrived" with the clergyman Mr. Williams to send her packet of letters to her parents. Contrivance is the only
means of deliverance in this section of the novel. Living by her wits and
having no proper place of her own leads Pamela to ruses of various shorts;
she must hide a "Pen . . . here, and another there, and a little . . . Ink in a
broken China cup, and a little in another Cup; and a Sheet of Paper here
and there among [her] Linen; with a little Wax and a few Wafers in several
Places." Hopefully, she thinks, "I . . . might happen to open a Way for . . .
Deliverance, by these or some other Means" (I, 149; I, 96). Contrivance is
allied at this point with both the writing process—and its requisite pens,
paper, and so forth—and the delivery (deliverance) of letters. Arranging
with Mr. Williams to send out letters by first hiding them beneath the tiles
by the sunflower in the garden, Pamela cautions the innocent cleric:
"Study, good Sir, and contrive for me. . . . I say no more, but commit this
to the happy Tiles, in the Bosom of the Earth, where I hope my Deliverance will take Root, and bring forth such Fruit, as may turn to my inex-
pressible Joy" (I, 166; I, 107).

There are hints, of course, that contrivance is not wholly positive, that it
can signal pride. When Pamela takes a prideful joy in her own ruses, she
suffers a fitting comedown from Mrs. Jewkes, who has tricks of her own to
play. Even the sunflower connected with the burial of the letters may have
its negative side; in order to avert the suspicions of Mrs. Jewkes, Pamela
uses the ruse of the "great nasty worm" to explain her own behavior as she
retrieves a letter from its hiding place.

Contrivance, ruse, imagination are, on their own, really inadequate to release. The bull episode demonstrates that the isolated imagination may even hinder escape. Here, where Pamela counters her "strong temptations" to follow the route of her letters (which Mr. Williams has by this time taken away) with her fear of the bull, "ugly, grim, surly creature, that hurt the poor cook-maid," she first laments her own solitude: "tis sad," she says, "to have nobody to advise with" (I, 203; I, 131). Alone only with imagination, her perceptions are not to be trusted. She begins to see the "horrid bull" as specially delegated to watch her. Wandering even further from reality, she queries: "Do you think there are such things as Witches and Spirits?" (I, 204; I, 131). Clarissa-like she agonizes: "What can I do?"

Whatever isolation Pamela describes here, however, is heightened in the to-the-moment technique that isolates points in time as well; the style of *The Portuguese Letters* is adapted to a much more homely situation but with a similar effect of intensified emotion and imaginative force. Richardson stretches his to-the-moment technique to the limits of credibility in an attempt to capture the movements of Pamela's mind. We move from future tense—"I'll see if this Bull be still there!"—to present tense—"Well, here I am, come back again!"—to past tense: "O how terrible every thing appears to me! I had got twice as far again as I was before." The ending of the episode is especially relevant to what Pamela learns about imagination: "When I had got the Door in my Hand, I ventur'd to look back, to see if these supposed Bulls were coming; and I saw they were only two poor Cows grazing in distant Places, that my Fears had made all this Rout about" (I, 205; I, 132). Released from the immediacy of the experience, Pamela comes back to the moment of writing and reflects: "O why are poor foolish Maidens try'd with such Dangers, when they have such weak Minds to grapple with them!" (I, 206; I, 133). "I am persuaded," she says, "that fear brings one into more dangers, than the caution which goes along with it delivers one from."

Deliverance for Pamela must take other forms. Frightened now from trying escape through the pasture, she decides upon one final attempt at freedom: she hides her journal by the rosebush and sneaks out the bedroom window while her keeper Mrs. Jewkes is sleeping. As for Clarissa, however, the "way out" is difficult and complex. "For if I could have got out of the Chamber door," says Pamela, "there were two or three Passages, and Doors to them all, double-lock'd and barr'd, to go thro' into the great Garden; so that, to escape, there was no Way, but out of the Window" (I, 238; I, 153). Hence Pamela resorts to the window, just as Clarissa does in her attempt to get out of Mrs. Sinclair's house; but the height of the garden wall yet remains. The gate is locked, the servant girl does not have the key, and the wall is too high to climb: "alas for me! nothing but ill Luck!—no Escape for poor *Pamela*!" (I, 231; I, 149). Down she comes, bricks and all, into awful despondency—and contemplation of suicide in the pond. It is only at this point that the "ray of grace" darts "upon the benighted mind" (I, 233; I, 149). Divine mercies bring about true deliverance, and hence escape takes on new meaning when Pamela explains to her parents:

> But, Oh! my dear Parents, rejoice with me, even in this low Plunge of my Distress; for your poor *Pamela* has escap'd from an Enemy worse than any she ever met with; an enemy she never thought of before, and was hardly able to stand against; I mean the Weakness and Presumption . . . of her own mind. (I, 230; I, 148)

Just as Clarissa's escape from Mrs. Sinclair's house after the rape is the point of transition in her story, so is Pamela's unsuccessful suicide attempt a point of crisis that signals a change in the young heroine's mode of dealing with her confinement. Pamela can give up contrivance only after she has, in her terms, escaped her "worse Enemy," the "Weakness and Presumption of her own mind."

When Pamela escapes confinement in the "monster self" and achieves spiritual deliverance then physical barriers are ultimately irrelevant. So too is imagination on its own: although she has not yet won her battle with Mr. B., Pamela rises up again, assuring Mrs. Jewkes, "all my Contrivances . . . [are] at an End" (I, 241; I, 155). The letter written for the self and encapsulating imagination is destined to comprise a larger form: a public, structured self, a self within the tale that Mr. B. will read. Pamela's spiritual release then looks toward the end of isolated letters and letter writing. The letters have after all been gathering, buried "in the Bosom of the Earth," where their writer hopes her deliverance "will take Root, and bring forth . . . Fruit" (I, 166; I, 107). Pamela has never really wavered in her faith in her letters and the life she expects them to produce:

> Of all the Flowers in the Garden, the Sun-flower, sure, is the loveliest!—It is a propitious one to me! How nobly my Plot succeeds! But I begin to be afraid my Writings may be discover'd; for they grow large: I stitch them hitherto in my Undercoat next my Linen. (I, 174; I, 113)

The plot succeeds, the writings grow large. Using the excuse of planting bean seeds in order to deposit her letter under the tile, Pamela has told Mrs. Jewkes, "I will plant Life, if I can, while you are destroying it." The "planting of life" is really a recreation of life. The packet of letters "grows large" because each letter is a piece of a growing epistolary structure: Pamela's own story. The servant girl may now even wear her letters stitched next to her body, but later they will emerge, separated from the self, as the public embodiment of Pamela's private experience.

In order for these created documents to effect the social transformation of Pamela and her instatement as Mrs. B., however, they must find their appropriate audience in Mr. B., learner as well as lover.[46] Preceding Mr. B.'s own arrival in Lincolnshire, we remember, Pamela has sent out, with Mr. Williams, a packet of letters; and though the unfortunate parson has been set upon by thieves, he has not been robbed of his precious charge. Then follows the bull episode, the hiding of the journal by the rosebush, and the climactic suicide attempt. At this point, Mr. B. arrives, only to fail in his last trick, the impersonation of Nan in Pamela's bedroom. It appears that Mr. B. is nearing the end of contrivance also. Cured of masquerade acts aimed at rape, he begins to show signs of reformation, and Pamela is softening toward him. Saying she fears the gardener will be working near the rosebush, she decides to dig up her letters from their hiding place—in fact making them available to a reader. About this time, too, Pamela also becomes unwittingly involved in the "contrivance" of the gypsy and the anonymous note; but contrivance is truly no longer Pamela's métier: she loses her letters to Mrs. Jewkes, who hands them over to Mr. B. "Now he will see all my private thoughts of him, and all my secrets," says Pamela.

Mr. B. does indeed read the entries from the seventeenth to the twenty-seventh day of Pamela's confinement (the earlier entries having gone on to Pamela's parents), but he does not have the details of the near suicide. Pamela still wears those entries stitched up in her clothing. Here is the most significant segment of the story, its gravity underlined not only by its hiding place but by the fact that Mr. B. is not yet a reader appropriate to it. He is still capable of that anger and jealousy that he duly exhibits when, reacting rashly to Pamela's apparent reluctance to accept even an honorable relationship, he sends her away. Only when she is physically distanced on her way home does he read the remainder of the journal/letter that Pamela has handed over to him shortly before. Only then is his pride overcome to the point that he can send for Pamela to come back to him.

Events at Lincolnshire demonstrate that the major shift in *Pamela* is from writing to reading, or to release to readers. The letters emerge from their earthy burial place to assert a moral, public message as the tale of Pamela's suffering and ultimate victory. Mr. B. is finally transformed by the "moving tale." As a reader, he is enabled to put the letters together according to the form Pamela (directed by Richardson) has provided; the packet of letters is now an epistolary structure. Neither is Mr. B. the only reader. Richardson spends many pages of *Pamela* establishing his heroine not only within the social circle but also within the pages of her story. The circle of readers widens as Pamela takes her place in society. If the tension in *Pamela* mitigates considerably in the second part when she is Mrs. B., a pattern we have noted in Clarissa as well, that is because Pamela and her letters are no longer vulnerable to the machinations, contrivances, and of course, seductions that threaten isolated characters, enclosed imaginations, and individuated letter texts. In *Pamela*, Richardson firmly grounds the fruits of imagination in epistolary documents. He fuses transcendent vision and, of course, language with a concrete world and real readers. Pamela acquires not only a space, even an estate, of her own, but a public, social status—and an authentic story—of her own. The solitary becomes the social.

The servant girl achieves the status of Mrs. B., the Christian sufferer that of a divine personage; the room becomes a unit in a structure, the letter a component in a novel. The Puritan John Beadle's dichotomy of private and public, considered particularly as a question of readers and spatially designated texts, enables Richardson's characters to transcend what Henry James called the "terrible fluidity of self-revelation."[47] In a story, the letter-writing heroine finds a fixed identity.

To some degree, the questions of *Clarissa* are still with us. A writer like Doris Lessing has constructed in *The Golden Notebook*, for example, a novel composed of four seprate notebooks that also purport to differentiate the public and private dimensions of experience.[48] If two diaries were sufficient for John Beadle, Lessing accounts for four levels of experience, including the realm of dream and that of the fiction her own character writes. It is the function of the novel, however, to transform and transcend its own separate parts: "publick matters" and those of private-personal experience are interwoven into a whole.

I cite Lessing in the present context—though aware of the inadequacy of one paragraph to discuss a work like *The Golden Notebook*—because the care with which Lessing's Anna Wulf keeps her notebooks, allocates the writing time, closes her door, and chooses her audience derives from a long tradition of introspective literature. The moment of transition or publicization begins with the creation of the written document: the letter written by the confined Clarissa and supposedly publicized by her editor or the complex novel of the twentieth-century "free woman." Like Clarissa, what the epistolarian Lipsius called the "breaking of walls," the achievement of insight into self, comes for Anna Wulf from the interior place: for Richardson's heroine, within the nightmare interior of Mrs. Sinclair's house; for Anna Wulf, within consciousness and the realm of dream.

Yet this is not to argue that Clarissa is really the predecessor of Lessing's free woman. It may rather be said that as the novel celebrating the image of the chaste woman *Clarissa* speaks for the status quo: the solidification of the family, the withdrawal of the woman from the political-social community.[49] *Clarissa* is, in this sense, the celebration of the private. To locate the public in Richardson's novel we can only return to our original questions, citing the problem of describing form without recourse to identifying the community of which it is the reflection and to which it speaks. I have already argued here that acknowledging Richardson's personal letter and novel-reading coterie does not spell the only community available in *Clarissa*, and that readers do not know fictional characters only as one of themselves. This would be, once again, to read letters only as letters, to negate Clarissa's history as a story; it is to be attentive to all the details, as Richardson surely demanded, but to overlook the importance of waiting for (attending) the ending: to be drawn into the separate room and neglect to see the whole house. Mr. B. we have seen, must read all of Pamela's story. Similarly, at the end of *Clarissa*, in the conclusion "supposed to have written by Mr. Belford," we see the reactions of the Harlowe parents upon reading "large extracts from some of the letters that compose this history" (VIII, 278; IV, 532). The family now view with abhorrence the "majesty" of Clarissa's virtue; they see, after the fact, in the "large extracts" what they could not, or would not, perceive in Clarissa's individuated letters.

Raymond Williams has said of the flowering of the nineteenth-century novel in the 1840s that its strength lay in its addressing itself to the problem of the "knowable community" and how individuals relate themselves to it.[50] It is the pattern of relationships communicated in part through arrangements of textual space and the effect of such arrangements on readers that I have tried to account for in this study. Clearly community, a knowable public, does not assert itself in *Clarissa* as, for example, in *Middlemarch*; but what interests us so much in Richardson's novel is that a public is defined through the individually written texts that, within the novel, are made available to readers: a smaller community perhaps than that of Eliot or Dickens, but a community of readers that is available to Clarissa's own injunction, "Let my story be a warning to all."

Notes

Introduction

1. On the notion of "reception," or the importance of letter readers to letter writers, see Janet Gurkin Altman, *Epistolarity: Approaches to a Form*, especially chap. 3, "The Weight of the Reader," pp. 87–115. Valuable summaries of the varieties of epistolary structure appear in Bertil Romberg, *Studies in the Narrative Technique of the First-Person Novel*, p. 52, and Jean Rousset, "Une Forme littéraire: le roman par lettres," in *Forme et signification*, pp. 65–108.

2. Samuel Richardson, *Clarissa: Preface, Hints of Prefaces, and Postscript*, p. 5.

3. Ian Watt, *The Rise of the Novel: Studies in Defoe, Richardson, and Fielding*, p. 176.

4. Elizabeth Eisenstein, "Some Conjectures about the Impact of Printing on Western Society and Thought: A Preliminary Report."

5. John Carroll, Introduction, *Selected Letters of Samuel Richardson*, ed. John Carroll, p. 30.

6. Forster Collection, XI, ff. 240–41 (April 21, 1758) (hereafter cited as *FC*).

7. Malvin R. Zirker, "Richardson's Correspondence: The Personal Letter as Private Experience," p. 77.

8. Carroll, *Selected Letters*, pp. 33–34.

9. Michel Głowinski, "On the First-Person Novel," pp. 103–14.

10. Watt, *Rise of the Novel*, p. 192. Watt's reading of *Clarissa*, and his confidence in letter language, have been sharply attacked by William Warner, who challenges what he calls the "humanist" effort to make the reader feel "admiration for the good in others" and to see the novel as a "unified whole." See William Warner, *Reading Clarissa*, pp. 220, 235. One may, of course, question Watt's assertion that letters are the "most direct material evidence for the inner life of their writers" without sharing Warner's claims.

11. John Preston, *The Created Self: The Reader's Role in Eighteenth-Century Fiction*, pp. 46–49. Preston writes that letters are a "medium for those who have lost the syntax of experience" (p. 49).

12. Alan Dugald McKillop, *Epistolary Technique in Richardson's Novels*.

13. Anthony Kearney, "*Clarissa* and the Epistolary Form."

14. Mark Kinkead-Weeks, *Samuel Richardson: Dramatic Novelist*, p. 459.

15. James Swearingen, *Reflexivity in Tristram Shandy*, p. 141.

16. Leslie Stephen, "Richardson's Novels," *Hours in a Library*, 1:89.

17. McKillop, "Epistolary Technique," p. 139; McKillop, *Samuel Richardson Printer and Novelist*, p. 138; McKillop, *The Early Master of English Fiction*, pp. 61–62.

18. The influence of drama upon Richardson's work is well-covered ground and will be explored further here in chapter 3. See particularly Kinkead-Weekes, chapter 10, "The Novel as Drama," pp. 395 ff.

19. Frederick W. Hilles, "The Plan of *Clarissa*."

20. Altman, chapter 6, "The Epistolary Mosaic," pp. 167–84.

21. Rousset, "Une Forme littéraire," p. x.

22. Lionel Trilling, *Sincerity and Authenticity*, pp. 24–25.

23. Watt, *Rise of the Novel*, pp. 176–77; Margaret Anne Doody, *A Natural Passion: A Study of the Novels of Samuel Richardson*, pp. 188 ff. "Space, or the lack of it," writes Doody, "is important in suggesting the emotional condition of a character" (p. 188).

24. Raymond Williams uses the term "shaping principle" in "Formalist," in *Keywords: A Vocabulary of Culture and Society*, p. 113; Jonathan Culler, *Structuralist Poetics*, p. 189.

25. Williams, "Formalist," p. 253.

26. Eric Rabkin, "Spatial Form and Plot."

27. Quoted in Rudolf Wittkower, *Architectural Principles in the Age of Humanism*, pp. 74–75. Because of this theory, Wittkower points out, Palladio's using a temple front for a private building "appears to him a legitimate regression to an ancient custom" (p. 75).

28. For the Augustan view of man-created space and community, see Paul Fussell, *The Rhetorical World of Augustan Humanism*, pp. 173–77.

29. Lawrence Stone, *The Family, Sex, and Marriage in England, 1500–1800*, p. 253. Those changes that Richard Sennett attributes to the social and economic transformations of the nineteenth century I would seek in the eighteenth century as well: see *The Fall of Public Man*, pp. 19 ff.

30. David H. Flaherty, "The Meaning of Privacy," in *Privacy in Colonial New England*, pp. 1–21; John Curtis Raines, *Attack on Privacy*, p. 55.

31. Elizabeth Stirredge, *Strength in Weakness Manifest*, p. 8.

32. Philippe Ariès, *Centuries of Childhood: A Social History of Family Life*, pp. 398–99.

33. Mark Girouard, *Life in the English Country House*. See for example the plan of the state apartments of Chatsworth, fig. 11, p. 155.

34. Katherine Mansfield, *Journal of Katherine Mansfield*, p. 16.

35. [Marianna Alcoforado], *Five Love-Letters from a Nun to a Cavalier with the Cavalier's Answers* (hereafter cited as *Portuguese Letters*). For a discussion of setting in this work see Jean Rousset, *Narcisse romancier*, p. 58.

36. Since there is no edition of *Clarissa* that is both standard and generally ac-

cessible, I follow the precedent of other studies in quoting from the Shakespeare Head edition and providing double citations. The *first* indication of volume and page refers to the eight volume Shakespeare Head *Clarissa or, The History of a Young Lady* (Stratford-upon-Avon, 1930); the *second*, to the less accurate but more accessible four-volume *Everyman* (London, 1962). The citation for the quotation under consideration here is I, 74; I, 50.

37. Leo Braudy, "The Form of the Sentimental Novel."

38. John Hughes, trans., *The Letters of Abelard and Heloise*, p. 4. The work first appeared in 1713.

39. Northrop Frye, "Towards Defining An Age of Sensibility," pp. 311–18.

40. Carroll, *Selected Letters*, p. 289.

41. See note 11.

42. For a discussion of the proliferation of the "sentimental tradition" in the twentieth century, see R. F. Brissenden, *Virtue in Distress*, chapter 6.

43. Ronald Rosbottom discusses the ambiguity of reader role in eighteenth-century fiction, in "A Matter of Competence: The Relationship between Reading and Novel-Making in Eighteenth-Century France."

44. Compare Richardson's statement: "Attentive Leaders have found, and will find, that the Probability of all Stories told, or of Narrations given, depends upon small Circumstances" (Richardson, *Clarissa: Preface*, p. 5).

45. Preston, *The Created Self*, p. 78.

46. Hugh Blair stressed the importance of formal divisions and the "natural sequence of arguments" in "fixing" attention. Quoted in Rolf P. Lessenich, *Elements of Pulpit Oratory in Eighteenth-Century England*, p. 98. James Fordyce recommended using "leading Truths . . . which shall run through [the sermon] from beginning to end, and serve to collect the several Parts together": *The Eloquence of the Pulpit*, p. 23.

47. John Locke, *Essay Concerning Human Understanding*, III, x, 34; quoted in Swearingen, *Reflexivity*, p. 183.

48. John Wesley, *Works*, 2:503. Wesley's attitudes toward rhetoric are also discussed in James L. Golden, "John Wesley on Rhetoric and Belles Lettres." See also Anthony Ashley Cooper, 3d Earl of Shaftesbury, *Characteristics of Men, Manners, Opinions, Times*, p. 27; and Edward Young, *Conjectures on Original Composition*, p. 37.

49. Fordyce, *Eloquence*, p. 38.

50. Ibid., p. 26.

51. Lawrence Stone, "The Rise of the Nuclear Family in Early Modern England: The Patriarchal Stage."

52. On the importance of the transformation from private to public in epistolary literature, see Altman, *Epistolarity*, pp. 106–12.

53. Irwin Gopnik, *A Theory of Style and Richardson's Clarissa*, pp. 81 ff.

54. Wolfgang Iser, "The Generic Control of the Aesthetic Response: An Examination of Smollett's *Humphry Clinker*."

55. Geoffrey Hartman, "Structuralism: The Anglo-American Adventure."

Chapter 1

1. The importance of the temporal and spatial position of the narrator in the fictitious memoir, diary novel, and epistolary novel has been discussed by Bertil Romberg, *Studies in the Narrative Technique*, pp. 38–39.

2. R. W. Stallman, "Some Rooms from 'The Houses that James Built,'" pp. 37–44. Ian Watt has noted (*Rise of the Novel*, p. 26) that in Richardson's work "considerable attention is paid to interiors," but he does not point out that the highly detailed description of Grandison Hall, in *Sir Charles Grandison*, differs greatly from the paucity of physical detail in Harlowe Place.

3. I take the term "epistolarity" from Altman's *Epistolarity*.

4. Maurice Blanchot, *L'Espace littéraire*, p. 46.

5. Clarissa's use of "retirement" is not to be confused with that of the *beatus ille* ("happy man") tradition wherein one "retires" from the city to enjoy good friendship and tranquil state of mind in a rural setting. See Maren-Sofie Røstvig, *The Happy Man: Studies in the Metamorphoses of a Classical Ideal*, 1:230 ff.

6. Altman, *Epistolarity*, pp. 13–15.

7. Frances, Countess of Hertford, and Henrietta Louisa, Countess of Pomfret, *Correspondence . . . Between the Years 1738 and 1741*, 3:286 (hereafter cited as *Hertford and Pomfret*).

8. On the economic aspects of marriage for a family like the Harlowes see Christopher Hill, "Clarissa Harlowe and Her Times."

9. Compare the plan of Eltham House, Kent, in A. E. Richardson and H. Donaldson Eberlin, *The Smaller English House of the Later Renaissance, 1660–1830*, p. 54.

10. Robert Kerr, *The Gentleman's House; or, How to Plan English Residences, from the Parsonage to the Palace*, p. 48.

11. Sir John Vanbrugh, *The Complete Works*, p. 13.

12. Robert Morris, *Rural Architecture Consisting of Regular Designs of Plans and Elevations for Building in the Country*. Morris presented similar views in *Lectures on Architecture*. Contrast Kerr (*The Gentleman's House*): "The family constitutes one community, the servants another . . . [and] each class is entitled to shut its door upon the other and be alone" (p. 68).

13. Colen Campbell, *Vitruvius Britannicus; or, The British Architect, Containing the Plans, Elevations, and Sections of the Regular Buildings, both Publick and Private, in Great Britain*.

14. Campbell, *Vitruvius*, 2:31. When Dr. Richard Pococke visited Cholmondely Hall in 1750–51, the bedchamber had apparently been made into the "best drawing room." See Richard Pococke, *The Travels through England of Dr. R. Pococke*.

15. The late seventeenth and first quarter of the eighteenth centuries were periods of much alteration and enlargement of already existing houses. See Ralph Dutton, *The English Interior, 1500 to 1900*, p. 83; also Horace Walpole's comments on rebuilding in *Journals of Visits to Country Seats*, in *The Sixteenth Volume of the Walpole Society*, pp. 9–80.

16. Celia Fiennes, *Through England on a Side Saddle in the Time of William and Mary*, pp. 52–53.

17. Pococke, *Travels through England*, p. 261.

18. Quoted in Dutton, *The English Interior*, p. 75. For the notion of the family as a community in the Puritan context see William and Malleville Haller, "The Puritan Art of Love." The man is the "head," the woman the "heart, which is the most excellent part of the body next the head" (p. 250).

19. Kerr, *The Gentleman's House*, p. 155.

20. Richard Gwinnett and Elizabeth Thomas, *The Honourable Lovers: or, The Second and Last Volume of Pylades and Corinna*; Mary Davys, *The Works of Mrs. Davys*, vol. 2. *The Perfidious P—: Being Letters from a Nobleman to Two Ladies* (n.p., 1702), one of the more sophisticated examples of early epistolary fiction, also uses a country-to-city correspondence.

21. Cynthia Griffin Wolff, *Samuel Richardson and the Eighteenth-Century Puritan Character*, p. 95.

22. Kinkead-Weekes, *Samuel Richardson*, provides a detailed summary of all these events, pp. 123–276.

23. Daniel Defoe, *Religious Courtship: Being Historical Discourses on the Necessity of Marrying Religious Husbands and Wives Only*, p. 195.

24. Eliza Haywood, *The Female Spectator*, 4:315.

25. Raymond Williams, *Drama in Performance*, p. 182.

26. Preston, *The Created Self*, p. 40.

27. Robert Folkenflik has made a similar point for Pamela in "A Room of Pamela's Own."

28. Quoted in Maurice Blanchot, *L'Espace Littéraire*, p. 145.

29. Roland Barthes, *On Racine*, p. 4.

30. Ibid., p. 5.

31. Ariès, *Centuries of Childhood*, p. 375. At Coleshill and Eltham Lodge, both typically mid-seventeenth-century houses, a hall bisects the house from front to back so that a set of rooms is formed on either side. See John Summerson, *Architecture in Britain, 1530 to 1830*; Dutton, *The English Country House*, p. 74; N. B. L. Pevsner, *The Planning of the Elizabethan Country House*; and Girouard, *Life in the English Country House*.

Chapter 2

1. An exception is Judith Wilt, "He Could Go No Farther: A Modest Proposal about Lovelace and Clarissa," pp. 19–32. John Samuel Bullen does not really consider the epistolary implications of setting when he notes the lack of "full sensory details": *Time and Space in the Novels of Samuel Richardson*, p. 31.

2. For the destruction of the virgin as a theme in *Clarissa* see Mario Praz, *The Romantic Agony*.

3. Charles Johnson's *Caelia* is a dramatic example frequently noted for its simi-

larity to *Clarissa*: Caelia is duped by Wronglove and placed in a brothel, later to find herself in prison with the prostitutes. Eliza Haywood's *Female Spectator* and Jasper Goodwill's *The Ladies Magazine* are full of tales on this pattern.

4. Lady Mary Wortley Montagu, *The Complete Letters*, 1:446. Lady Mary tells her daughter (Lady Bute) in the same letter that she should teach her own daughters to "confine their Desires to Probabilitys . . . and think privacy . . . the happiest state of life." Charles Johnson, in *The Masquerade: A Comedy*, also presents a grim picture of the dangers of the city.

5. Sennett, *The Fall of Public Man*, pp. 50–51.

6. Ian Watt, *Rise of the Novel*, pp. 189–90. See also Mark Kinkead-Weekes, "Defoe and Richardson: Novelists of the City."

7. Pat Rogers, *Grub Street: Studies in Subculture*, and Aubrey Williams, *Pope's Dunciad: A Study of Its Meaning*, have eloquently demonstrated how in Pope, Gay, and Swift the actual names of streets and localities make their own statement on the relationship between the real and the ideal.

8. F. H. Sheppard, ed., *The Parish of St. James Westminster*, vol. 29 of *Survey of London*, p. 507.

9. Goodwill, *Ladies Magazine*.

10. John Stow, *A Survey of the Cities of London and Westminster*.

11. John Summerson, *Georgian London*, p. 26.

12. Ibid., p. 39.

13. T. C. Duncan Eaves and Ben D. Kimpel, *Samuel Richardson: A Biography*, pp. 6–18. This volume is the most recent and comprehensive biography of Richardson. For a description of Richardson's suburban retreat in Fulham, see F. E. Hansford and G. A. C. Evans, *The Story of the Grange, North End Crescent, Fulham*; and Angela Thirkell, *Three Houses*. The Grange, interestingly enough, was a double house; according to Hansford and Evans, the "two portions of The Grange were originally precisely alike."

14. Summerson, *Georgian London*, pp. 39–40.

15. See Summerson, *Georgian London*, p. 34, fig. 5, for a diagram of the floor plan of the typical London house of this period; also Crace Collection, Portfolio 9, 112 and 119, houses in Bishopsgate St. and Adam's Court; and G. H. Gater and W. H. Godfrey, *Parish of St. Martin-in-the-Fields*, pt. 1, vol. 16 of *Survey of London*. St. Martin-in-the-Fields, abutting St. James on the west, lies in the same part of the city that Clarissa is supposed to inhabit.

16. "Meditations," appended to Elizabeth Mascall, *Remnants of a Life. With Letters by Her Relatives and Friends*. The author of the poem is noted as Anne Laugher, who died at age twenty-eight in 1764.

17. Henry Fielding, *The Letter-Writers: Or, A New Way to Keep A Wife at Home*; Richard Steele, *The Theatre* (January 16, 1720).

18. Ronald Paulson, *Hogarth: His Life, Art, and Times*, pp. 263 ff.

19. This point is explored further in Kinkead-Weekes, "Defoe and Richardson," pp. 241–42. Fielding has great fun with the theme of the whore's putting on a cos-

tume and becoming the mirror image of "quality" in *The Covent Garden Tragedy*, III, xii. Here, clothes literally substitute for, and save, individuals: a lover escapes death in a duel because his coat saves him, and a prostitute who appears to have hanged herself for love turns out to have hanged, instead, only her gown.

20. A similar point is made in Emile Benveniste, "Language in Freudian Theory," in *Problems in General Linguistics*, p. 67.

21. François Jost, *Essais de littérature comparée*, p. 100. Jean-Luc Seylaz speaks of the "double image" in the epistolary novel, the distance between the "character narrated and the narrator," in Les Liaisons dangereuses *et la création romanesque chez Laclos*, p. 127.

22. Rousset, "Une Forme littéraire," p. 68.

23. Wolff, *Puritan Character*, p. 17. I will discuss these points in chapter 6.

24. The letter as "portrait" or "mask" is discussed in Altman, *Epistolarity*, pp. 194–95.

25. On the importance of editorial signs in *Clarissa* see Preston, *The Created Self*, pp. 42–43.

26. John A. Dussinger, "What Pamela Knew: An Interpretation."

27. Gaston Bachelard, *The Poetics of Space*, p. 75.

28. Rousset, "Une Forme littéraire," p. 68. Also see Malvin R. Zirker, "Richardson's Correspondence." According to Zirker, "the primary merit of the letter form in the novel lies in its power to convince us of the immediacy and authenticity of the subjective inner state of the writer" (p. 76).

29. Richardson, *Clarissa: Preface*, pp. 4–5, and *The Richardson-Stinstra Correspondence, and Stinstra's Prefaces to Clarissa*, ed. William C. Slattery, p. 156.

30. On the general plan of the action of Clarissa, see Frederick W. Hilles, "The Plan of *Clarissa*."

31. Seven days and more than forty pages of text elapse before Clarissa receives an answer from Anna. Time and space—in pages—both assert distance.

32. Erik Erikson discusses the "productive interior" in *Identity: Youth and Crisis*, p. 267. I do not think one must give Clarissa a psychological reading in order to find Erikson's term useful.

33. The Harlowes object to the "outsider" Belford as executor, but Belford's position is of course essential in making Clarissa a public example. On other epistolary editors see Altman, *Epistolarity*, pp. 110–12.

34. As I will discuss in chapter 6, death statements figure importantly in the spiritual biography and frequently are expressed in language that could be erotic. Consider Elizabeth Johnson's description in *An Account of Mrs. Elizabeth Johnson*: "In the night he came down—he filled me—he filled me—I had no distinct perception—but it was God diffusing himself through all my soul" (p. 23). The dying woman's final words: "Come—Lord—Come—Come" (p. 30).

35. J. Paul Hunter, *The Reluctant Pilgrim*, p. 86.

36. Wolff, *Puritan Character*, pp. 52–53.

37. Of the final 176 letters, only eight are written between Clarissa and Anna,

one the posthumous letter given in excerpt. The final letters stress Clarissa's role as an example to women and the necessity of arranging the letters for the wider audience. We no longer have the personal correspondence between two women.

Chapter 3

1. Edith Wharton and Ogden Codman, Jr., *The Decoration of Houses*, p. 103.

2. The letter-writing formularies explore this point in detail. See, for example, J. Hill, *The Young Secretary's Guide; or A Speedy Help to Learning*, pp. 96–97. I will discuss the formularies in chapter 4 below.

3. For a reading that stresses Richardson's "awareness of disturbing forces at work in his society," see William M. Sale, Jr., "From *Pamela* to *Clarissa*." Sale rightly argues that Clarissa's desire for a chance to "live more completely" cannot be achieved in the real world.

4. Robert M. Schmitz, "Death and Colonel Morden in *Clarissa*."

5. James Gibbs, *A Book of Architecture*, Plate XLIV.

6. While my own examination of proposed changes to already existent houses in the eighteenth century suggests little incidence of adding a bypassing corridor, a striking exception is William Hiorn's proposal for Gopsall, Leicestershire; the plan here, only partly executed, included a corridor running the entire length of the house. RIBA, Prints and Drawings Collection, Box K 10, particularly K 10/5 (dated 1749). An elaborate and later example of the bypassing corridor is seen at Wilton in the "gothic cloisters" that James Wyatt added to the Inigo Jones structure in 1814. The cloisters are a wide corridor which follows the shape of the four-sided interior courtyard. Doors from this corridor open into rooms that previously were accessible only by passing from one to the other. Suggestive of Wyatt's design, Colen Campbell submitted plans for changes to Goodwood House, Sussex, in which he proposed building two wings, each with full-length corridor. See RIBA collection, Box CA.

7. Fiennes, *Through England on a Side Saddle*, p. 44.

8. John Summerson, *Architecture in Britain, 1530 to 1830*, p. 329.

9. Mary Granville Delany, *The Autobiography and Correspondence of Mrs. Delany*, 1:281.

10. Mario Praz, *Conversation Pieces: A Survey of the Informal Group Portrait in Europe and America*, p. 56.

11. Frontispiece in Dutton, *The English Interior*.

12. Kerr, *The Gentleman's House*, p. 107.

13. Summerson, *Architecture*, p. 435.

14. *The Georgian Society Records of Eighteenth-Century Domestic Architecture and Decoration in Dublin*, 3:41. See also Ralph Dutton, *London Homes*. The houses of Bloomsbury Square were, for example, according to Dutton, "reticent without, but admirably appointed within" (p. 63).

15. Girouard, *Life in the English Country House*, pp. 155 ff.

16. John Cornforth and John Fowler, *English Decoration in the 18th Century*. See

chapter 3, "The Uses of Houses and their Arrangement," particularly p. 56. The connections between architectural plan and state ritual are lucidly described in Hugh Murray Baille, "Etiquette and the Planning of the State Apartments in Baroque Palaces."

17. The distinction between hall and other apartments is always prominent in eighteenth-century designs. See, for example, Gibbs, *A Book of Architecture*, Plate LIV, a design for a "person of quality": "From the Hall you enter between a double Stair-case into a Dining-Room richly adorn'd, having a handsome Apartment on each Hand."

18. For an earlier example of a didactic letter that uses elaborate visual detail in order to reform the addressee, see Thomas Cranley, *Amanda: or, The Reformed Whore.*

19. Frances A. Yates, *The Art of Memory*, explains Quintillian's memory system wherein the individual imprints on his memory a series of loci, each connected with one segment of what is to be remembered: "This done, as soon as the memory of the facts requires to be revived, all those places can be visited in turns and the various deposits demanded of their custodians" (p. 3).

20. The Hogarth illustrations were, however, not used, and are now lost. See T. C. Duncan Eaves and Ben D. Kimpel, "The Composition of *Clarissa* and Its Revisions before Publication," p. 127; and Marcia Epstein Allentuck, "Narration and Illustration: The Problem of Richardson's *Pamela*."

21. Wharton and Codman, *The Decoration of Houses.*

22. Ronald Paulson, *The Art of Hogarth*, pp. 9–16.

23. Quoted in Praz, *Conversation Pieces*, p. 68.

24. A similar example appears in *The Indian Empress; or, The Conquest of Mexico*, ibid., fig. 162.

25. Both Richardson and Hogarth use what we might call an inner stage for purposes of dramatization. Compare James Thornhill's drawings for the play, *Arsinoe Queen of Cyprus* [1705?], Drawings Collection, Victoria and Albert Museum, D25-1891 and D26-1891.

26. Compare the scenery of Inigo Jones, as discussed in Stephen Orgel, "The Poetics of Spectacle." Orgel points out that Jones's scenery consisted of partitions that could be dragged in and out and on which were represented churches, dwelling houses, palaces, and so forth. See also Lily B. Campbell, *Scenes and Machines on the English Stage during the Renaissance.*

27. Emmett L. Avery and Arthur H. Scouten, Introduction, *The London Stage, 1660–1800*, p. lxxxvi.

28. Richard Southern, *The Georgian Playhouse*, p. 21.

29. Southern, *Changeable Scenery*, pp. 146–52.

30. See Martin, "From Forestage to Proscenium: A Study of Restoration Staging Techniques." Martin concludes that the result of using the inner stage was an increase in the "scope of the action and realism" of the play (p. 26).

31. Southern, *Changeable Scenery*, p. 152.

32. McKillop, *Samuel Richardson Printer and Novelist*, p. 105; Ira Konigsberg, *Samuel Richardson and the Dramatic Novel*, pp. 33 ff.

33. Charles Gildon, *The Post-Boy Robb'd of his Mail: or The Pacquet Broke Open*; Gildon, *Love's Victim: or, The Queen of Wales*.

34. Arnold Hauser, "The Origins of Domestic Drama."

35. Hauser, "Origins," pp. 407–8.

36. Nicholas Rowe, *The Fair Penitent: A Tragedy*.

37. Denis Diderot, "*Eloge de Richardson*," in *Oeuvres complètes de Diderot*, pp. 217–18.

38. Adam Smith, *The Theory of Moral Sentiments*, p. 202.

39. The resemblance between *Clarissa* and *Caelia* should not, however, be overstated. See chapter 2, note 3.

40. Charles Johnson, *The Force of Friendship*. The importance of witnessing visually the "well wrought Scene" is commensurate with Shaftesbury's notion of "moral sense": that the mind has an eye and ear to discern proportion, distinguish sound, and scan each sentiment or thought that comes before it. "No sooner are actions viewed . . . human affections discerned and felt . . . (than) straight an inward eye distinguishes, and sees the fair and shapely, amiable and admirable . . . apart from the foul, the odious, or the despicable," *Inquiry Concerning Virtue*, bk. 1, pt. 3, sec. 2, quoted in William E. Alderman, "Shaftesbury and the Doctrine of Moral Sense in the Eighteenth Century."

41. Doody, *A Natural Passion*, discusses *The Country Lasses*, particularly in reference to *Pamela*, pp. 37–41.

42. It remains unclear why Aura has to go such lengths to achieve the proof; but the text allows Johnson to emphasize the importance of social duties befitting the best "custom of the manor."

43. *Caelia* was not a box office success, apparently because the audience objected to the scene of Madame Lupine and her strumpets. See M. Maurice Shudofsky, "Charles Johnson and Eighteenth-Century Drama."

44. Compare also Richard Steele's *The Lying Lover, or, The Ladies Friendship*, a comedy described by its author as "not improper entertainment in a Christian Commonwealth." Since Steele's aim is to "strip Vice of the gay Habit in which it has too long appear'd, and cloath it in its native Dress of Shame, Contempt, and Dishonor," he includes in the fifth act the familiar contrition scene where the previously debauched character awakes with "compunction and remorse." Such awakening in the prison enclosure suggests once again the ending of *Barnwell*, and the framed picture.

45. Quoted in George Bush Rodman, "Sentimentalism in Lillo's *The London Merchant*." I have used here the 1792 edition of *The London Merchant*, retitled *George Barnwell*.

46. The notion of pictures within pictures, with the suggestion of various time dimensions, is particularly apparent in Hogarth's "progresses." See Plate III of *The Harlot's Progress*, where, as Ronald Paulson points out, a central group of characters

represents the present, a second group in the rear of the picture, the next step in the action (*Hogarth: His Life, Art, and Times*, p. 265).

Chapter 4

1. Thomas Forde, "Preface to Reader," *Foenestra in Pectore or, Familiar Letters.*

2. Quoted in Wesley Trimpi, *Ben Jonson's Poems: A Study of the Plain Style*, p. 62. The italicized phrase is taken by Lipsius from Horace's *Satires*.

3. Samuel Richardson, Preface, *Letters Written to and for Particular Friends On the Most Important Occasions* (hereafter *Familiar Letters*).

4. Georges Gusdorf, "Conditions et limites de l'autobiographie," p. 119.

5. Roman Jakobson, "Two Aspects of Language and Two Types of Aphasic Disturbances," in *Fundamentals of Language*, pp. 55–82.

6. Jakobson, "Two Aspects," p. 73.

7. Hughes, *Abelard and Heloise*, p. 4.

8. Robert Adams Day, *Told in Letters: Epistolary Fiction before Richardson*, pp. 91–92.

9. Thomas Brown and Charles Gildon, *Familiar Letters: Written by the Right Honourable John late Earl of Rochester, and several other Persons*. See also Day, p. 260.

10. Teresia Constantia Phillips, *An Apology for the Conduct of Mrs. Teresia Constantia Phillips*, p. 49. Richardson discussed the *Apology* in a letter to Lady Bradshaigh disapproving of Mrs. Phillips.

11. Charles Walker, *Authentick Memoirs of the Life, Intrigues, and Adventures of Sally Salisbury*.

12. Daniel Defoe, *The Storm: or, a Collection of the most Remarkable Casualties and Disasters which happen'd in the Late Dreadful Tempest, Both by Sea and Land.*

13. Anon, *Love's Posie, Or, A Collection of Seven and Twenty Love-Letters, Both in Verse and Prose, that Lately Pass'd Betwixt A Gentleman and A Very Young Lady in France*, p. 15.

14. Wolfgang Iser, *The Implied Reader*, p. 58.

15. Jane Austen, *Lady Susan, The Watsons, Sanditon*, p. 101. On Jane Austen's own use of epistolary form, see Ian Jack, "The Epistolary Element in Jane Austen," pp. 173–86.

16. Introductory Letter, *Love's Posie*.

17. François Jost, *Essais*, p. 143.

18. Altman, *Epistolarity*, points out that "winning *confiance*" (confidence) from the addressee is part of the epistolary subject (pp. 48 ff).

19. Day, *Told in Letters*, p. 25; Charles E. Kany, *The Beginnings of the Epistolary Novel in France, Italy, and Spain*, pp. 50 ff; Godfrey Frank Singer, *The Epistolary Novel: Its Origin, Development, Decline, and Residuary Influence*, pp. 17–18.

20. Lord Berners (Johan Bowrchier), *The Castell of Love*. The work is a translation from the Spanish of Diego de San Pedro. Epistolary irony is also present when Lauerola says to Lereano, in her letter: "no creature knows of this letter, but thy self and the bearer."

21. The specific identification of the reader in a fiction like *Clarissa* marks the contrast between the letter and the diary: the latter, according to Robert A. Fothergill, is addressed to a "certain kind of responsiveness" (see his work, *Private Chronicles: A Study of English Diaries*, p. 84). For other discussions of audience role in monologic narrative see Martin Price, "The Other Self: Thoughts about Character in the Novel," and John Preston, *The Created Self*, pp. 38 ff.

22. Robert Scholes and Robert Kellogg, *The Nature of Narrative*, p. 256.

23. Walter J. Ong, S. J., "The Writer's Audience Is Always a Fiction."

24. See Doody, *A Natural Passion*, pp. 28–33.

25. Samuel Richardson, *Pamela or, Virtue Rewarded*, 3 : 408–9; *Pamela*, 2 : 211–12. See Introduction, note 36. I refer to the continuation of *Pamela* as *Pamela II*.

26. Katherine Gee Hornbeak, *The Complete Letter Writer in English, 1568–1800*, pp. 3–4.

27. Hill, *The Young Secretary's Guide*, p. 15.

28. Day, *The English Secretorie*, p. 164.

29. Hill, *The Young Secretary's Guide*, p. 16.

30. Barbara Herrnstein-Smith, "Poetry as Fiction."

31. Hornbeak, *The Complete Letter Writer*," p. 33.

32. Stone, *The Family, Sex, and Marriage*, p. 253. The split between the outer world and the "inner world of feeling" would be, of course, even more pronounced in the nineteenth century; see Eli Zaretsky, *Capitalism, the Family, and Personal Life*, p. 30.

33. William Fulwood, Preface, *The Enimie of Idlenesse*.

34. Preface, *The Secretarie's Studie*. The author is noted as "S. S."

35. *The Wits Academy or, The Muses Delight*, pp. 134–35. The author is noted as "W. P."

36. Day, *Told in Letters*, p. 20; Hornbeak, *The Complete Letter Writer*, p. 33.

37. Nicholas Breton, *A Poste with a Packet of Mad Letters*, p. 38.

38. Day, *The English Secretorie*, pp. 144–45.

39. Day's persuasive letter (in ibid.) uses visual detail in a manner similar to Cranley's *Amanda*, where, in attempting to reform the "whore," the writer creates a Hogarthian scene through minute listing of detail (pp. 51 ff).

40. Hill, *The Young Secretary's Guide*, p. 14.

41. Day, *The English Secretorie*, p. 1.

42. Forde, *Foenestra in Pectore*, p. 6.

43. Fulwood, Preface, *Enimie*; Hill, *The Young Secretary's Guide*, p. 100.

44. Watt, *Rise of the Novel*, p. 32.

45. I refer here to Roman Jakobson's statement that "an outline [of the functions of language] demands a concise survey of the constitutive factors in any speech event, in any act of verbal communication. The ADDRESSOR sends a MESSAGE to the ADDRESSEE." See "Concluding Statement: Linguistics and Poetics," pp. 350–77.

46. Abraham Flemming, *Panoplie of Epistles*.

47. Leo Braudy, in "The Form of the Sentimental Novel," draws attention to the importance of the fragment in sentimental literature.

48. Gildon, *The Post-Boy*, p. 6.

49. Richardson, of course, was always interested in style, both in *Familiar Letters* and other correspondence. "Answers in general" (Hill, *The Young Secretary's Guide*, p. 13) would not do. In discussing the letters of Madame Sévigné to her daughter, he remarked that he should like to have seen the daughter's replies: "I shd. then have been better able to judge of the Propriety of the Mother's Stile in hers." *FC*, XI, f. 209 (July 12, 1757).

50. Margaret Cavendish, *Sociable Letters*.

51. Elizabeth Rowe, *Friendship in Death in Twenty Letters from the Dead to the Living*, p. 7. See also chapter 6.

Chapter 5

1. Rousset, *Narcisse romancier*, p. 17.

2. Hill, in *The Young Secretary's Guide*, includes a long section on making out wills and legal documents. Significantly, the writing of a familiar letter is associated in the same text with other forms of documentation.

3. Dorothy Van Ghent overstates the importance of the juxtaposition of sex and violence in *Clarissa*, in *The English Novel: Form and Function*, p. 50. Ian Watt discusses sexually violent dreams in *Clarissa*, p. 232.

4. Altman, *Epistolarity*, pp. 167 ff.

5. Raymond Williams, *The English Novel from Dickens to Lawrence*, p. 133.

6. Benveniste, *Problems in General Linguistics*, p. 197. In a primitive way, the letter pairs in the epistolary manual also share context. In *The Young Secretary's Guide*, for example, "A Letter of Reproof" is answered by "The Answer of Excuse" (p. 45): *a* letter gives rise to *the* answer, the change in article signaling the establishment of context.

7. Williams, *The English Novel*, pp. 69–71.

8. Forde, Preface, *Foenestra in Pectore*.

9. Brown and Gildon, *Familiar Letters*, p. 189.

10. Diderot, "*Eloge de Richardson*," p. 218.

11. For the Richardson-Lady Bradshaigh correspondence, see *FC*, XI.

12. Mrs. Elizabeth Carter, *Letters from Elizabeth Carter to Mrs. Montagu*. For an example of the sharing of phrases and subjects, see pp. 139 ff.

13. Richardson, *Selected Letters*, p. 30.

14. Samuel Richardson, *The Correspondence of Samuel Richardson*, 3:166.

15. Ibid., 6:122.

16. *FC*, XIV, ff. 25–26 (March 12, 1758).

17. *Pamela II*, 3:408–9; 2:211–12.

18. Richardson, *Correspondence of Samuel Richardson*, 6:138.

19. Similarly, the Anna Howe–Mr. Hickman plot in *Clarissa* gains importance if we consider that it renders Anna not only an advice giver but also a young person herself requiring good counsel and good example. The Clarissa-Anna correspondence is to provide many instances of each young woman "setting right the other" (Preface).

20. This does not mean, however, that characters read in fiction are assumed to be real; or that such reader response would be in any way adequate to the reading of *Clarissa*.

21. Richardson, *Selected Letters*, p. 30.

22. *FC*, XI, f. 27 (November 8, 1753).

23. *FC*, XI, f. 85 (February 22, 1754).

24. Altman, *Epistolarity*, pp. 87 ff.; Preston, *The Created Self*, p. 45.

25. Nathalie Sarraute, *Tropisms* and *The Age of Suspicion*, p. 109.

26. Lady Mary Wortley Montagu, *The Complete Letters of Lady Mary Wortley Montagu*, 1:5.

27. Altman points out that as a means of seduction the letter attempts to break down distance; although Richardson does not focus upon a correspondence between seducer and seduced, Lovelace's frenzied attempts to break down physical space through the act of rape do mirror, on a grotesque level, a stock epistolary concern with overcoming space. When the rake accomplishes his design, Clarissa tells him, "[The rape has caused me to be] where you are" (V, 335; III, 211). After conquering the physical distance, however, Lovelace's energy is depleted: he is no longer the active force in the novel.

28. Preston argues that as a reader Anna Howe is "denied entry into the action" of the novel; there is always the "barrier of the words on the page" (*The Created Self*, p. 58). Preston overlooks, however, the epistolary dynamic between writer and correspondent: Anna Howe is a writer too.

29. Day, *The English Secretorie*, p. 54.

30. Madame Du Noyer, *Letters from a Lady at Paris*, p. 54.

31. Cavendish, *Sociable Letters*.

32. Mary Hearne, *The Lover's Week: or, The Six Days Adventures of Philander and Amaryllis*. The letters are all specifically dated and are all written by Amaryllis to Emilia. While Amaryllis apparently feels she should justify her behavior to the world by explaining herself to her friend, the main object seems rather to provide an "entertaining Amusement."

33. Davys, *Familiar Letters Betwixt a Gentleman and a Lady*.

34. Richardson, *Familiar Letters*, p. 115.

35. A. R. Humphreys, "Richardson's Novels: Words and the 'Movements Within.'"

36. In the terms of Jean Rousset, *Narcisse romancier*, such "counterplay" of "reported speech and internal monologue" serves to point up the presence of the narrator within his own narration.

37. Examples of this type of dialogue are numerous in *Pamela* too, as Humphreys has pointed out. For example, a reported statement from Pamela's keeper, Mrs. Jewkes, is followed by the heroine's comment "Could anything in womanhood be so vile?"

38. Eliza Haywood, *Love-Letters on All Occasions Lately Passed Between Persons of Distinction*, Letters XIX and XX.

39. Lyly, *Euphues*, p. 178.

40. For example, Hester Chapone, *Letters on the Improvement of the Mind by Mrs. Chapone*, bound in the same volume with Dr. Gregory, *A Father's Legacy to His Daughters*; Lady Pennington, *A Mother's Advice to Her Absent Daughters*; and Catherine Talbot, *Reflections on the Seven Days of the Week*. Mrs. Chapone (1727–1801) met Richardson in 1748 and was introduced by him to her husband. Her *Letters* are addressed to her niece for "private instruction"—but also to be kept for future perusal. The principal virtues of a woman must be, according to Mrs. Chapone, "Of a private and domestic kind" (p. 69).

Chapter 6

1. Laurent Versini, *Laclos et la tradition*, p. 246.

2. Jean Hagstrum has observed that "Ovid continued to teach the learned classes of the eighteenth century the *ars amatoria*," but the Bible remained a "truly effective"—if somewhat ambiguous—instructor in love. See Hagstrum, *Sex and Sensibility: Ideal and Erotic Love from Milton to Mozart*, pp. 19 ff. The letter writers in Ovid's *Heroides*, which I will discuss in more detail below, are perhaps the most famous examples of the "solitary." The *Heroides* are love letters representing seventeen mythological heroines and the historical character Sappho. Robert Adams Day has called the volume "one of the most important sources or models for the emotional layer in the structure of modern fiction" (in *Told in Letters*, p. 12); and Ovid, the "father of epistolary, sentimental, and psychological fiction" (p. 11). Other discussions of the *Heroides* appear in Kany, *The Beginnings of the Epistolary Novel*, pp. 3–4; and Charlotte E. Morgan, *The Rise of the Novel of Manners: A Study of English Prose Fiction Between 1600 and 1750*, pp. 72 ff.

3. Richardson was writing to Lady Bradshaigh when he used the term. *FC*, XI, f. 156 (October 6, 1748).

4. Montagu, *Letters of Lady Mary Wortley Montagu*, 1:16.

5. Carter, *Letters . . . to Mrs. Montagu*, 2:83; Hertford, *Hertford and Pomfret*, 1:126.

6. Carter, *Letters . . . to Mrs. Montagu*, 1:153–54.

7. Richardson, *Correspondence of Samuel Richardson*, 5:204.

8. Carter, *Letters . . . to Mrs. Montagu*, 1:195.

9. Hertford, *Hertford and Pomfret*, 1:103.

10. Delany, *Autobiography and Correspondence*, 1:351.

11. Smith, *The Theory of Moral Sentiments*, p. 202.

12. Carter, *Letters . . . to Mrs. Montagu*, 1:64.

13. Frye, "Towards Defining an Age of Sensibility," pp. 312–13; 316.

14. Edward W. Copeland, "*Clarissa* and *Fanny Hill*: Sisters in Distress."

15. See particularly Wolff, *Puritan Character*, p. 17.

16. *Pamela*, 1, 149; 1, 96.

17. On the congruence of the isolation of the individual and that of the moment see Georges Poulet, *Etudes sur le temps humain*, vol. 3, *Le Point de Départ*, p. 218, quoted in Preston, *The Created Self*, p. 41.

18. Frank Kermode, *The Sense of an Ending: Studies in the Theory of Fiction*, p. 123.

19. Blanchot, *L'Espace littéraire*, p. 19.

20. Mrs. Housman, *The Power and Pleasure of the Divine Life Exemplify'd in the Late Mrs. Housman*, p. 77.

21. Stirredge, *Strength in Weakness*, p. 8.

22. Mary Penington, *A Brief Account of my Exercises from my Childhood*, pp. 2–3.

23. Elizabeth Johnson, *An Account of Mrs. Elizabeth Johnson*, p. 39.

24. Elizabeth Rowe, *Devout Exercises of the Heart in Meditation and Soliloquy, Prayer and Praise*. William M. Sale, Jr., in *Samuel Richardson: Master Printer*, p. 200, indicates that Richardson printed the second volume of Mrs. Rowe's *Miscellaneous Works* (1739) as well as the 1740 and 1743 editions of *Friendship in Death*. It is certainly likely that Richardson would have known the *Devout Exercises* as well.

25. Rowe, *Devout Exercises*, p. 56.

26. Elizabeth Rowe, Soliloquy 9, *Miscellaneous Works in Prose and Verse*.

27. Rowe, *Devout Exercises*, pp. xv, xvi.

28. Ibid., p. 96. Another possible reading here is, however, that the editor knows his readers will be interested in the language of passion on both the spiritual and erotic levels.

29. "Life of Mrs. Elizabeth Rowe," in Rowe, *Miscellaneous Works*, p. xxxvi.

30. Housman, *The Power and the Pleasure*, p. 114. According to the account of the death, Mrs. Housman's words are also those of Clarissa at her death: "Come Lord Jesus, Come quickly." See also Mrs. Johnson, p. 52, where the final words are reported as "Come—Lord—Come—Come."

31. Hunter, *The Reluctant Pilgrim*, p. 86; Wolff, *Puritan Character*, p. 47.

32. Prefatory Letter to the Reader, *God's Mighty Power Magnified as Manifested and Revealed in His Faithful Handmaid Joan Vokins*.

33. While I do not intend to equate diary and journal keeping with autobiography, the critical discussion of autobiography is nonetheless relevant particularly within the Puritan context. See Paul Delany, *British Autobiography in the Seventeenth Century*, who stresses the self-conscious publicization of private experience (p. 55); Roy Pascal, *Design and Truth in Autobiography*, argues for private, personal motivation; Barrett John Mandel, "Bunyan and the Autobiographer's Artistic Purpose," sees in the use of conventional form a didactic (public) purpose.

34. John Beadle, *The Journal or Diary of a Thankful Christian*, p. 14.

35. The language of love-letter fiction in the Ovidian tradition is often remarkably close to that of the spiritual diary. Compare, for example, Clarinda's romantic outburst, "I yield, I yield, my rising Heart owns your victory," in *The Perfidious P—*, p. 38, with Mrs. Johnson's diary entry: "Jesus, come now I beseech thee to fill the mighty void. My body, and all are thine," *An Account of Mrs. Elizabeth Johnson*, p. 47. John Richetti has discussed what he calls the "religious decoration" in amatory rhetoric, in *Popular Fiction before Richardson*, pp. 209–10.

36. Justus Lipsius, *Institutio Epistolica*, quoted in Trimpi, *Ben Jonson's Poems*, p. 62.

37. Ovid, *Epistles: With His Amours Translated into English Verse by the Most Eminent Hands*, p. 48.

38. Morgan, *The Rise of the Novel of Manners*, p. 70; Day, *The English Secretorie*, p. 33.

39. *Portuguese Letters*, p. 7.

40. Day, *The English Secretorie*, p. 33, questions the authenticity of the Nun's letters, but earlier commentators were more prepared to accept it. See Morgan, pp. 72 ff., and Singer, *The Epistolary Novel*, pp. 36 ff.

41. David L. Anderson, "Abelard and Heloise: Eighteenth Century Motif." In a general study of the epistolary novel in England, Ruth Perry has also considered the locked up heroine: *Women, Letters, and the Novel*, p. 107.

42. Hughes, *Abelard and Heloise*, p. 68.

43. Haywood, *Love-Letters*, p. 100.

44. Haywood, *Female Spectator*, 4:78.

45. Folkenflik, "A Room of Pamela's Own," p. 585.

46. This point has also been made by Richard H. Costa, "The Epistolary Monitor in Pamela." Although Costa deals with the "softening effect" of the letters on Mr. B., he does not consider the important role of the reader in helping Pamela escape her confinement.

47. Henry James, *Art of the Novel*, p. 321.

48. Doris Lessing, *The Golden Notebook*.

49. See Marlene LeGates, "The Cult of Womanhood in Eighteenth-Century Thought," pp. 21–39.

50. Williams, *The English Novel*, p. 10.

Selected
Bibliography

Unpublished Sources

Crace Collection. British Museum.
Forster Collection. Victoria and Albert Museum.
Prints and Drawings. RIBA.
Prints and Drawings. Victoria and Albert Museum.

Richardson's Published Writing

Clarissa or, The History of a Young Lady. Shakespeare Head ed. 8 vols. Stratford-upon-Avon, 1930.

Clarissa or, The History of a Young Lady. Everyman ed. 4 vols. London, 1962.

Clarissa: Preface, Hints of Prefaces, and Postscript. Edited by R. F. Brissenden. Augustan Reprint Society, no. 103. Los Angeles, 1964.

Letters Written to and for Particular Friends, On the Most Important Occasions. Directing not only the Requisite Style to be Observed in Writing Familiar Letters; But How to Think and Act Justly and Prudently in the Common Concerns of Human Life. London, 1741.

Pamela or, Virtue Rewarded. Shakespeare Head ed. 4 vols. Stratford-upon-Avon, 1929.

Pamela. Everyman ed. 2 vols. London, 1962.

The Richardson-Stinstra Correspondence, and Stinstra's Prefaces to Clarissa. Edited by William C. Slattery. Carbondale, Ill., 1969.

Selected Letters of Samuel Richardson. Edited by John Carroll. Oxford, 1964.

Sir Charles Grandison. 3 vols. London, 1972.

Epistolary Sources

[Alcoforado, Marianna]. *Five Love-Letters from a Nun to a Cavalier with the Cavalier's Answers.* Translated by Sir Roger L'Estrange. London, 1714.

Behn, Aphra. *All the Histories and Novels Written by the Late Ingenious Mrs. Behn.* 9 vols. London, 1705.

——. *Love-Letters Between A Noble-Man and his Sister.* 3 vols. London, 1694.

——. *The Lover's Watch. The Histories and Novels of the Late Ingenious Mrs. Behn.* London, 1686.

Berners, Lord (Johan Bowrchier). *The Castell of Love.* N.p., [1549?].

Boscawen, Mrs. Edward. *Admiral's Wife: Being the Life and Letters of the Honourable Mrs. Edward Boscawen from 1719 to 1761*. New York, 1940.

Breton, Nicholas. *A Poste with a Packet of Mad Letters*. London, 1633.

Brown, Thomas. *Letters from the Dead to the Living*. London, 1702.

———. *The Lover's Secretary or, the Adventures of Lindamira, A Lady of Quality*. London, 1713.

———, and Charles Gildon. *Familiar Letters: Written by the Right Honourable John late Earl of Rochester, and several other Persons of Honour and Quality*. London, 1697.

Carter, Elizabeth. *Letters from Mrs. Elizabeth Carter to Mrs. Montagu*. Edited by Montague Pennington, London, 1817.

Cavendish, Margaret. *Sociable Letters*. 1664. Facsimile reprint. Menston, England, 1969.

Cranley, Thomas. *Amanda: or, The Reformed Whore*. London, 1635.

Davys, Mary. *Familiar Letters Betwixt a Gentleman and a Lady*. In *The Works of Mrs. Davys*. 2 vols. London, 1725.

Day, Angel. *The English Secretorie. Wherein is contayned, a Perfect Method, for the inditing of all manner of Epistles and Familiar Letters*. London, 1586.

Defoe, Daniel. *The Storm: or, a Collection of the most Remarkable Casualties and Disasters which happen'd in the Late Dreadful Tempest, Both by Sea and Land*. London, 1704.

Delany, Mary Granville. *The Autobiography and Correspondence of Mrs. Delany*. Edited by Sarah Chauncey Woolsey. Boston, 1879.

Dorat, Claude Joseph. *Lettre de Barnvelt dans sa prison à Truman son ami*. Paris, 1766.

Du Noyer, Anne Marguerite. *Letters from a Lady at Paris to a Lady at Avignon*. London, 1716.

Eland, G., ed. *The Purefoy Letters: 1735–1753*. London, 1931.

The Fatal Amour Between a Beautiful Lady and a Young Nobleman. In *The Secret History of the Prince of the Nazarenes and Two Turks*. London, 1719.

Flemming, Abraham. *Panoplie of Epistles*. London, 1576.

Forde, Thomas. *Foenestra in Pectore or, Familiar Letters*. London, 1660.

Fulwood, William. *The Enimie of Idlenesse*. London, 1568.

Gildon, Charles. *Ovidius Britannicus: Or, Love Epistles in Imitation of Ovid*. London, 1703.

———. *The Post-Boy Robb'd of his Mail: or, The Pacquet Broke Open*. London, 1706.

Gwinnett, Richard, and Elizabeth Thomas. *The Honourable Lovers: or, The Second and Last Volume of Pylades and Corinna*. London, 1731.

Haywood, Eliza. *The Female Spectator*. 4 vols. London, 1745.

———. *Love in Excess; or the Fatal Enquiry*. 3 vols. London, 1719–20.

———. *Love-Letters on All Occasions Lately Passed Between Persons of Distinction*. London, 1730.

——— [?]. *Some Memoirs of the Amours and Intrigues of a Certain Irish Dean*. London, 1728.

Hearne, Mary. *The Lover's Week: or, The Six Days Adventures of Philander and Amaryllis.* London, 1718.

Hertford, Frances, Countess of, and Henrietta Louisa, Countess of Pomfret. *The Correspondence Between Frances, Countess of Hertford, and Henrietta Louisa, Countess of Pomfret, Between the Years 1738 and 1741.* 3 vols. London, 1805.

Hill, J. *The Young Secretary's Guide: or A Speedy Help to Learning.* 7th ed. London, 1696.

Hughes, John, trans. *Letters of Abelard and Heloise.* London, 1722.

"I. W." *A Speedie Poste With certaine New Letters.* London, 1629.

James, Henry. *A Bundle of Letters.* Boston, [n.d.].

————. *The Siege of London, The Pension Beaurepas,* and *The Point of View.* Boston, 1883.

Love's Posie; or, A Collection of Seven and Twenty Love-Letters, both in Verse and Prose, That Lately Pass'd Betwixt a Gentleman and a Very Young Lady in France. London, 1686.

Lyly, John. *Euphues. The Anatomy of Wit.* Edited by Edward Archer. London, 1868.

Manly, Mrs. *Court Intrigues, in a Collection of Original Letters.* London, 1711.

Marlborough, Sarah, Duchess of. *Letters of a Grandmother, 1732–1735.* Edited by Gladys Scott Thomson. London, 1943.

Montagu, Lady Mary Wortley. *The Complete Letters of Lady Mary Wortley Montagu.* Edited by Robert Halsband. Oxford, 1967.

"M. R." *A President for Young Pen-Men, or The Letter Writer.* London, 1615.

Osborn, Emily F. D., ed. *Political and Social Letters of a Lady of the Eighteenth Century.* New York, 1891.

Ovid. *Epistles: With His Amours Translated into English Verse by the Most Eminent Hands.* London, 1748.

Perfidious P——, The: Being Letters from a Nobleman to Two Ladies. [1702?].

Piccolomini, Aeneas Sylvius. *The Goodli History of the most noble and beautiful Ladye Lucres and her lover Eurialus.* [n.p.], 1550.

Rowe, Elizabeth. *Friendship in Death in Twenty Letters from the Dead to the Living.* London, 1733.

Suffolk, Henrietta, Countess of. *Letters to and from Henrietta, Countess of Suffolk, and Her Second Husband, The Hon. George Berkeley, From 1712 to 1767.*

"S. S." *The Secretarie's Studie.* London, 1652.

Trotter, Catherine. *Olinda's Adventures: Or the Amours of a Young Lady.* 1718. Reprinted in *Augustan Reprint Society Publications,* no. 138. Los Angeles, 1969.

Voiture, V. *The Words of Monsieur Voiture Containing His Familiar Letters to Gentlemen and Ladies With Three Collections of Letters on Friendship . . . Written by John Dryden, William Wycherly, William Congreve.* London, 1705.

Walker, Charles. *Authentick Memoirs of the Life, Intrigues, and Adventures of Sally Salisbury.* London, 1723.

"W. P." *The Wits Academy or, The Muses Delight.* London, 1677.

Diary and Autobiography

Beadle, John. *The Journal or Diary of a Thankful Christian*. London, 1656.

Cavendish, Margaret. *A True Relation of the Birth, Breeding, and Life of Margaret Cavendish, Duchess of Newcastle*. Edited by Egerton Brydges. Kent, England, 1814.

Fell, Margaret. *A Brief Collection of Remarkable Passages and Occurrences Relating to the Birth, Education, Life, Conversation, Travels, Services, and Deep Suffering of Margaret Fell*. London, 1710.

Hayes, Alice. *A Legacy, or Widow's Mite; Left by Alice Hayes to Her Children and Others*. London, 1723.

Housman, Mrs. *The Power and Pleasure of the Divine Life Exemplify'd in the Late Mrs. Housman*. Edited by Richard Pearsall. London, 1755.

Hutchinson, Lucy. "The Life of Mrs. Lucy Hutchinson, Written by Herself. A Fragment." In *Memoirs of the Life of Colonel Hutchinson*. London, 1810.

Johnson, Elizabeth. *An Account of Mrs. Elizabeth Johnson*. Bristol, England, [1799?].

Mascall, Elizabeth. *Remnants of a Life. With Letters by her Relatives and Friends*. Edited by A. W. Matthews. London, 1902.

Penington, Mary. *A Brief Account of my Exercises from my Childhood*. Philadelphia, 1848.

Phillips, Teresia Constantia. *An Apology for the Conduct of Mrs. Teresia Constantia Phillips*. London, 1748–1749.

Raper, Elizabeth. *The Receipt Book of Elizabeth Raper*. Edited by Bartle Grant. London, 1924.

Stirredge, Elizabeth. *Strength in Weakness Manifest*. London, 1711.

Thornton, Alice. *The Autobiography of Mrs. Alice Thornton. Publications of the Surtees Society* 62 (1875).

Trapnel, Anna. *A Legacy for Saints*. London, 1654.

Turner, Anne. *Choice Experiences of the Kind Dealings of God before, in, and after Conversion*. London, 1653.

Vokins, Joan. *God's Mighty Power Magnified as Manifested and Revealed in His Faithful Handmaid Joan Vokins*. London, 1691.

Drama

Addison, Joseph. *The Drummer; or, the Haunted-House*. London, 1716.

Cibber, Colly. *The Careless Husband*. In *Plays Written by Mr. Cibber*. 2 vols. London, 1721.

Cibber, Theophilus. *The Harlot's Progress; or, The Ridotto al Fresco: A Grotesque Pantomime Entertainment*. London, 1733.

Fielding, Henry. *The Covent-Garden Tragedy*. London, 1732.

———. *The Letter-Writers: Or, A New Way to Keep A Wife at Home*. London, 1731.

———. *The Masquerade: A Comedy*. London, 1728.

Gildon, Charles. *Love's Victim: or, The Queen of Wales*. London, 1701.

Haywood, Eliza. *The Fair Captive: A Tragedy*. London, 1721.

Hill, Aaron. *The Tragedy of Zara*. Dublin, 1737.

Johnson, Charles. *Caelia*. London, 1733.

———. The *Country Lasses: Or, the Custom of the Manor*. London, 1715.

———. *The Force of Friendship*. London, 1710.

———. *The Masquerade*. London, 1719.

———. *The Tragedy of Medea*. London, 1731.

Lillo, George. *The Works of Mr. George Lillo*. 2 vols. London, 1775.

———. *George Barnwell*. London, 1792.

Moore, Edward. *The Foundling*. London, 1748.

Pix, Mary. *The Double Mistress*. London, 1701.

Rowe, Nicholas. *The Ambitious Step-Mother*. London, 1701.

———. *The Fair Penitent: A Tragedy*. London, 1742.

———. *Tamerlane: A Tragedy*. London, 1744.

Steele, Richard. *The Conscious Lovers*. London, 1723.

———. *The Lying Lover, or The Ladies Friendship*. London, 1704.

Sturgess, Keith, ed. *Three Elizabethan Domestic Tragedies*. Middlesex, England, 1969.

Decoration and Architecture

Baille, Hugh Murray. "Etiquette and the Planning of the State Apartments in Baroque Palaces." *Archaeologia* 101 (1967): 167–99.

Campbell, Colen, *Vitruvius Britannicus; or, The British Architect, Containing the Plans, Elevations, and Sections of the Regular Buildings, both Publick and Private, in Great Britain*. London, 1717.

Cornforth, John, and John Fowler. *English Decoration in the 18th Century*. London, 1974.

Dutton, Ralph. *The English Country House*. London, 1962.

———. *The English Interior, 1500 to 1900*. London, 1948.

———. *London Houses*. London, 1952.

Fiennes, Celia. *Through England on a Side Saddle In The Time of William and Mary*. London, 1888.

Gater, G. H., and W. H. Godfrey. Parish of St. Martin-in-the-Fields. Pt. 1. Vol. 16 of *Survey of London*. London, 1935.

Georgian Society. *Records of Eighteenth-Century Domestic Architecture and Decoration in Dublin*. Vol. 3. Dublin, 1911.

Gibbs, James. *A Book of Architecture*. London, 1728.

Girouard, Mark. *Life in the English Country House*. New Haven, 1978.

Hibbard, G. R. "The Country House Poem of the Seventeenth Century." In *Essential Articles for the Study of Alexander Pope*, edited by Maynard Mack. London, 1964.

Hussey, Christopher. *English Country Houses: Early Georgian, 1715–1760*. London, 1965.

Kerr, Robert. *The Gentleman's House; or, How to Plan English Residences, From the Parsonage to the Palace*. London, 1865.

Langley, Batty. *The Builders Compleat Assistant; or a Library of Arts and Sciences Absolutely Necessary to be Understood by Builders and Workmen in General*. London, 1738.

Morris, Robert. *Lectures on Architecture*. London, 1734.

————. *Rural Architecture Consisting of Regular Designs of Plans and Elevations for Buildings in the Country*. London, 1750.

Pevsner, N. B. L. *The Planning of the Elizabethan Country House*. London, 1960.

Pococke, Richard. *The Travels through England of Dr. R. Pococke*. Edited by James Joel Cartwright. 2 vols. 1888–1889.

Richardson, A. E. and H. Donaldson Eberlin. *The Smaller English House of the Later Renaissance, 1660–1830*. London, 1925.

Sheppard, F. H. ed. *The Parish of St. James Westminster*. Vol. 29 of *Survey of London*. London, 1960.

Summerson, John. *Architecture in Britain, 1530 to 1830*. Baltimore, 1970.

————. *Georgian London*. London, 1945.

Stow, John. *A Survey of the Cities of London and Westminster*. Edited by John Strype. London, 1720.

Stratton, Arthur. *The English Interior: A Review of the Decoration of English Homes from Tudor Times to the XIXth Century*. London, [n.d.].

Thirkell, Angela. *Three Houses*. London, 1931.

Vanbrugh, Sir John. *The Complete Works*. Edited by Bonamy Dobree and Geoffrey Webb. 4 vols. London, 1928.

Walpole, Horace. *Journals of Visits to Country Seats*. In *The Sixteenth Volume of the Walpole Society*. Oxford, 1928.

Wharton, Edith, and Ogden Codman, Jr. *The Decoration of Houses*. London, 1898.

Wittkower, Rudolf. *Architectural Principles in the Age of Humanism*. New York, 1971.

General Background and Critical Sources

Alderman, William E. "Shaftesbury and the Doctrine of Moral Sense in the Eighteenth Century." *PMLA* 46 (1931): 1087–94.

Allentuck, Marcia Epstein. "Narration and Illustration: The Problem of Richardson's *Pamela*." *PQ* 51 (1972): 874–86.

Altman, Janet Gurkin. *Epistolarity: Approaches to a Form*. Columbus, Ohio, 1982.

Anderson, David L. "Abelard and Heloise: Eighteenth Century Motif." *Studies on Voltaire and the Eighteenth Century* 84 (1971): 7–51.

Ariès, Philippe. *Centuries of Childhood: A Social History of Family Life*. Translated by Robert Baldick. New York, 1965.

Austen, Jane. *Lady Susan, The Watsons, Sanditon*. London, 1975.

Avery, Emmett L., and Arthur H. Scouten. *The London Stage, 1660–1800*. 5 vols. Carbondale, Ill., 1960–68.

Bachelard, Gaston. *The Poetics of Space*. Translated by Maria Jolas. New York, 1964.

Barthes, Roland. *On Racine*. Translated by Richard Howard. New York, 1964.

Beer, Gillian. "Richardson, Milton, and the Status of Evil." *RES* 75 (1968): 261–70.

Benveniste, Emile. *Problems in General Linguistics*. Translated by Mary Elizabeth Meek. Coral Gables, Fla., 1971.

Black, Frank Gees. *The Epistolary Novel in the Late Eighteenth Century*. Eugene, Ore., 1940.

Blanchot, Maurice. *L'Espace littéraire*. Paris, 1955.

Blondel, Jacques. "On 'Metaphysical Prisons.'" *Durham University Journal* 32 (1970–71): 133–38.

Booth, Wayne. *The Rhetoric of Fiction*. Chicago, 1961.

Braudy, Leo. "The Form of the Sentimental Novel." *Novel* 7 (1973): 5–13.

————. "Penetration and Impenetrability in *Clarissa*." In *Selected Papers from the English Institute*, edited by Phillip Harth. New York, 1974.

Bredvold, Louis I. *The Natural History of Sensibility*. Detroit, 1962.

Briggs, Asa. *How They Lived: An Anthology of Original Documents Written Between 1700 and 1815*. Oxford, 1969.

Brissenden, R. F. *Virtue in Distress*. New York, 1974.

Brophy, Elizabeth Bergen. *Samuel Richardson: The Triumph of Craft*. Knoxville, Tenn., 1974.

Bullen, John Samuel. *Time and Space in the Novels of Samuel Richardson*. Utah State University Monograph Series, vol. 12, no. 2. Logan, Utah, 1965.

Campbell, Lily B. *Scenes and Machines on the English Stage during the Renaissance*. Cambridge, England, 1923.

Chapone, Hester. *Letters on the Improvement of the Mind by Mrs. Chapone*. Edinburgh, 1823.

Clay, Christopher. "Marriage, Inheritance, and the Rise of Large Estates in England, 1660–1815." *The Economic History Review* 21 (1968): 503–18.

Collingwood, R. G. "The Expression of Emotion." In *The Problems of Aesthetics*, edited by Eliseo Vivas and Murray Krieger, pp. 343–58. New York, 1960.

Cooper, Anthony Ashley. See Shaftesbury, Earl of.

Copeland, Edward W. "*Clarissa* and *Fanny Hill*: Sisters in Distress." *Studies in the Novel* 4 (1972): 343–52.

————. "Samuel Richardson and Naive Allegory: Some Beauties of the Mixed Metaphor." *Novel* 4 (1971): 231–39.

Costa, Richard H. "The Epistolary Monitor in *Pamela*." *MLQ* 31 (1970): 38–47.

Culler, Jonathan. *Structuralist Poetics*. Ithaca, 1975.

Day, Robert Adams. *Told in Letters: Epistolary Fiction before Richardson*. Ann Arbor, 1966.

Defoe, Daniel. *Religious Courtship: Being Historical Discourses on the Necessity of Marrying Religious Husbands and Wives Only*. London, 1722.

Delany, Patrick. *Fifteen Sermons Upon Social Duties*. London, 1744.

————. *Revelation Examined with Candour*. Dublin, 1732.

Delany, Paul. *British Autobiography in the Seventeenth Century*. London, 1969.

Diderot, Denis. "Eloge de Richardson." In *Oeuvres complètes de Diderot*, edited by J. Assezat. Paris, 1875.

Donovan, Robert Alan. *The Shaping Vision: Imagination in the English Novel from Defoe to Dickens*. Ithaca, 1966.

Doody, Margaret Anne. *A Natural Passion: A Study of the Novels of Samuel Richardson*. Oxford, 1974.

Drew, Elizabeth. *The Literature of Gossip: Nine English Letter Writers.* New York, 1964.

Duchène, Roger. *Réalité vécue et art epistolaire: Madame de Sévigné et la lettre d'amour.* Paris, 1970.

Dussinger, John A. "Conscience and the Pattern of Christian Perfection in *Clarissa.*" *PMLA* 81 (1966): 236–45.

———. "What Pamela Knew: An Interpretation." *JEGP* 69 (1970): 377–93.

Eaves, T. C. Duncan, and Ben D. Kimpel. "The Composition of *Clarissa* and Its Revisions before Publication." *PMLA* 83 (1968): 416–28.

———. *Samuel Richardson: A Biography.* Oxford, 1971.

Eisenstein, Elizabeth. "Some Conjectures about the Impact of Printing on Western Society and Thought." *Journal of Modern History* 40 (1968): 1–56.

Erikson, Erik. *Identity: Youth and Crisis.* New York, 1968.

Fairchild, Hoxie Neale. *Protestantism and the Cult of Sentiment.* Vol. 1 of *Religious Trends in English Poetry.* 1939. Reprint. New York, 1964.

Farrel, William J. "The Style and the Action in *Clarissa.*" *SEL* 3 (1963): 363–75.

Fielding, Henry. *The Criticism of Henry Fielding.* Edited by Ioan Williams. London, 1970.

Flaherty, David H. *Privacy in Colonial New England.* Charlottesville, 1972.

Folkenflik, Robert. "A Room of Pamela's Own." *ELH* 39 (1972): 585–96.

Fothergill, Robert A. *Private Chronicles: A Study of English Diaries.* London, 1974.

Frank, Joseph. "Spatial Form in Modern Literature." In *Criticism: The Foundations of Modern Literary Judgment,* edited by Mark Schorer, Josephine Miles, and Gordon McKenzie, pp. 379–92. New York, 1958.

Friedman, Norman. "Point of View in Fiction: The Development of a Critical Concept." *PMLA* 70 (1955): 1160–84.

Frye, Northrop. "Towards Defining An Age of Sensibility." In *Eighteenth Century English Literature,* edited by James L. Clifford, pp. 311–18. New York, 1959.

Fussell, Paul. *The Rhetorical World of Augustan Humanism.* New York, 1969.

Głowinski, Michel. "On the First-Person Novel." *NLH* 9 (1977): 103–14.

Golden, James L. "John Wesley on Rhetoric and Belles Lettres." *Speech Monographs* 28 (1961): 250–64.

———. "The Rhetorical Theory of Adam Smith." *Southern Speech Journal* 23 (1968): 200–15.

Goodwill, Jasper. *The Ladies Magazine.* 3 vols. 1749–52.

Gopnik, Irwin. *A Theory of Style and Richardson's* Clarissa. The Hague, 1970.

Gouge, William. *The Works of William Gouge.* 2 vols. London, 1627.

Gusdorf, Georges. "Conditions et limites de l'autobiographie." In *Formen der Selbstdarstellung,* edited by Gunter Reichenkron and Erich Haase, pp. 105–23. Berlin, 1956.

Hagstrum, Jean. *Sex and Sensibility: Ideal and Erotic Love from Milton to Mozart.* Chicago, 1980.

Haller, William and Malleville. "The Puritan Art of Love." *HQ* 5 (1942): 235–72.

Hansford, R. E. and G. A. C. Evans. *The Story of The Grange, North End Crescent, Fulham.* Fulham History Society Publications, no. 1. London, 1953.

Hartman, Geoffrey. "Structuralism: The Anglo-American Adventure." *Yale French Studies* 36–37 (1966): 148–67.

Hauser, Arnold. "The Origins of Domestic Drama." In *The Theory of the Modern Stage: An Introduction to Modern Theatre and Drama,* edited by Eric Bentley, pp. 403–19. Middlesex, England, 1968.

Havens, Raymond D. "The Sentimentalism of *The London Merchant.*" *ELH* 12 (1945): 187–97.

Hemlow, Joyce. "Fanny Burney and the Courtesy Books." *PMLA* 65 (1950): 732–61.

Herrnstein-Smith, Barbara. "Poetry as Fiction." *NLH* 2 (1970–71): 259–81.

Hervey, James. *Meditations and Contemplations.* London, 1748.

Hill, Christopher. "Clarissa Harlowe and Her Times." *Essays in Criticism* 5 (1955): 314–40. Reprinted in *Samuel Richardson: A Collection of Critical Essays,* edited by John Carroll, pp. 102–23. Englewood Cliffs, N.J., 1969.

Hilles, Frederick W. "The Plan of *Clarissa.*" *PQ* 45 (1966): 236–48. Reprinted in *Samuel Richardson: A Collection of Critical Essays,* edited by John Carroll, pp. 80–91. Englewood Cliffs, N.J., 1969.

Hornbeak, Katherine Gee. *The Complete Letter Writer in English, 1568–1800.* Smith College Studies in Modern Language, nos. 3–4. Northampton, 1934.

Hughes, Helen S. "Characterization in *Clarissa Harlowe.*" *JEGP* 13 (1914): 110–23.

Humphreys, A. R. "Richardson's Novels: Words and 'Movements Within.'" *Essays and Studies* 23 (1970): 34–51.

Hunter, J. Paul. *The Reluctant Pilgrim.* Baltimore, 1966.

Iser, Wolfgang. "The Generic Control of the Aesthetic Response: An Examination of Smollett's *Humphry Clinker.*" *Southern Humanities Review* 3 (1969): 243–57. Reprinted in *The Implied Reader,* Wolfgang Iser, pp. 57–81. Baltimore, 1974.

Jack, Ian. "The Epistolary Element in Jane Austen." In *English Studies Today,* edited by G. A. Bonnard, pp. 173–86. Bern, 1961.

Jakobson, Roman. "Concluding Statement: Linguistics and Poetics." In *Style in Language,* edited by Thomas A. Sebeok, pp. 350–77. Boston, 1960.

———. "Two Aspects of Language and Two Types of Aphasic Disturbances." In *Fundamentals of Language,* pp. 55–82. Pt. 2. The Hague, 1956.

James, Henry. *The Art of the Novel.* Edited by Richard P. Blackmur. London, 1935.

Johnson, Samuel. *The Rambler.* Vols. 3–5. *The Yale Edition of the Works of Samuel Johnson.* New Haven, 1969.

Joseph, Stephen. *Scene Painting and Design.* London, 1964.

———. *The Story of the Playhouse in England.* London, 1963.

Jost, François. *Essais de littéraire comparée.* Fribourg, 1968.

Kany, Charles E. *The Beginnings of the Epistolary Novel in France, Italy, and Spain.* University of California Publications in Modern Philology, no. 21. Berkeley, 1937.

Kearney, Anthony. "*Clarissa* and the Epistolary Form." *Essays in Criticism* 16 (1966): 44–56.

———. *Samuel Richardson*. London, 1968.

Kermode, Frank. *The Sense of an Ending: Studies in the Theory of Fiction*. New York, 1967.

Kinkead-Weekes, Mark. "Defoe and Richardson—Novelists of the City." In *Dryden to Johnson*, edited by Roger Lonsdale. Vol. 4 of *Sphere History of Literature in the English Language*. London, 1971.

———. *Samuel Richardson: Dramatic Novelist*. Ithaca, 1973.

Konigsberg, Ira. *Samuel Richardson and the Dramatic Novel*. Lexington, 1968.

Law, William. *The Grounds and Reasons of Christian Regeneration, or the New-Birth*. London, 1742.

———. *A Serious Call to a Devout and Holy Life*. London, 1729.

Le Gates, Marlene. "The Cult of Womanhood in Eighteenth-Century Thought." *ECS* 10 (1976): 21–39.

Lerner, L. D. "Puritanism and the Spiritual Autobiography." *Hibbert Journal* 55 (1957): 373–86.

Lessenich, Rolf P. *Elements of Pulpit Oratory in Eighteenth-Century England*. Köln, 1972.

Lessing, Doris. *The Golden Notebook*. New York, 1970.

MacCarthy, B. G. *Women Writers: Their Contributions to the English Novel, 1621–1744*. Cork, 1944.

McBurney, William H. *Chronological Check List of English Prose Fiction, 1700–1739*. Cambridge, Mass., 1960.

McKillop, Alan Dugald. *The Early Masters of English Fiction*. Lawrence, Kans., 1956.

———. "Epistolary Technique in Richardson's Novels." *Rice Institute Pamphlet* 38 (1951): 36–54. Reprinted in *Samuel Richardson: A Collection of Critical Essays*, edited by John Carroll, pp. 139–51. Englewood Cliffs, N.J., 1969.

———. *Samuel Richardson Printer and Novelist*. Chapel Hill, 1936.

Mandel, Barrett John. "Bunyan and the Autobiographer's Artistic Purpose." *Criticism* 10 (1968): 225–43.

Mansfield, Katherine. *Journal of Katherine Mansfield*. Edited by J. Middleton Murry. New York, 1946.

Martin, Lee. "From Forestage to Proscenium: A Study of Restoration Staging Techniques." *Theatre Survey* 4 (1963): 3–28.

Mish, Charles C. *English Prose Fiction, 1600–1700: A Chronological Checklist*. Charlottesville, 1967.

Morgan, Charlotte E. *The Rise of the Novel of Manners: A Study of English Prose Fiction between 1600 and 1740*. New York, 1911.

Mylne, Vivienne. *The Eighteenth-Century French Novel: Techniques of Illusion*. New York, 1965.

Nicoll, Allardyce. *A History of English Drama, 1660–1900*. Vols. 1 and 2. Cambridge, England, 1952.

Ong, Walter J., S. J. "The Writer's Audience Is Always a Fiction." *PMLA* 90 (1975): 9–21.

Orgel, Stephen. "The Poetics of Spectacle." *NLH* 2 (1970–71): 367–89.

Pascal, Roy. *Design and Truth in Autobiography*. London, 1960.

Paulson, Ronald. *The Art of Hogarth*. New York, 1975.

———. *Hogarth: His Life, Art, and Times*. 2 vols. New Haven, 1971.

Perry, Ruth. *Women, Letters, and the Novel*. New York, 1980.

Phillips, Ambrose. *The Free-Thinker*. 3 vols. London, 1718–22.

Poulet, Georges. *La Distance intérieure*. Paris, 1952.

———. *The Metamorphoses of the Circle*. Baltimore, 1966.

Praz, Mario. *Conversation Pieces: A Survey of the Informal Group Portrait in Europe and America*. University Park, Pa., 1971.

———. *The Romantic Agony*. London, 1951.

Preston, John. *The Created Self: The Reader's Role in Eighteenth-Century Fiction*. New York, 1970.

Price, Martin. "The Other Self: Thoughts about Character in the Novel." In *Imagined Worlds*, edited by Maynard Mack and Ian Gregor. London, 1968.

Rabkin, Eric. "Spatial Form and Plot." *Critical Inquiry* 4 (Winter, 1977): 253–70.

Raines, John Curtis. *Attack on Privacy*. Valley Forge, N.Y., 1974.

Richetti, John. *Popular Fiction before Richardson: Narrative Patterns 1700–1739*. London, 1969.

Rodman, George Bush. "Sentimentalism in Lillo's *The London Merchant*." *ELH* 12 (1945): 45–61.

Rogers, Pat. *Grub Street: Studies in Subculture*. London, 1972.

Romberg, Bertil. *Studies in the Narrative Techniques of the First-Person Novel*. Stockholm, 1962.

Rosbottom, Ronald. "A Matter of Competence: The Relationship between Reading and Novel-Making in Eighteenth-Century France." In vol. 6 of *Studies in Eighteenth-Century Culture*, edited by Ronald Rosbottom. Madison, 1977.

Røstvig, Maren-Sofie. *The Happy Man: Studies in the Metaphormoses of a Classical Ideal*. 2 vols. Oslo, 1962, 1971.

Rousset, Jean. *Forme et signification: Essais sur les structures littéraires de Corneille à Claudel*. Paris, 1962.

———. *Narcisse romancier*. Paris, 1973.

Rowe, Elizabeth. *Devout Exercises of the Heart in Meditation and Soliloquy, Prayer and Praise*. London, 1738.

———. *Miscellaneous Works in Prose and Verse*. London, 1739.

Sale, William M., Jr. "From *Pamela* to *Clarissa*." In *The Age of Johnson: Essays Presented to Chauncey Brewster Tinker*, edited by Frederick W. Hilles, pp. 127–38. New Haven, 1949.

———. *Samuel Richardson: Master Printer*. Ithaca, 1950.

Sarraute, Nathalie. *Tropisms* and *The Age of Suspicion*. Translated by Maria Jolas. London, 1963.

Schmitz, Robert M. "Death and Colonel Morden in Clarissa." *South Atlantic Quarterly* 69 (1970): 346–53.

Scholes, Robert, and Robert Kellogg. *The Nature of Narrative*. New York, 1966.

Sennet, Richard. *The Fall of Public Man*. New York, 1978.

Seylaz, Jean-Luc. Les Liaisons dangereuses *et la création romanesque chez Laclos*. Paris, 1958.

Shaftesbury, Anthony Cooper, Earl of. *Characteristics of Men, Manners, Opinions, Times*. Edited by John M. Robertson. London, 1900.

Sharrock, Roger. "Richardson's *Pamela*: The Gospel and the Novel." *The Durham University Journal* 58 (1966): 67–74.

Sherbo, Arthur. *English Sentimental Drama*. East Lansing, Mich., 1957.

———. "Time and Place in Richardson's *Clarissa*." *Boston University Studies in English* 3 (1957): 139–46.

Shudofsky, M. Maurice. "Charles Johnson and Eighteenth-Century Drama." *ELH* 10 (1943): 131–58.

Singer, Godfrey Frank. *The Epistolary Novel: Its Origin, Development, Decline, and Residuary Influence*. Philadelphia, 1933.

Smith, Adam. *The Theory of Moral Sentiments*. London, 1774.

Southern, Richard. *Changeable Scenery: Its Origin and Development in the British Theatre*. London, 1952.

———. *The Georgian Playhouse*. London, 1948.

Stallman, R. W. "Some Rooms from 'The Houses the James Built.'" In *Twentieth Century Interpretations of* The Portrait of a Lady, edited by Peter Buitenhuis, pp. 37–44. Englewood Cliffs, N.J., 1968.

Starr, G. A. *Defoe and Spiritual Autobiography*. Princeton, 1965.

Steele, Richard. *The Theatre*. London, 1720.

Stephen, Leslie. "Richardson's Novels." In *Hours in a Library*. 4 vols. London, 1907.

Stevick, Philip. *The Chapter in Fiction: Theories of Narrative Division*. Syracuse, 1970.

Stone, Lawrence. *The Family, Sex, and Marriage in England, 1500–1800*. New York, 1977.

———. "The Rise of the Nuclear Family in Early Modern England: The Patriarchal Stage." In *The Family in History*, edited by Charles E. Rosenberg, pp. 13–58. Philadelphia, 1975.

Swearingen, James. *Reflexivity in* Tristram Shandy. New Haven, 1977.

Tillyard, E. M. W. *Some Mythical Elements in English Literature*. London, 1961.

Trimpi, Wesley. *Ben Jonson's Poems: A Study of the Plain Style*. Stanford, 1962.

Van Ghent, Dorothy. *The English Novel: Form and Function*. New York, 1961.

Versini, Laurent. *Laclos et la tradition*. Paris, 1968.

Warner, William. *Reading* Clarissa: *The Struggles of Interpretation*. New Haven, 1979.

Watt, Ian. *The Rise of the Novel: Studies in Defoe, Richardson, and Fielding*. Berkeley, 1967.

Wickham, Glynne. *Early English Stages 1300–1660*. Vol. 2. Pt. 1. London, 1963.

Williams, Aubrey L. *Pope's Dunciad: A Study of Its Meaning*. London, 1955.

Williams, Raymond. *Drama in Performance*. New York, 1968.

——. *The English Novel from Dickens to Lawrence*. New York, 1973.

——. *Keywords: A Vocabulary of Culture and Society*. New York, 1976.

Wilt, Judith. "He Could Go No Farther: A Modest Proposal about Lovelace and Clarissa." *PMLA* 92 (1977): 19–32.

Wolff, Cynthia Griffin. *Samuel Richardson and the Eighteenth-Century Puritan Character*. Hamden, Conn., 1972.

Wright, Louis B. *Middle-Class Culture in Elizabethan England*. Chapel Hill, 1935.

Yates, Frances A. *The Art of Memory*. Chicago, 1966.

Young, Edward. *The Complaint, and the Consolation; or Night Thoughts*. London, 1797.

——. *Conjectures on Original Composition*. Edited by Edith J. Morley. Manchester, 1918.

Zeraffa, Michael. "The Novel as Literary Form and as Social Institution." In *Sociology of Literature and Drama*, edited by Elizabeth and Tom Burns, pp. 35–55. Harmondsworth, England, 1973.

Zirker, Malvin R. "Richardson's Correspondence: The Personal Letter as Private Experience." In *The Familiar Letter in the Eighteenth Century*, edited by Howard Anderson, Philip Daghlian, and Irvin Ehrenpreis, pp. 71–91. Lawrence, Kans., 1966.

Index

169

UNIVERSITY OF FLORIDA MONOGRAPHS
Humanities

The Paradox of Privacy

University of Florida Monographs
Humanities No. 54